IMAGES of America

Crown Hill Cemetery

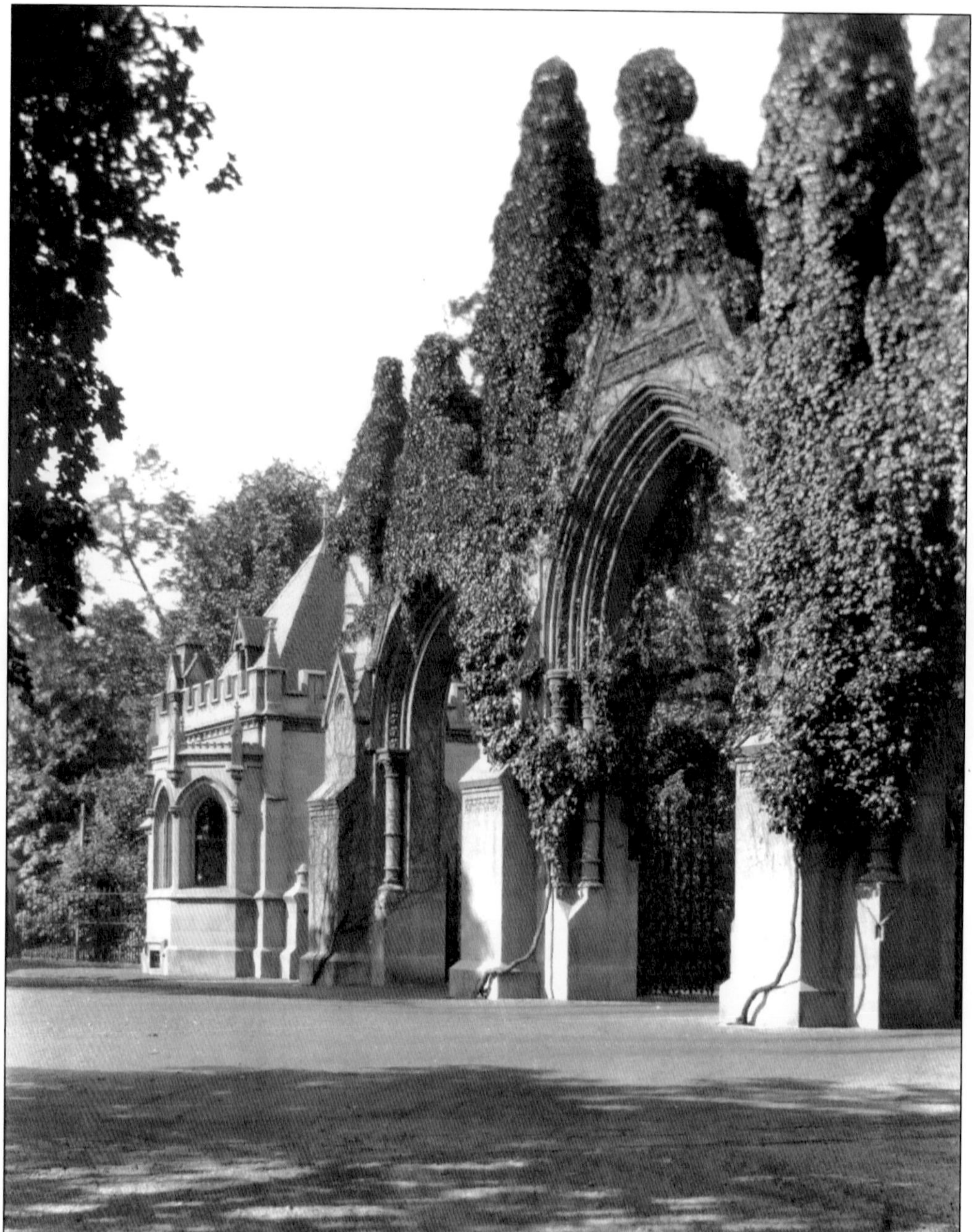

The Gothic gate at 34th Street and Boulevard Place was the main gate for Crown Hill Cemetery when this photo was taken in 1928. At the time, it was overgrown with ivy, which has since been removed. (Photo courtesy of Crown Hill Cemetery.)

IMAGES
of America

CROWN HILL CEMETERY

W.C. Madden

ARCADIA
PUBLISHING

ISBN 978-0-7385-3250-9

Published by Arcadia Publishing
Charleston, South Carolina

Printed in the United States of America

Library of Congress Catalog Card Number: 2004100275

For all general information contact Arcadia Publishing at:
Telephone 843-853-2070
Fax 843-853-0044
E-Mail sales@arcadiapublishing.com
For customer service and orders:
Toll-Free 1-888-313-2665

Visit us on the Internet at www.arcadiapublishing.com

Cover photo courtesy of Marty Davis, Crown Hill Cemetery.

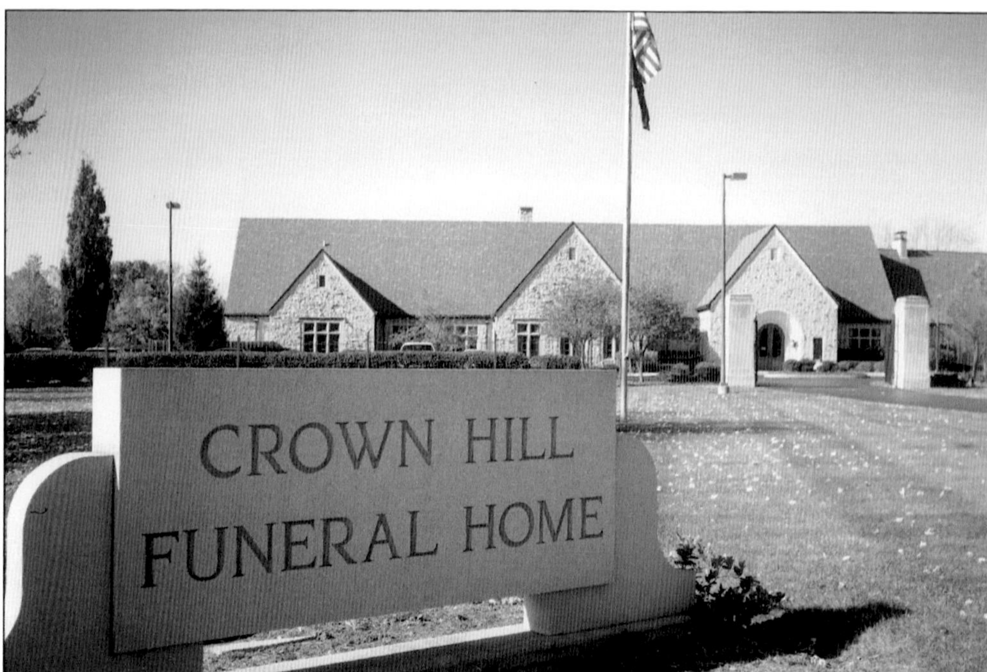

The Funeral Home entrance to Crown Hill Cemetery is located on 38th Street.

Contents

ACKNOWLEDGMENTS

Some years ago, on the fourth of March, I visited Crown Hill Cemetery for the first time in honor of my father. He is not buried there, but my wife's mother is, so we went and visited her grave on the occasion of my father's birthday. It was cold that day and we didn't spend much time at the gravesite. Janice hadn't seen her mother's grave in quite some time, so it was a moving moment for both of us. In any case, I was very impressed with the cemetery and little did I know at the time that I would some day write a book about Crown Hill. I'm honored that cemetery officials and my publisher met this project with open arms. Many thanks to the workers at Crown Hill, particularly Marty Davis and Marianne Randjelovic. Also, thanks to George Mitchell, Tom Davis, the Indianapolis Colts, Butler University, Indiana Historical Bureau, and others who provided information and photos for this book.

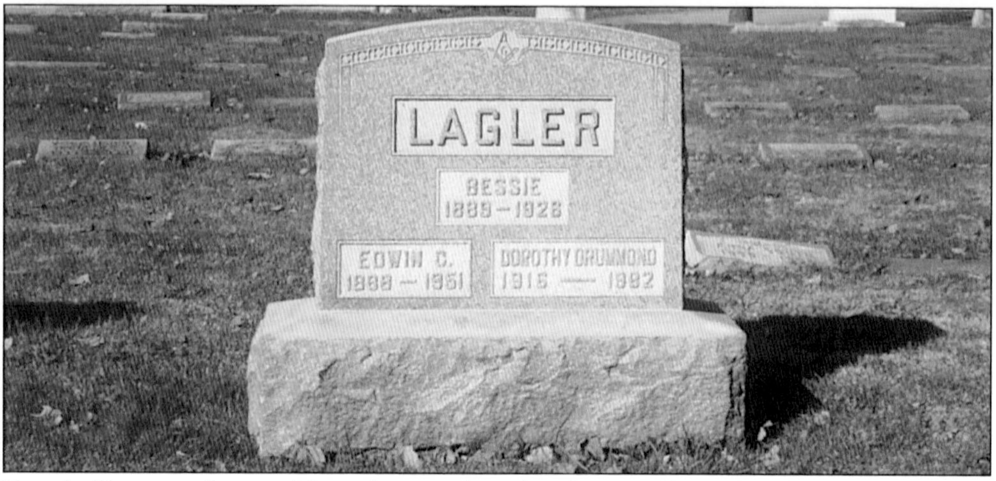

Dorothy Drummond, my wife's mother, was buried on January 12, 1982 in Section 62.

INTRODUCTION

Crown Hill Cemetery is one of the largest cemeteries in the world, housing the remains of some 200,000 souls from the richest of the rich to the poorest of the poor. That's the way it was meant to be. At the dedication of the cemetery, former Senator Albert S. White said the cemetery would be for "the rich and the poor, the proud and the humble, alike may enter here." People from all walks of life are buried there from the homeless to a United States President.

Besides being one of the largest cemeteries in the world, the heritage of those buried there can be traced to every part of the world. So Crown Hill has established some parts for people from different cultures. The latest additions are sections for those of the Muslim faith and Latinos. There are also sections for Greeks, Estonians, military, churches, anatomical donations, and cremations. Some of the international flavor of Crown Hill is reflected in different languages on the monuments, including German, Chinese, Arabic, and others. Some stones refer to a person's birth in Ireland, Scotland, Germany, or other foreign countries.

The Crown Hill Heritage Foundation was established in 1984 to perpetuate family memories, cultural heritage, and historic landmarks at the cemetery. The foundation has created extensive education programs through public tours. More than 250 school groups tour Crown Hill each year and over 1,000 students participate annually in the Spirit of Freedom program. Many come to view the 130 species of trees which were inventoried and catalogued as part of the Sallie E. Gould Tree Preservation Program.

The foundation was responsible for creating the Heroes of Public Safety section in an effort to reflect Indianapolis' recognition of and appreciation for the special group of Public Safety professionals who protect the community on a daily basis. The cemetery also provides free burial space for public safety officials and free services for those who are killed in the line of duty. The cemetery further provides a contribution to the Jason Baker Scholarship Fund for each burial space. The fund was established to assist individuals seeking a career in public safety. Discounts are also provided to veterans of the Armed Services.

The Crown Hill Heritage Foundation was also responsible for many activities surrounding the 140th anniversary of the cemetery, which began in 2003. The foundation presented a contemporary sculpture walk by Hoosiers artists. Visitors to the cemetery will vote on their favorite sculpture and the best sculpture will be named in 2004. Other special activities are planned for 2004 when the cemetery turns 140 on June 1. For more information about the cemetery, go their website at www.crownhill.org or call one of the following numbers: Cemetery (317-925-8231), Funeral Home (317-925-3800), Heritage Foundation (317-920-4165), tours (317-920-2644), or events line (317-920-2726).

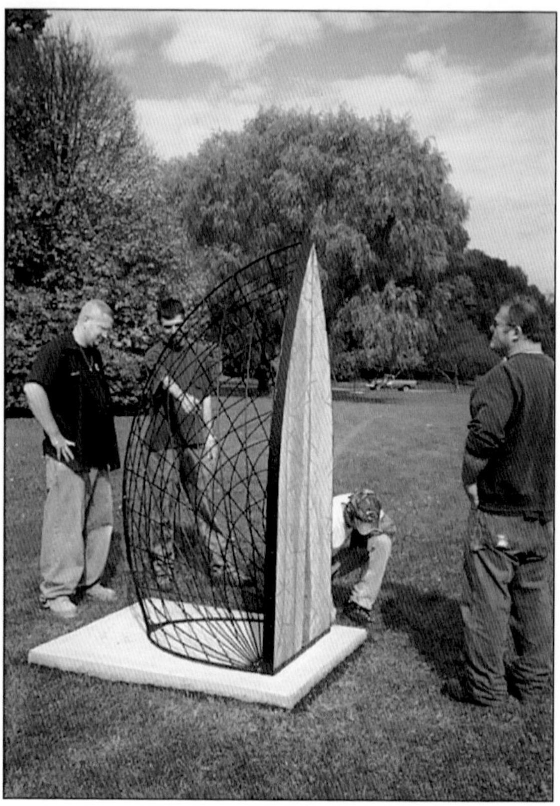

Crown Hill Cemetery workers install a geodetic by artist Jay C. Dougan. Ten contemporary Hoosier sculptures were installed in 2003 at Crown Hill Cemetery to honor the 140th anniversary. Visitors to the cemetery were asked to pick their favorite sculpture by May 15, 2004.

One

The History of Crown Hill Cemetery

In 1863, Indianapolis was quite small compared to today. Only about 20,000 residents lived in the Circle City. City leaders were concerned over the limited acreage and condition of Greenlawn Cemetery, the city cemetery located seven blocks southwest of Monument Circle. This led to the idea of establishing a rural cemetery in Indianapolis.

A meeting was held at the Indiana State Bank building at Pennsylvania and Washington Streets to discuss the possibility. Nine city leaders met with John Chislett, the superintendent of Allegheny Cemetery in Pittsburgh, Pennsylvania. He and three others—Gen. Thomas A. Morris, James Blake, and Calvin Fletcher—were appointed to selected the land and make its purchase. Fletcher said the old city cemetery had become a "public disgrace."

Chislett went to several possible sites, but when he saw Martin Williams' farm, a common picnic site for townspeople, he told the others, "Buy those grounds at whatever price you have to pay." The committee selected the area, which was 2.8 miles northwest of downtown Indianapolis. At the time, the city limits extended to 22nd Street. A total of 240 acres was purchased from five persons for a combined cost of $51,000, a considerable sum of money at the time. Money was advanced to the new cemetery corporation by Fletcher Bank.

Crown Hill was incorporated as a not-for-profit organization on September 25, 1863. Frederick W. Chislett, John's son, was hired as the superintendent. He would design, develop, and oversee the cemetery during its formative years. Chislett held the post until his death in 1899.

On June 1, 1864, a dedication ceremony was held on the gentle slope west of where the Gothic Chapel now stands. The first burial took place the next day when Lucy Ann Seaton was laid to rest. The wife of Capt. John L. Seaton died of consumption (tuberculosis) on May 31, 1864. The cemetery's original main entrance was opened on July 30 along the west side, which is now Dr. Martin Luther King Jr. Street. John Pattison built the gate for $2,300. It consisted of a main central gate flanked by two narrower gates. That gate was used until 1900, when another gate was built at the southwest corner of the cemetery. Indianapolis architect Herbert Foltz designed that gate. The archway was built of Bedford limestone. That entrance was closed in 1965.

Two years later, 708 Union soldiers who died during the Civil War and were buried at Greenlawn Cemetery were removed to Crown Hill and interred. The United States government purchased this 1.37-acre lot to become the second of three national cemeteries in Indiana. Two years later the first Decoration Day service was celebrated at Crown Hill. The traditional ceremony recurs each May on Memorial Day. The cemetery soon became a popular place to spend a few relaxing hours away from the city. Families would go to Crown Hill with their picnic baskets and spend the afternoon.

The first home for the superintendent was built on the grounds in 1869 and it stood until 1917. The second was erected in 1914 and was removed in 1950. Other buildings were also constructed for employees, horses, and equipment. Today, only the service yard constructed in the early 1920s remains.

In 1875, Diedrich A. Bohlen designed the Gothic Chapel. The limestone chapel was built by German craftsmen at the center of the cemetery. Originally a temporary storage vault for the dead, the chapel is now used for funeral services, tours, and special events. It was restored in 1971.

The principal entryway to Crown Hill was established in 1885 at 34th Street and Boulevard Place to replace the former western entrance located around 32nd Street and Dr. Martin Luther King Jr. Street. Adolph Scherrer designed the elaborate limestone archway as a companion to a brick administration building that served as the cemetery office until 1969. Indianapolis architect Adolph Scherrer completed the 34th Street gate just in time for the funeral procession of Vice President Thomas A. Hendricks on November 30, 1885. A sentry house was constructed to the left of the entrance in 1904.

Just before the turn of the century, the cemetery began to expand onto the north side of Maple Road (now 38th Street). To avoid having to cross 38th Street to get to the north side, the cemetery had the Subway built under 38th Street to bypass the street. The underpass was designed by the architectural firm of D.A. Bohlen and Son and constructed by Edward Strathmann and Company at a cost of $170,000. It was completed in 1927.

The construction of a brick and wrought iron fence began in 1914 and wasn't completed until the late 1930s. It replaced one selected of Tennessee lumber by Dr. John M. Kitchen, one of the founding members of the cemetery's governing Board of Corporators. It surrounds three sides of the south grounds as well as the southernmost end of the north grounds. George E. Kessler designed the fence, which underwent restoration from 1985 to 1992.

Crown Hill was listed on the National Register of Historic Places in 1973. Today, the cemetery averages four burials every day and more than 190,000 are buried there. Additional acreage was purchased for the cemetery and the last buy came in 1911. The 555-acre cemetery still has room for many more and won't run out of space for another two centuries.

Crown Hill has a crematorium as well, so several hundred people choose it every year. Governor Frank O'Bannon was cremated there in 2003 after he died in Chicago. However, his ashes were not left at Crown Hill. Crown Hill has created a Cremation Memorial Garden where ashes can be left and the dead honored.

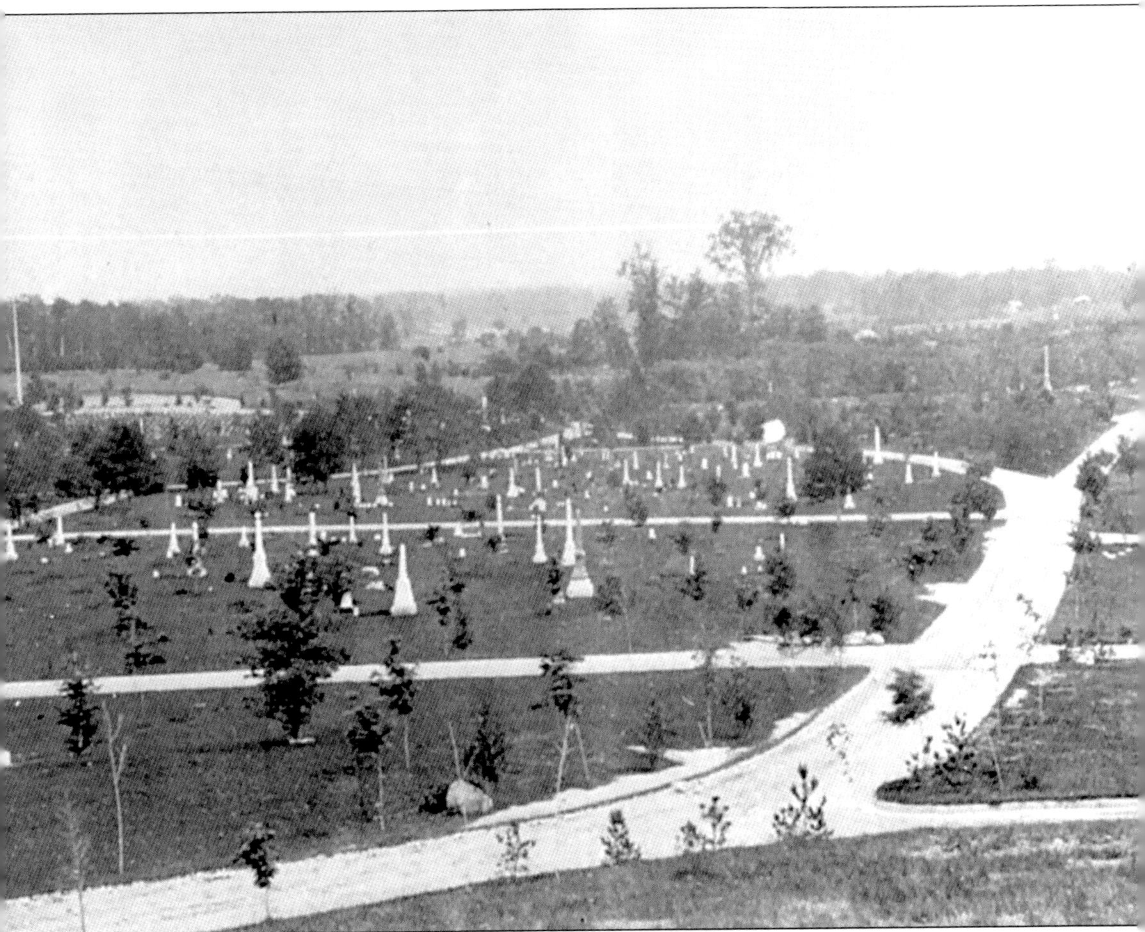

In 1875, when this photo was taken from the base of Crown Hill, the cemetery and the trees were quite small. The National Cemetery is located in the upper left of this photo. The tallest monument on the left belongs to the Almus Vinton family. The superintendent's home is in the upper right of the photo. (Photo courtesy of Crown Hill Cemetery.)

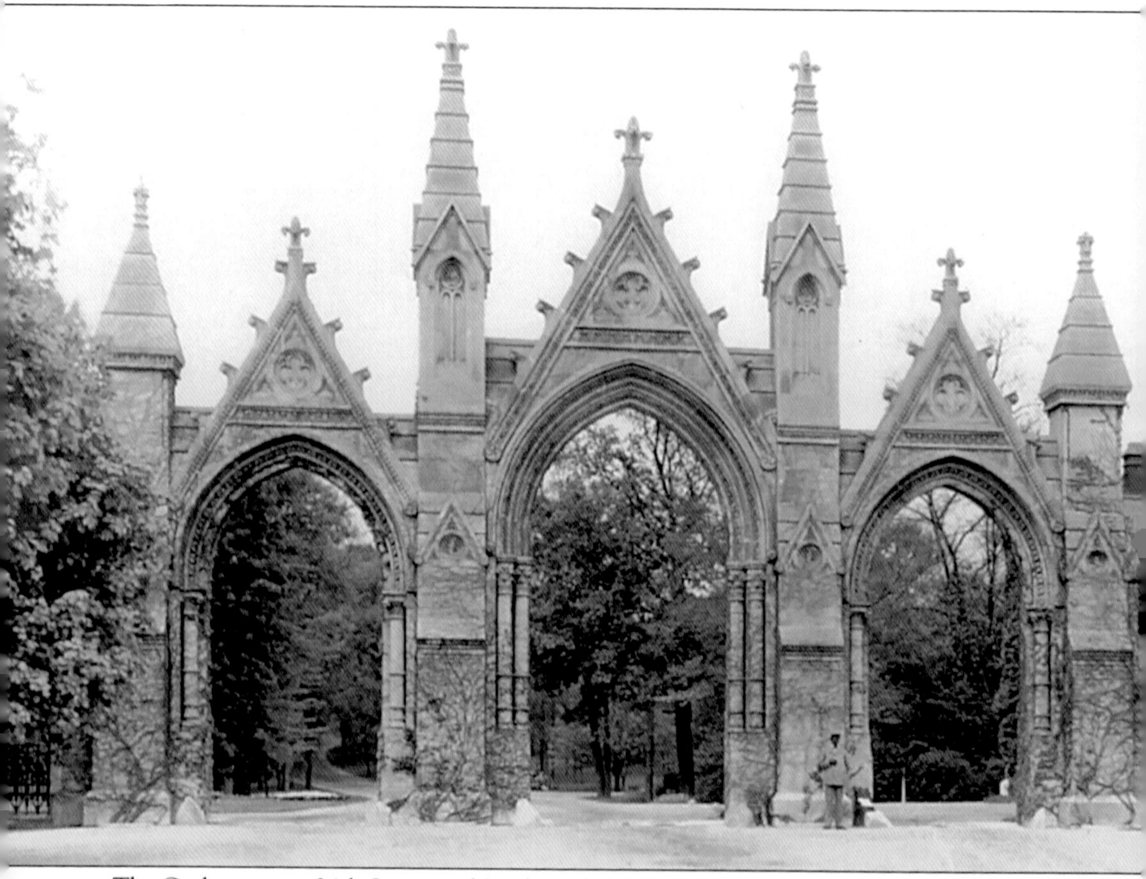

The Gothic gate at 34th Street and Boulevard Place was built in 1886 of Indiana limestone. For many years it was used as the cemetery's main entrance when the business office was located in the Waiting Station. It was designed by Adolph Scherrer, who also planned the Indiana State Capitol Building. This photo was taken in 1902. (Photo courtesy of Crown Hill Cemetery.)

Rhoads Cemetery was established in 1844 in southeastern Wayne Township in Marion County. In 1999, 12 adults and 34 children of the Rhoads, Rude, Foster, Foltz, and Johns families were moved to Crown Hill. This marker honors those pioneers.

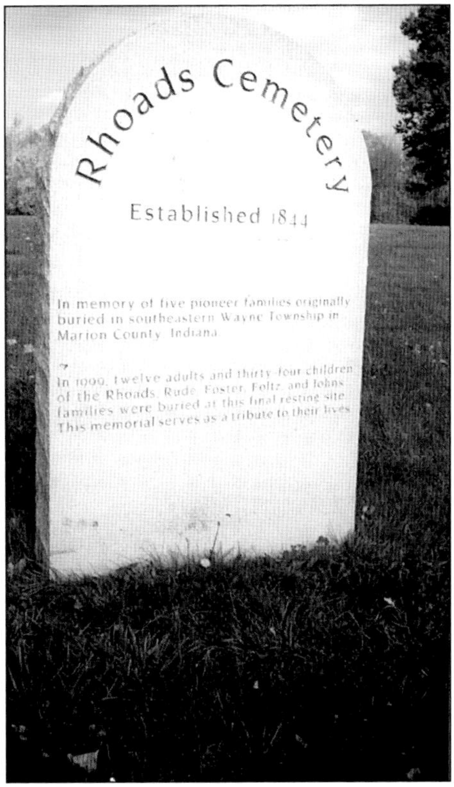

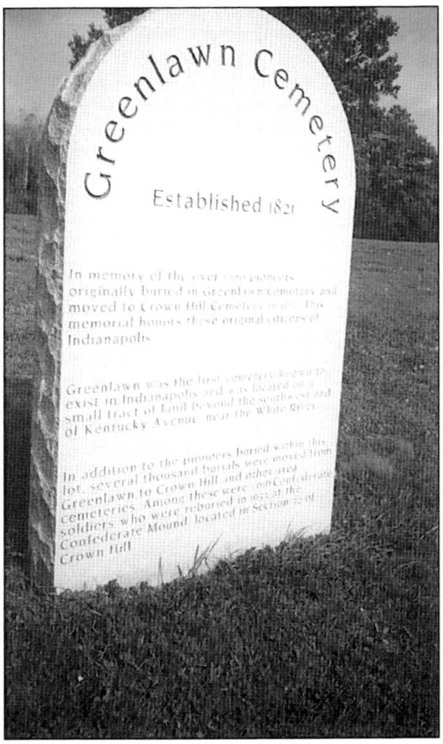

Greenlawn Cemetery was established in 1821 on a small tract of land beyond the southwest end of Kentucky Avenue near the White River. Several thousand burials at Greenlawn were later moved to Crown Hill. This monument is located in the north section of Crown Hill and honors them.

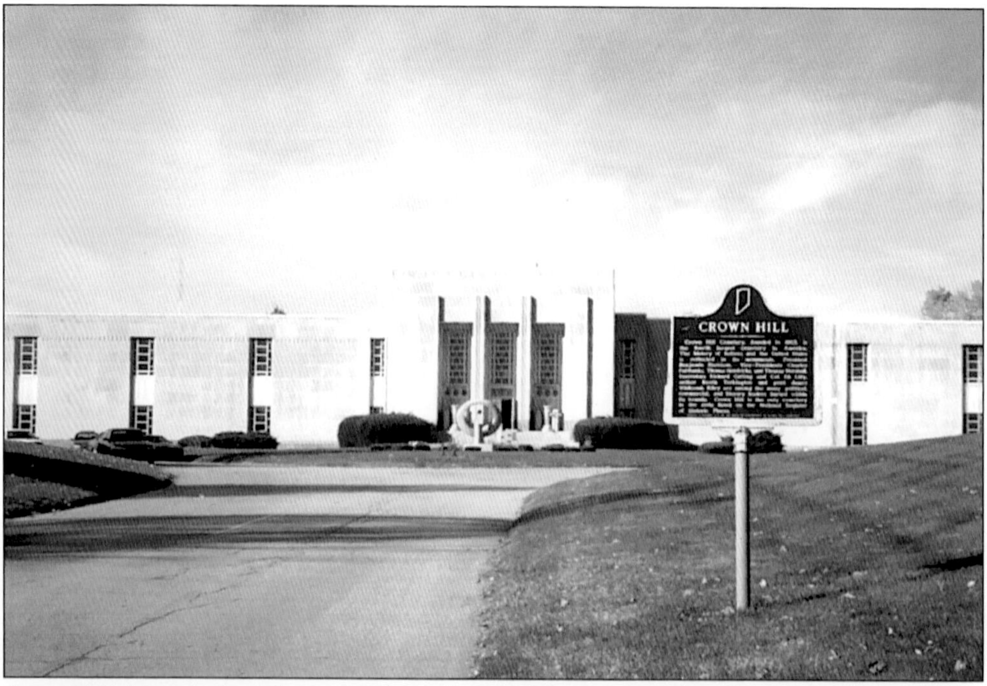

A roadside historical marker provides information to visitors about Crown Hill Cemetery. In the background is the Community Mausoleum, which also contains the Peace Chapel for memorial services.

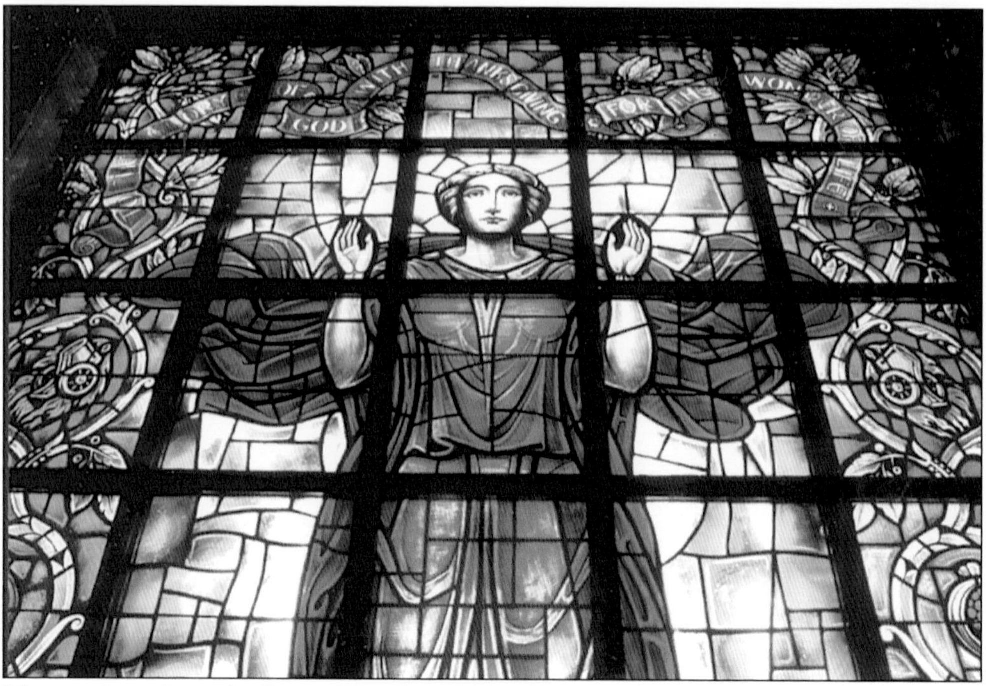

This window adorns the Peace Chapel inside the Community Mausoleum. (Photo courtesy of Marty Davis.)

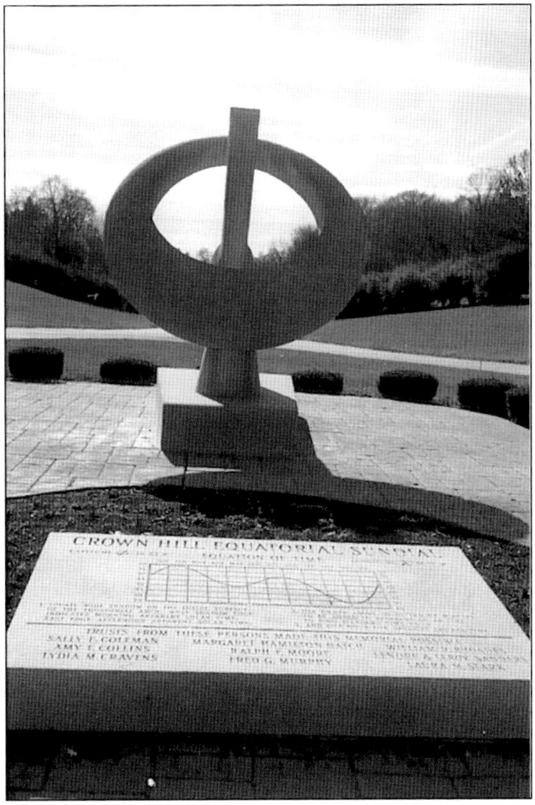

The Crown Hill Equatorial Sundial located in front of the Community Mausoleum was fabricated at Woolery Stone Company in Bloomington in 1986 and 1987. Sculptor David L. Rodgers completed the sundial on site in April 1987.

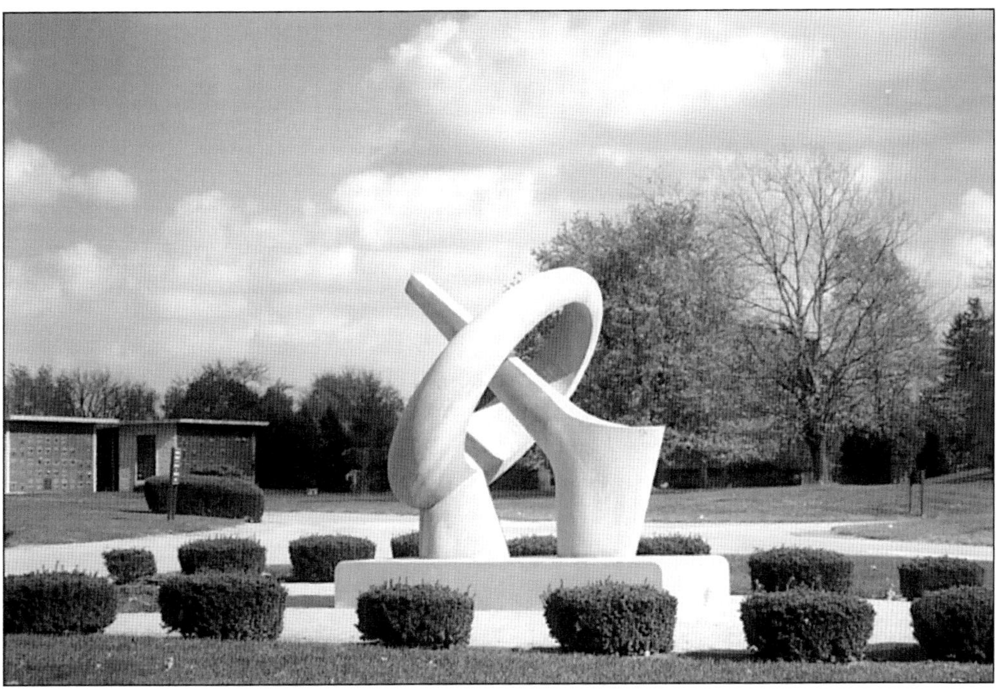

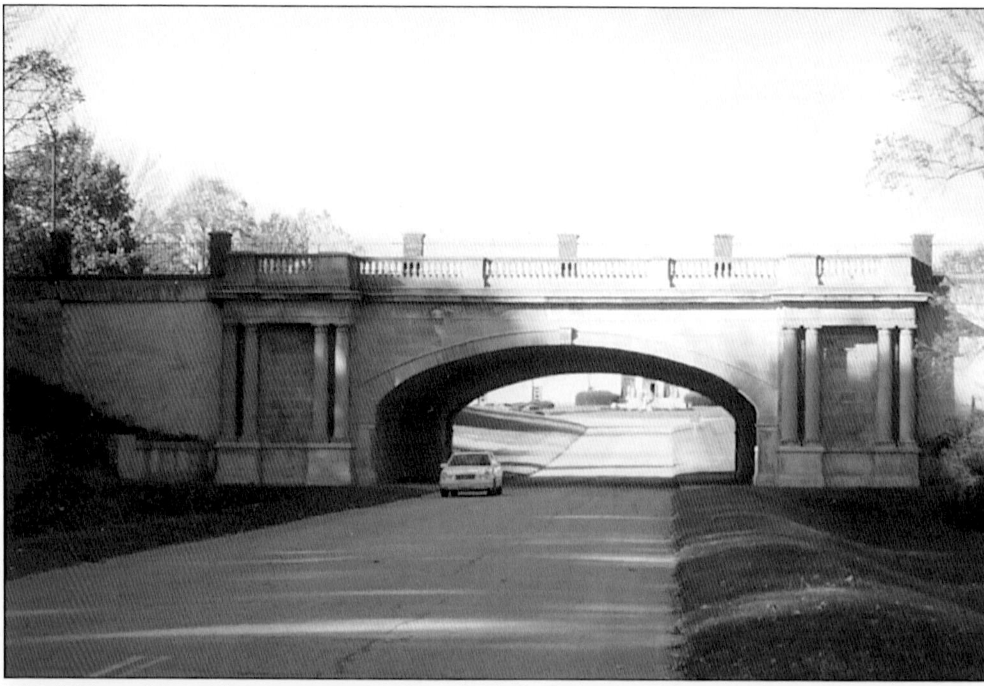

The "Subway" provides a passageway for vehicles in Crown Hill Cemetery under 38th Street. The roadway connects the southern section of the cemetery to the northern section.

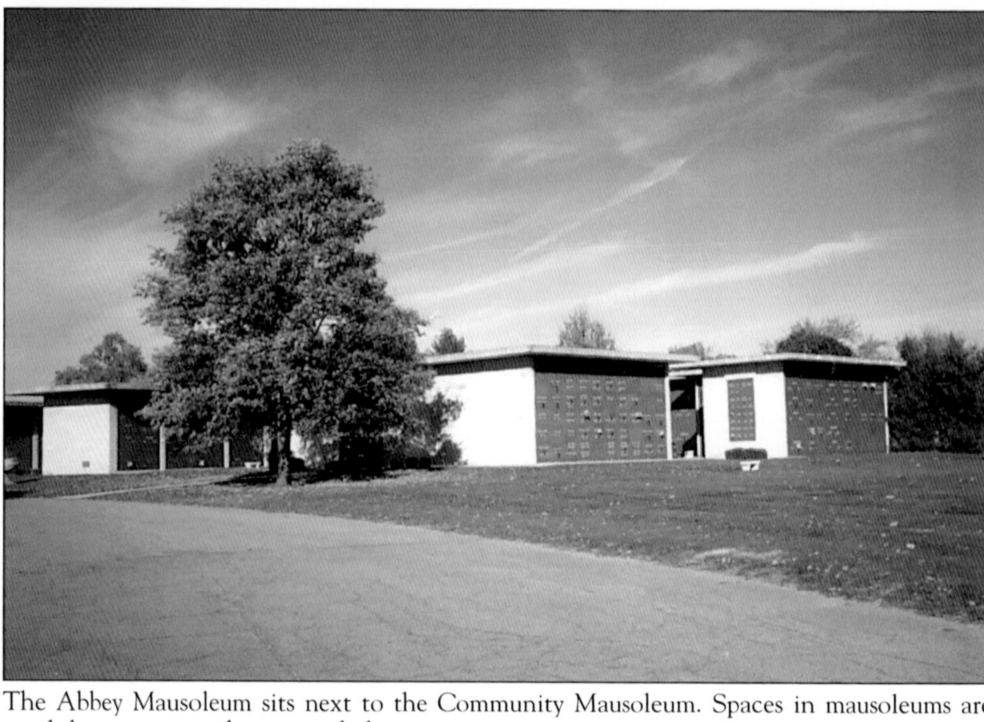

The Abbey Mausoleum sits next to the Community Mausoleum. Spaces in mausoleums are much less expensive than ground plots.

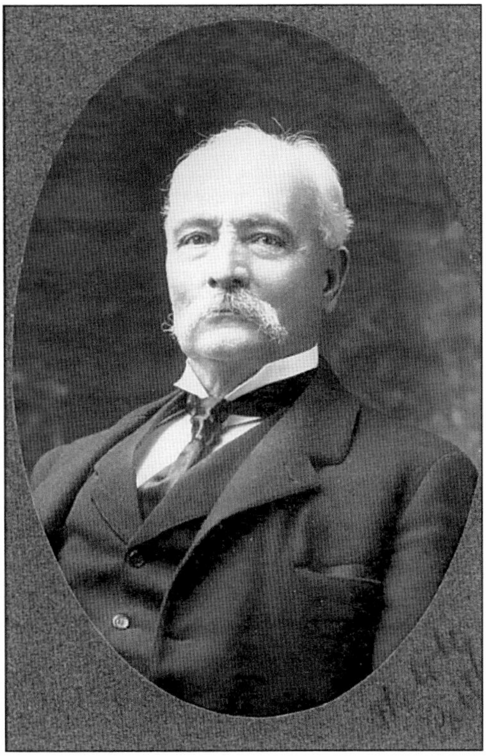

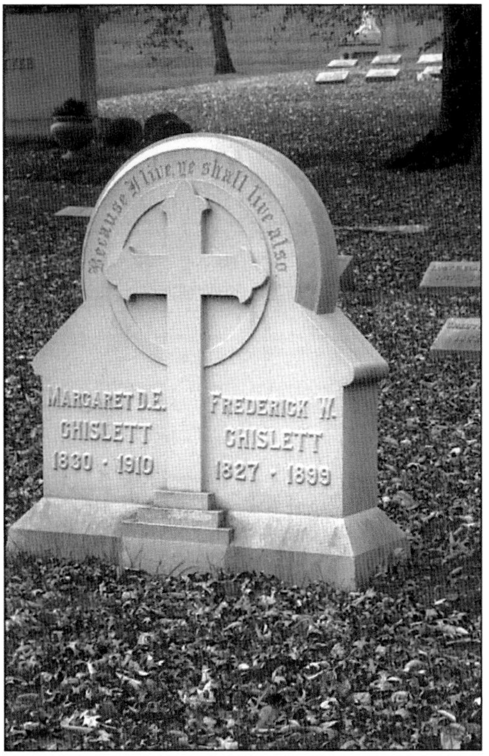

Frederick W. Chislett, 1827–1899, was Crown Hill's first superintendent and served for 36 years. Chislett was a landscape architect from Pittsburgh. He initially developed seven burial sections in the cemetery. In 1869, Crown Hill built him a residence on the grounds for him and his family. That home stood until 1917. A second residence was built in 1914 and was removed in 1950. His grave is located in Section 14. (Photo courtesy of Crown Hill Cemetery.)

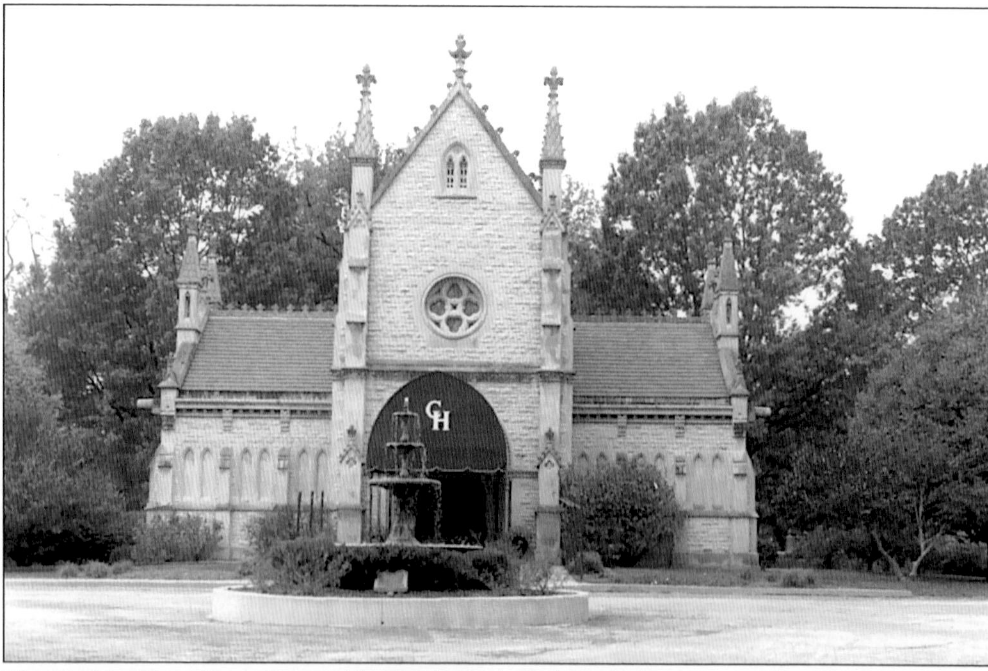

The Gothic Chapel was designed by Diedrich A. Bohlen and constructed by Peter Routiers in 1875 at a cost of $38,922.25. It was originally built to temporarily entomb the remains of as many as 96 bodies when burial was not immediately possible. This was due generally to a delay in burial arrangements or special requests by members of the deceased's family. Although the interior was designed for funeral services during inclement weather, the unpleasant surroundings and bleak interior made the "vault" an unpleasant place to visit. In 1971, it underwent restoration and became a place for services, lectures, and tours.

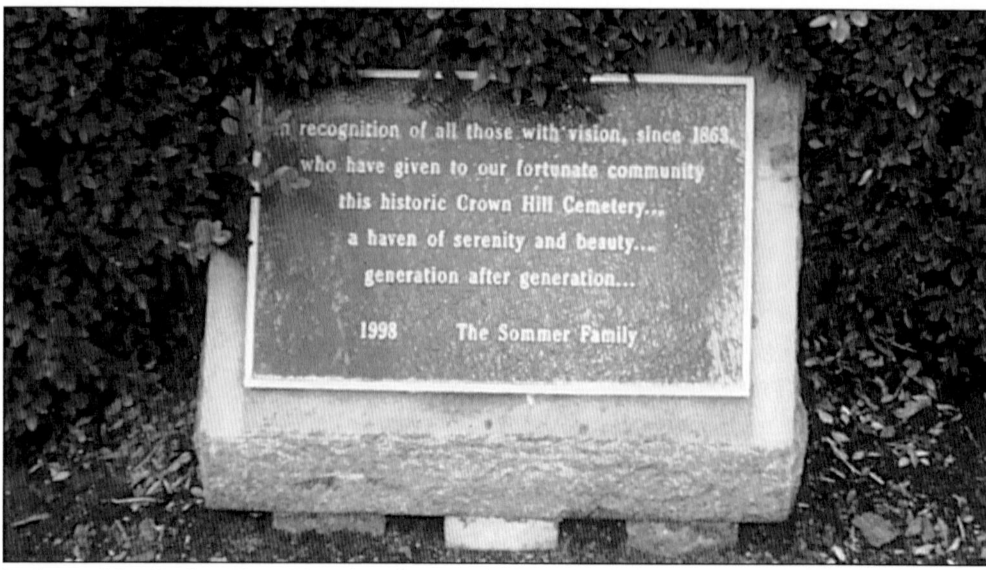

In front of the Gothic Chapel lies this plaque, which reads: "In recognition of all those with vision, since 1863, who have given to our fortunate community this historic Crown Hill Cemetery . . . a haven of serenity and beauty . . . generation after generation . . . 1998, The Sommer Family."

Crown Hill Cemetery acquired some of the statues from the old County Courthouse when the building was razed. This is one of them, a Greek goddess.

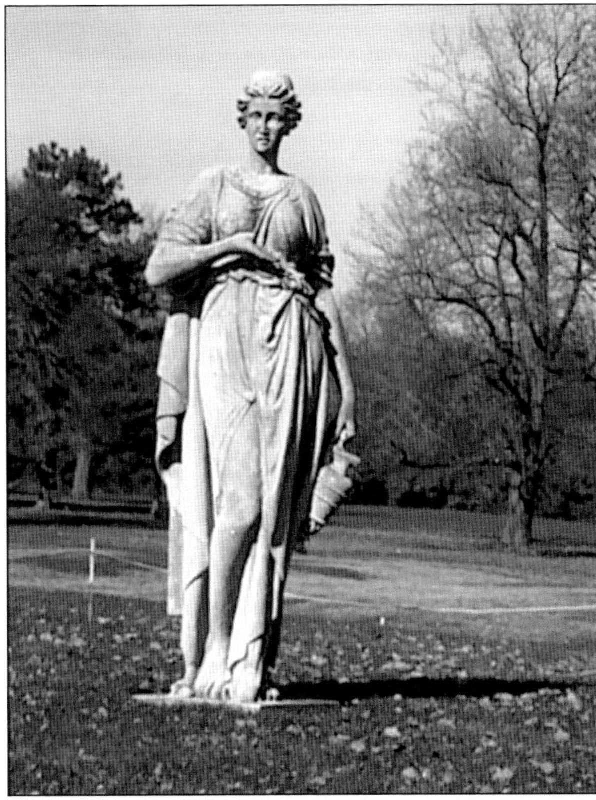

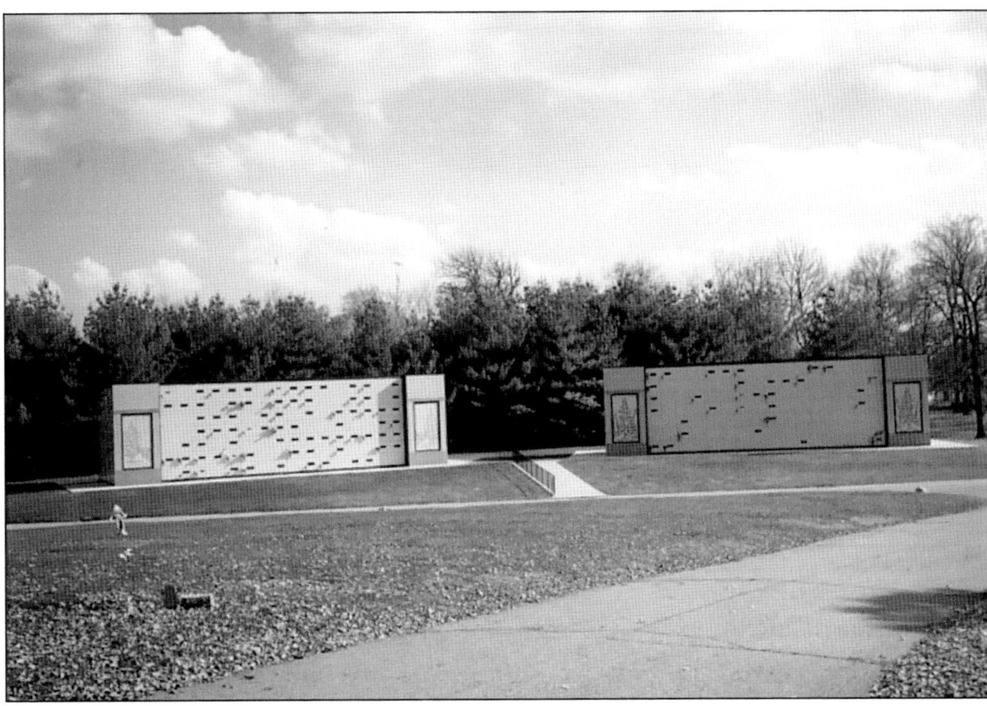

The Pine Mausoleum is located in the southernmost part of Crown Hill.

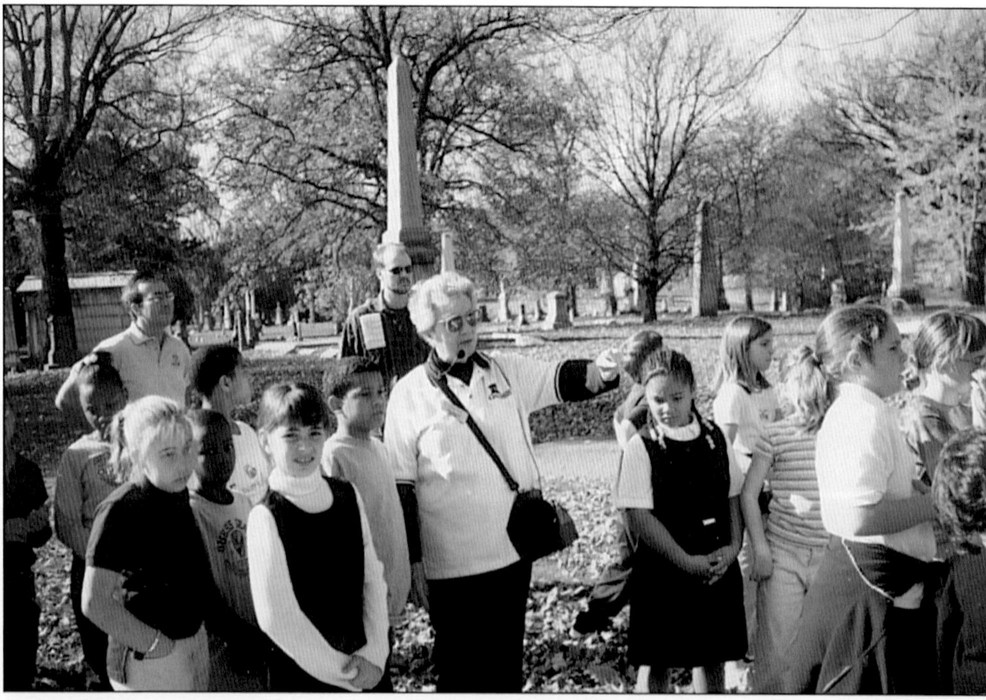

Crown Hill gives many tours to interested students like these. The cemetery also has several self-guided tours available to visitors.

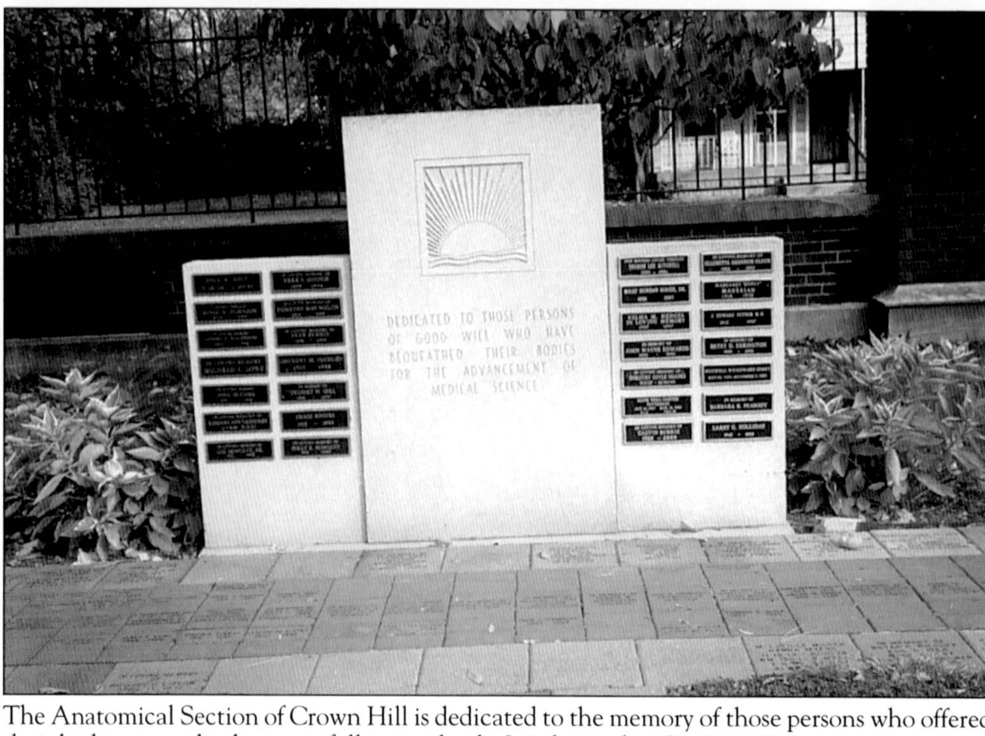

The Anatomical Section of Crown Hill is dedicated to the memory of those persons who offered their bodies to medical science following death. It is located in Section 41A.

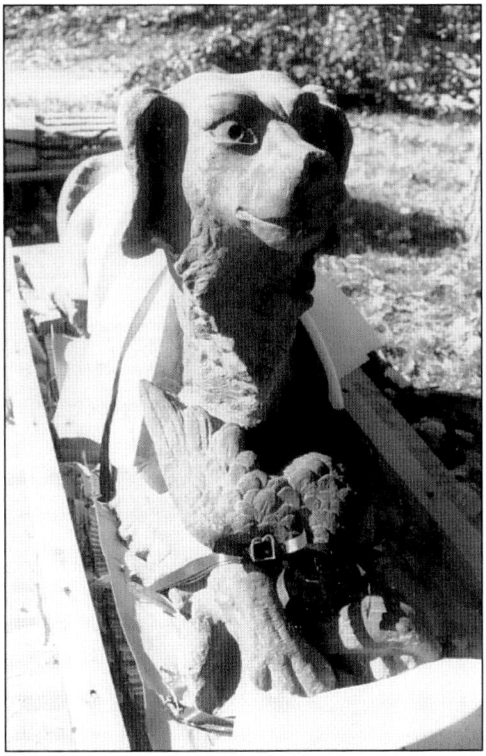

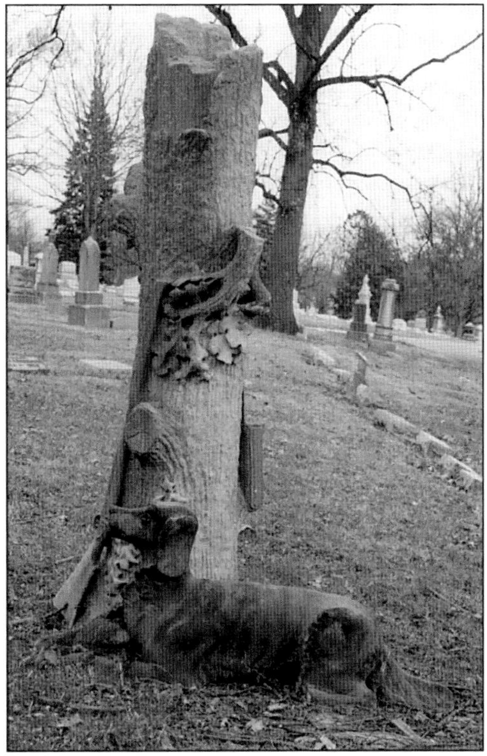

The Case of the Missing Dog. For more than 100 years, a hunting dog statue rested next to the grave of Charles Frese, 1834–1887, the owner of an Indianapolis hardware store. The dog sat at the side of the six-foot limestone monument carved in the shape of a tree stump, which symbolized that Frese's life was cut short. The only free standing animal in the cemetery weighed some 300 pounds! In 1995, Crown Hill officials noticed that the dog was missing. Fortunately, the cemetery had photos of the dog, so they were turned over to authorities for investigation. To make a long story short, the dog was discovered by police in Lake Placid, New York and shipped back to the Crown Hill. Thefts are rare at Crown Hill due to a full-time security force. (Photo courtesy of Marty Davis.)

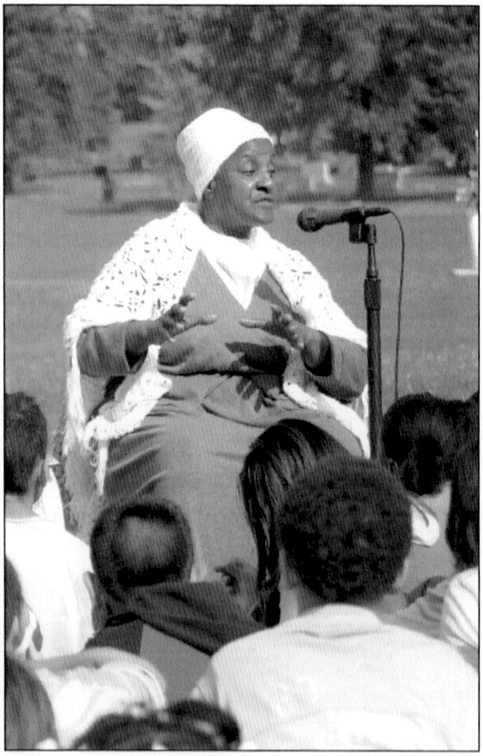

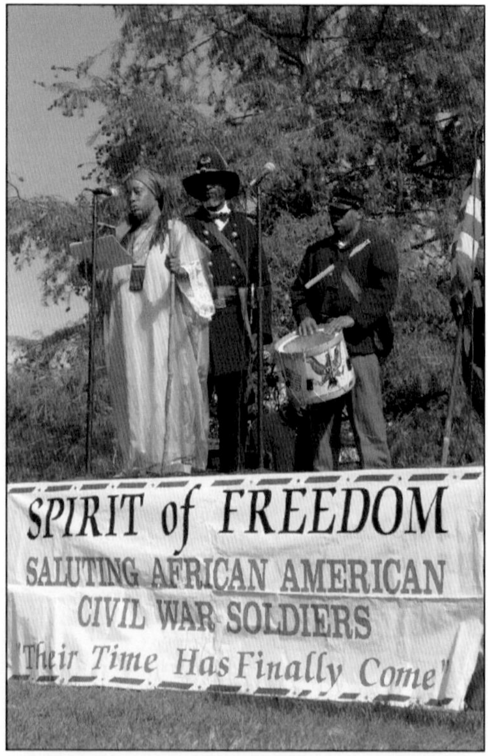

Re-enactors explain African-American history to Indianapolis Public Service students at Crown Hill in October each year at a ceremony called the Spirit of Freedom. The annual event, which is organized by the IPS Office of Multicultural Education and the Crown Hill Heritage Foundation, teaches fifth graders about the role African Americans played during the Civil War, including the Underground Railroad that passed through Indiana. Some of the descendants of those who actually fought in the war are also on hand each year. (Photos courtesy of Marty Davis.)

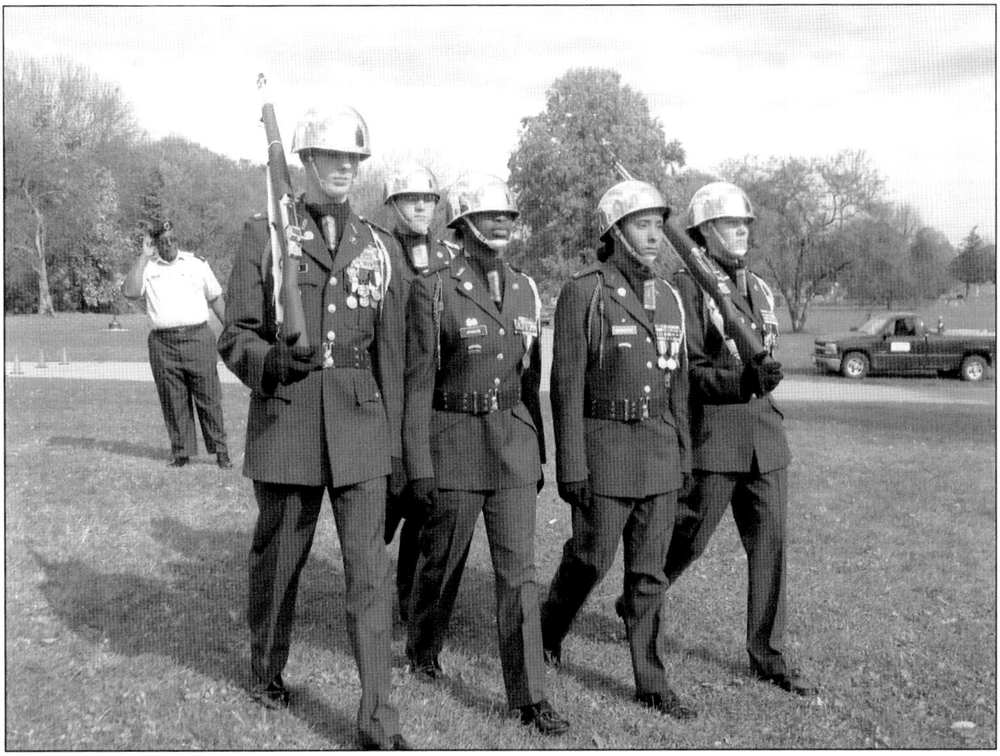

A color guard marches during the Spirit of Freedom celebration. (Photo courtesy of Marty Davis.)

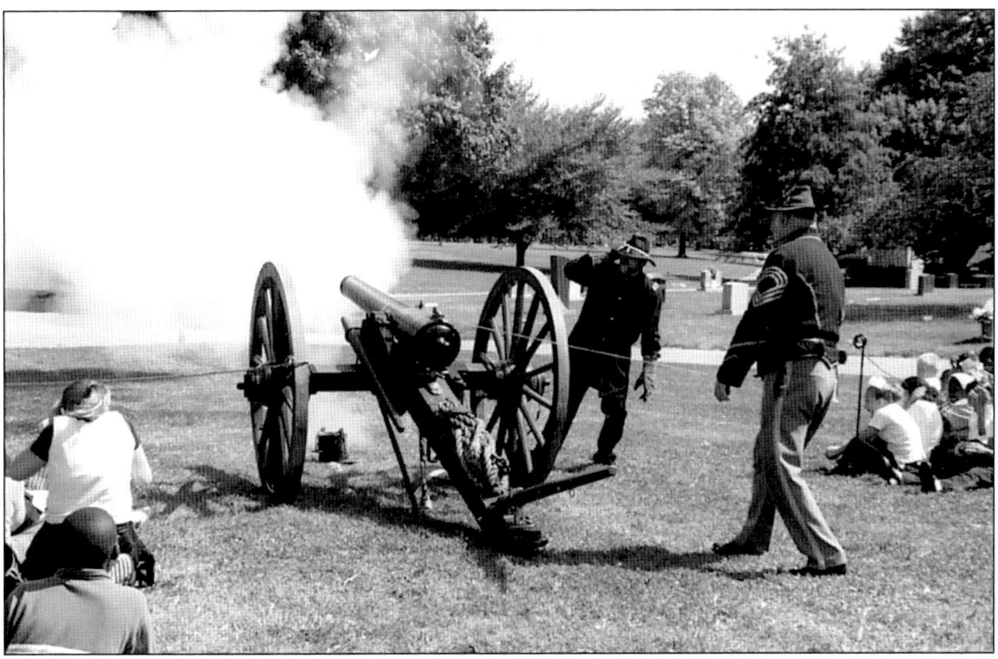

"Union soldiers" fire-off a cannon during the annual Spirit of Freedom Celebration, which honors the role of African Americans in the Civil War. Some 1,000 students from Indianapolis Public Schools come to the celebration. (Photo courtesy of Marty Davis.)

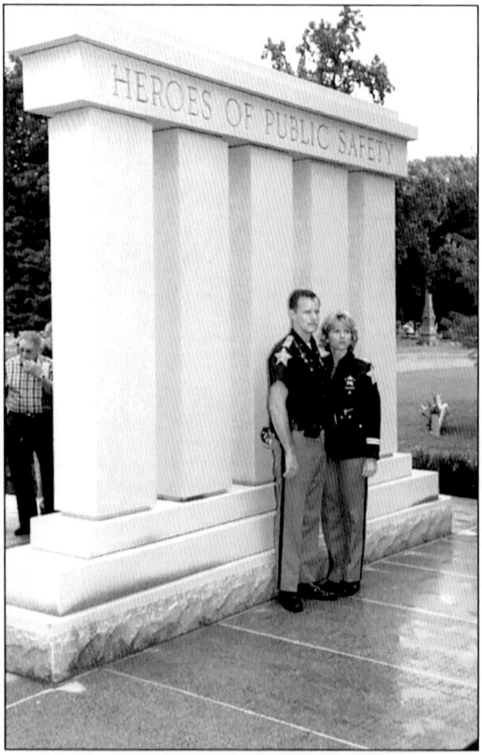

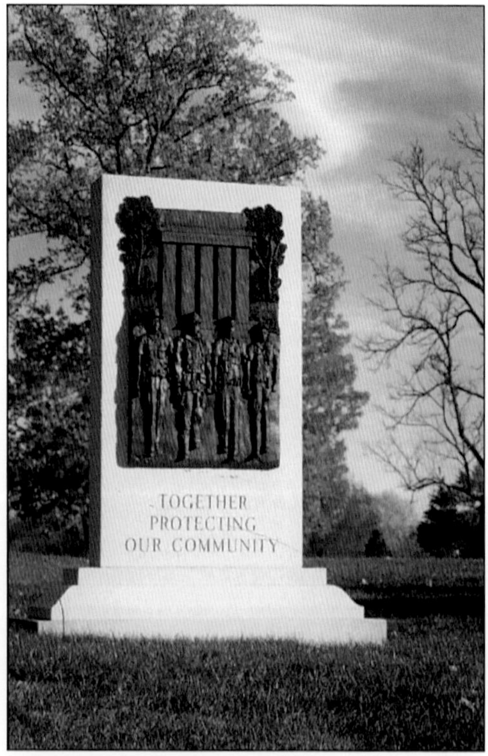

Sheriffs stand by the new Heroes of Public Safety memorial at Crown Hill after its dedication in 2001. The 14-foot monument of Romanesque design honors Indiana public safety professionals killed in the line of duty. (Photo by Banayote Photography.)

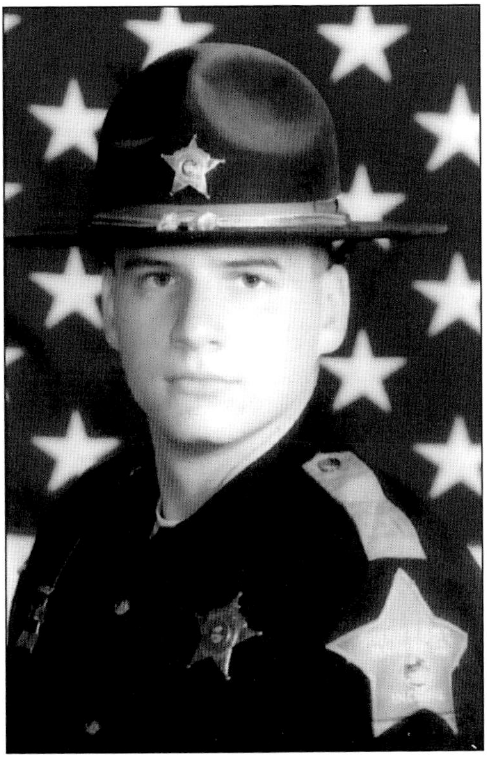

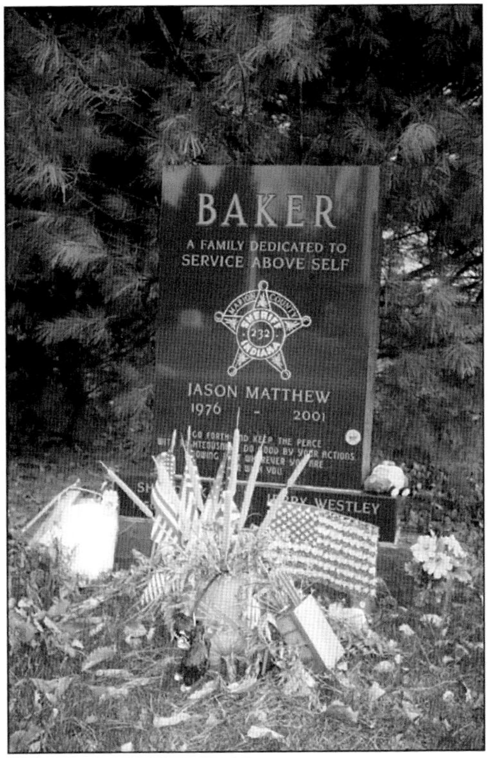

Jason Matthew Baker, 1976–2001, was a Marion County sheriff who died in the line of duty on September 17, 2001. Deputy Baker was en-route to a disturbance when his attention was diverted by a vehicle which he attempted to investigate. The driver of the vehicle refused to stop and Deputy Baker pursued. The chase reached the intersection of 32nd and Brouse Streets where suspects exited the vehicle and Deputy Baker was fatally wounded. By early the next day all suspects were located. Three were arrested and the fourth was found dead. On February 18, 2003, Michael Shannon pleaded guilty to killing Deputy Baker. In return for pleading guilty Shannon will not face the death penalty, but will be sentenced to life in prison without the possibility of parole. Because he confessed to the killing he will not be able to appeal. He also pleaded guilty to two counts of attempted murder and other charges. (Photo courtesy of Marion County Sheriff Dept.)

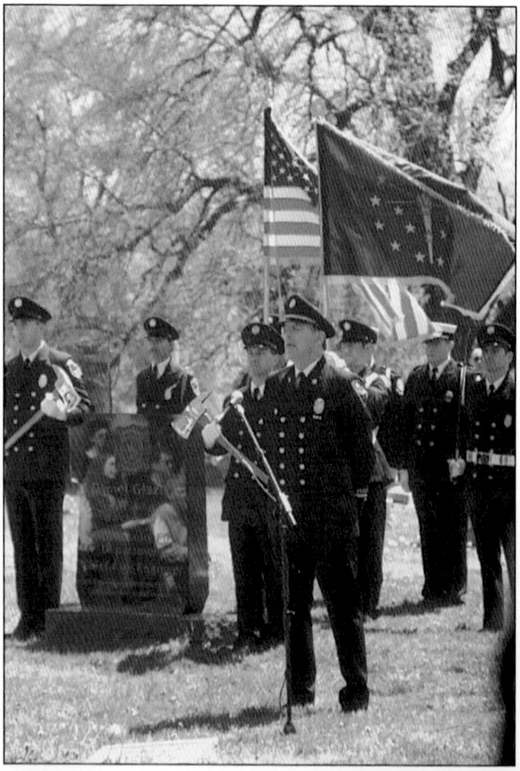

Firefighters dedicate the Daniel Glazier monument in a special ceremony. Glazier was the first Indiana firefighter to die in the line of duty. Glazer, 1835–1873, was killed and several firemen were injured when the wall of a building collapsed on top of him at the Woodburn Sarven Wheel Company. Two sons of Glazier went on to become firefighters as well. (Photo courtesy of Marty Davis.)

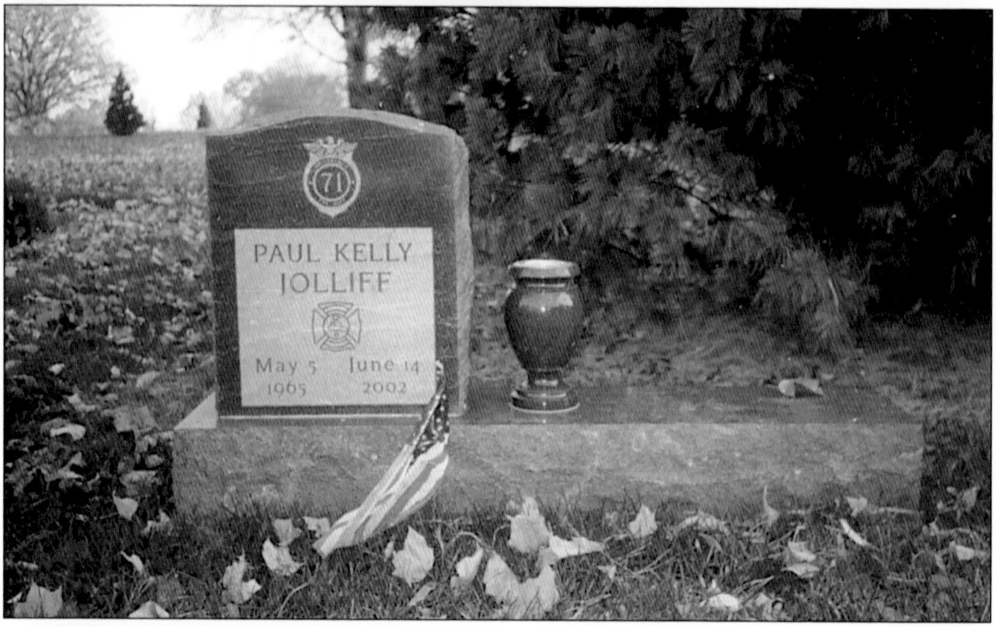

Paul Kelly Jolliff, 1965–2002, was an Indianapolis firefighter who drowned during diving rescue training on June 14, 2002. Private Jolliff was involved in an exercise to retrieve a concrete block when he lost contact with his partner, who went to the surface for help. Other divers searched for Jolliff and found him entangled in ropes. He died from gas expansion in the blood on ascent. He left behind a wife, Wendy, and two children.

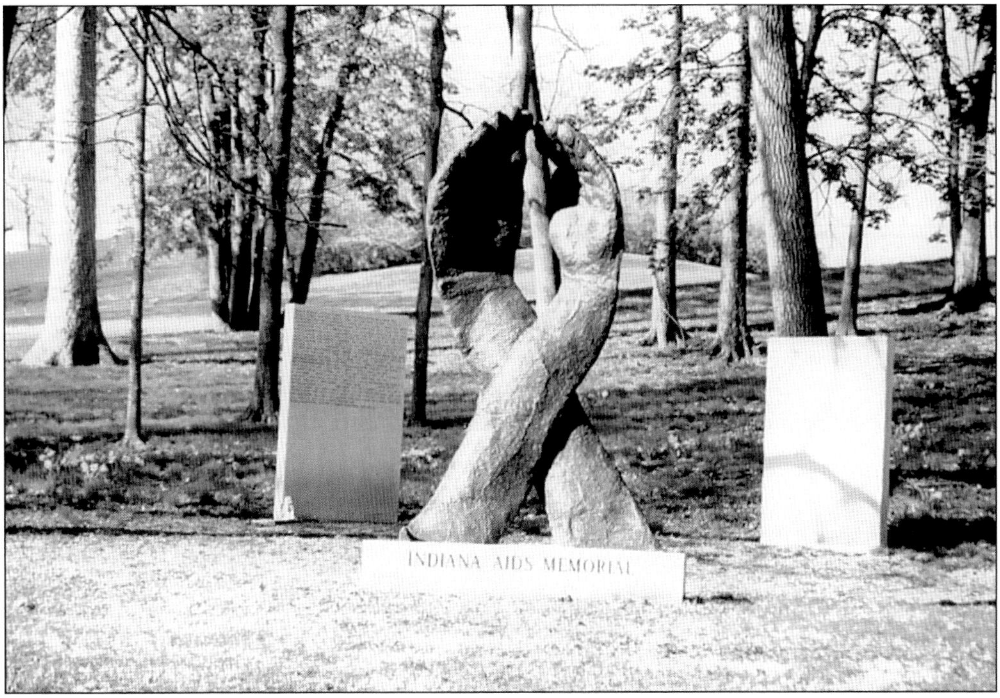

The Indiana AIDS Memorial was created in memory of people from Indiana who have died of the disease. (Photo courtesy of Marty Davis.)

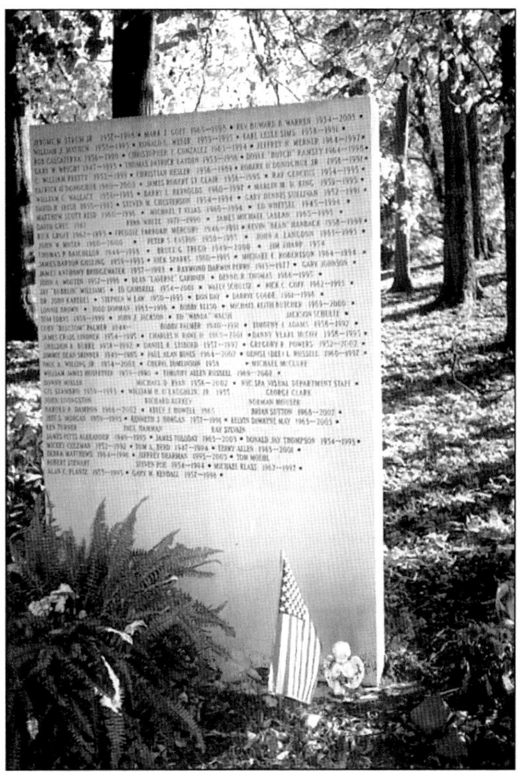

The names of those who have died of AIDS are inscribed on this monument.

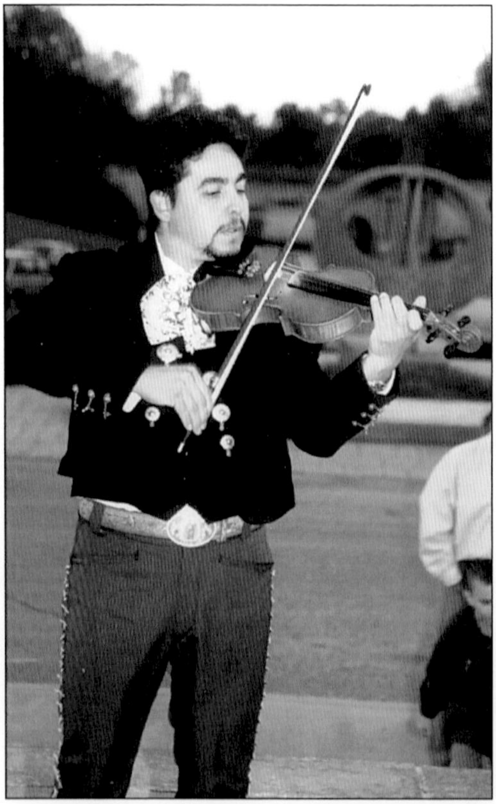

A violinist performs during the Day of the Dead service, which is held annually at Crown Hill. (Photo courtesy of Marty Davis.)

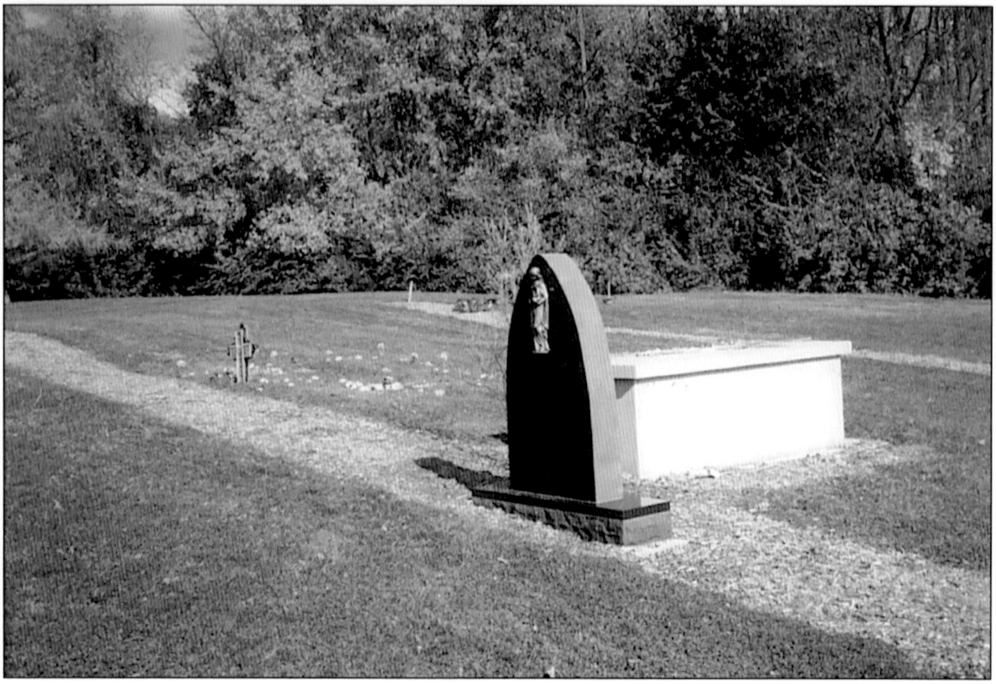

A new Hispanic Section has been created in the north section of Crown Hill Cemetery.

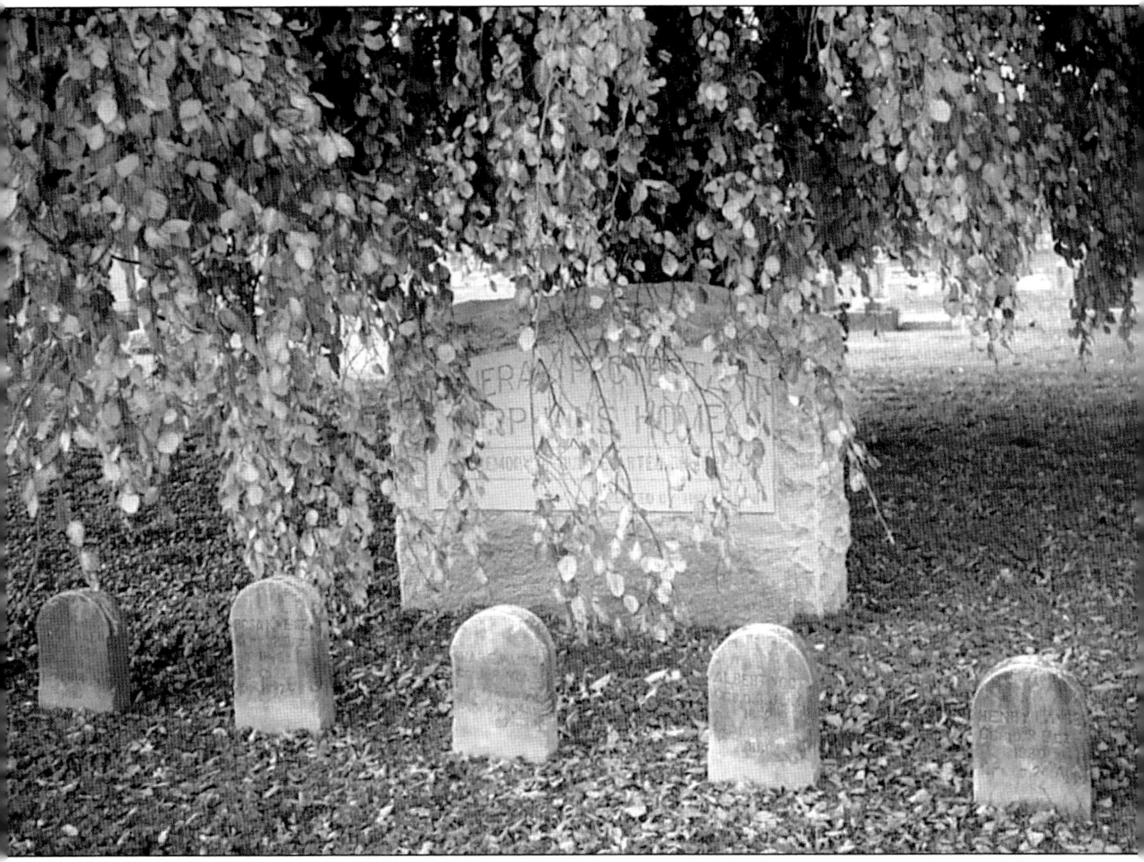

A large area in Section 31 is devoted to the General Protestant Orphans Home. In front of the monument are 23 headstones, but 181 burials actually occurred in this lot. Additional burials from this and other orphan facilities can be found in Section 37.

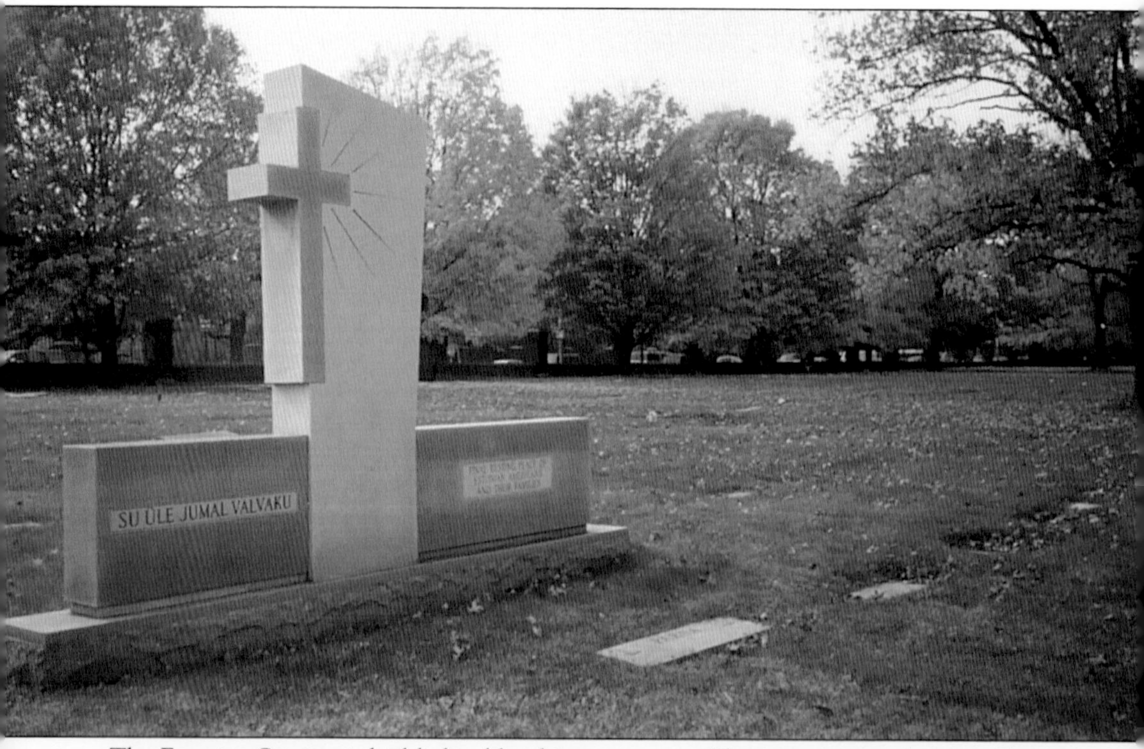

The Estonian Section is highlighted by this monument. The internments there are Estonians by heritage. Many migrated to the United States in 1918 following the Russian overthrow of Estonia in 1918. The monument is inscribed in English as well as the Estonian language. The first burial was made there in 1962. Names on the graves include Ehaste, Haas, Koots, Nurreots, Pihlak, Rikma, Truumaa, and Voosaar.

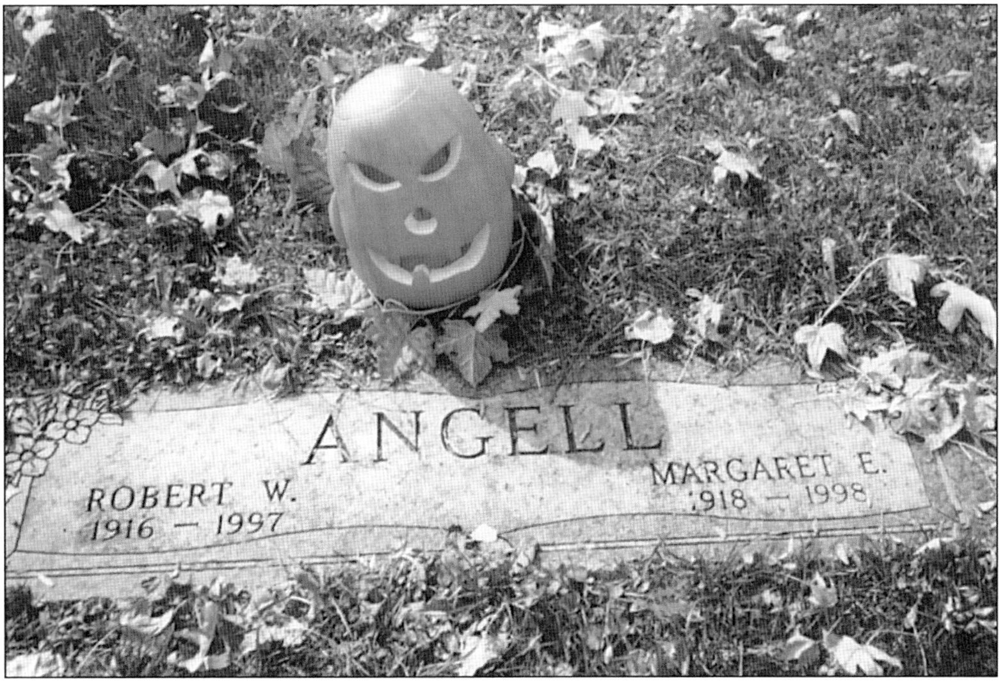

The Greek Section is located on the north side of the cemetery in Section 236. Church approval is required before burials can be made here by the Greek community. Interred in this section are members of the Holy Trinity Orthodox Church of Indianapolis. Graves in this area date from 1938. Buried there are members from many Greek families, such as Angell, Bisbecos, Cherpas, Diamantidis, Gianakos, Nikou, Speropoulos, Stratigakos, and Zoumis.

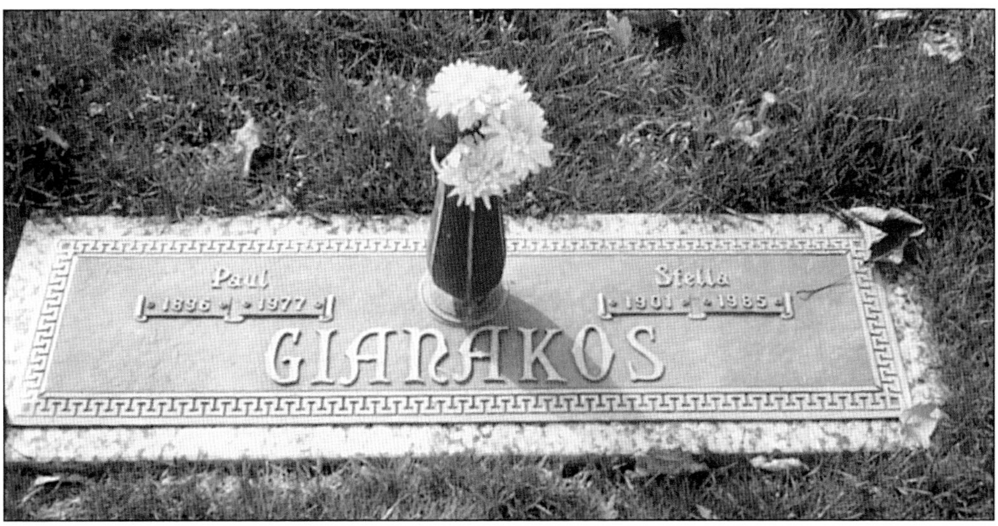

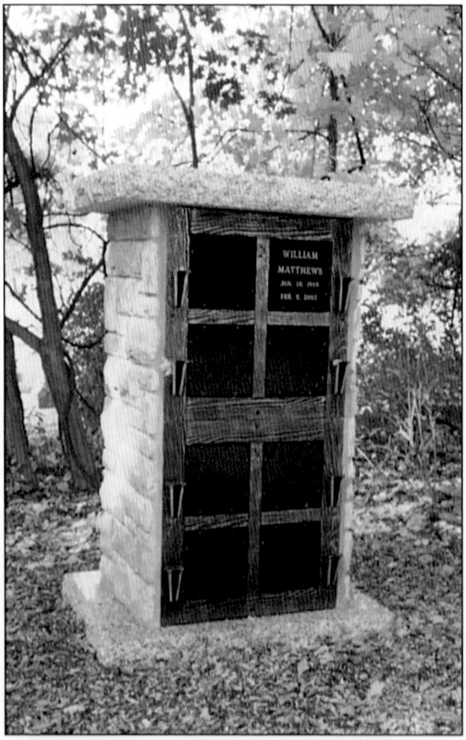

Crown Hill has created a Cremation Memorial Garden, which is located adjacent to Section A, near 38th Street. A new crematory replaced an older one in 1990 and is located in the lower level of the Community Mausoleum.

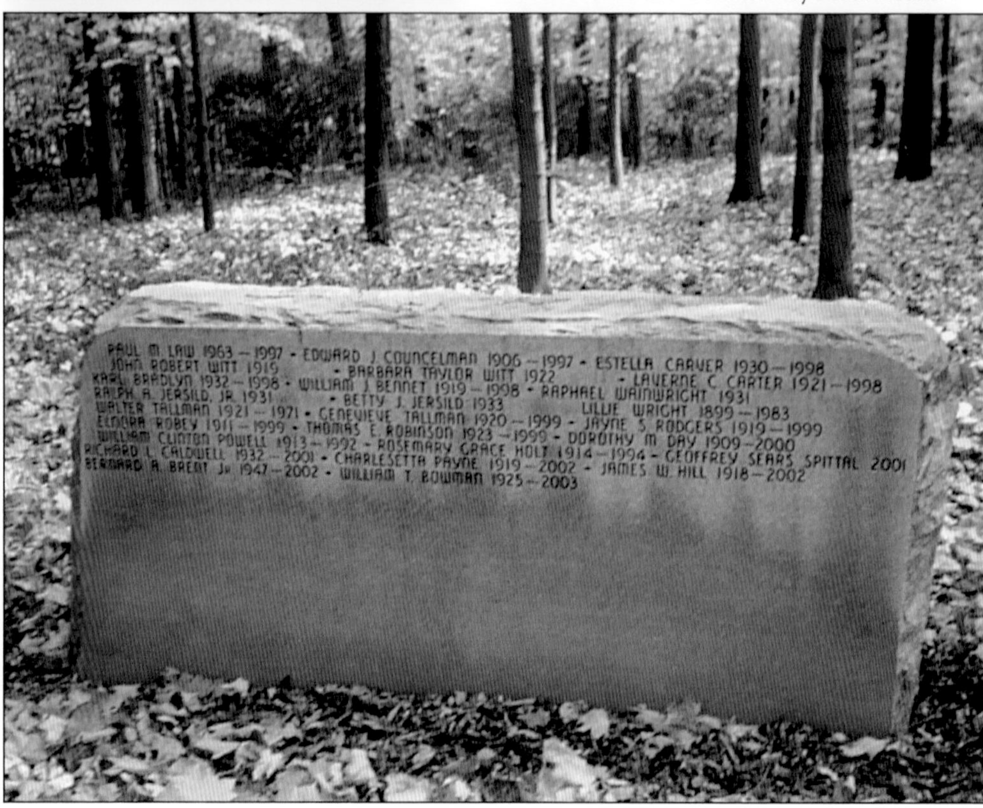

Two

POLITICAL FIGURES

Many political figures are buried at Crown Hill, including one United States president, three vice presidents, ten Indiana governors, one Kentucky governor, fourteen United States senators, fourteen Indianapolis mayors, congressmen, cabinet members, and other political offices.

Benjamin Harrison was the 23rd U.S. President and lived in Indianapolis before his death. He chose Crown Hill for his resting place along with his wife, Caroline, who died before him. The three vice presidents buried there are Charles Warren Fairbanks, Thomas A. Hendricks, and Thomas Riley Marshall.

Ten Indiana governors chose Crown Hill for their remains: Ira J. Chase, Winfield T. Durbin, Abram A. Hammond, Hendricks, Marshall, Oliver P. Morton, Noah Noble, Albert G. Porter, David Wallace, and James Whitcomb.

Fourteen U.S. senators are buried there, including: Albert Beveridge, Homer E. Capehart, John Worth Kern Sr., Harry S. New, Oliver H. Smith, Thomas Taggart, and David Turpie. Several U.S. congressmen are interned at Crown Hill, including: Ebenezer Dumont, William H. English, Hendricks, George W. Julian, Albert G. Porter, Caleb B. Smith, Oliver H. Smith, and Wallace.

Many of the mayors of Indianapolis are buried at Crown Hill, including: John Worth Kern Jr., Samuel D. Maxwell, James S. McCready, Thomas Taggart, and Henry F. West. Of course many other politicians are buried at Crown Hill.

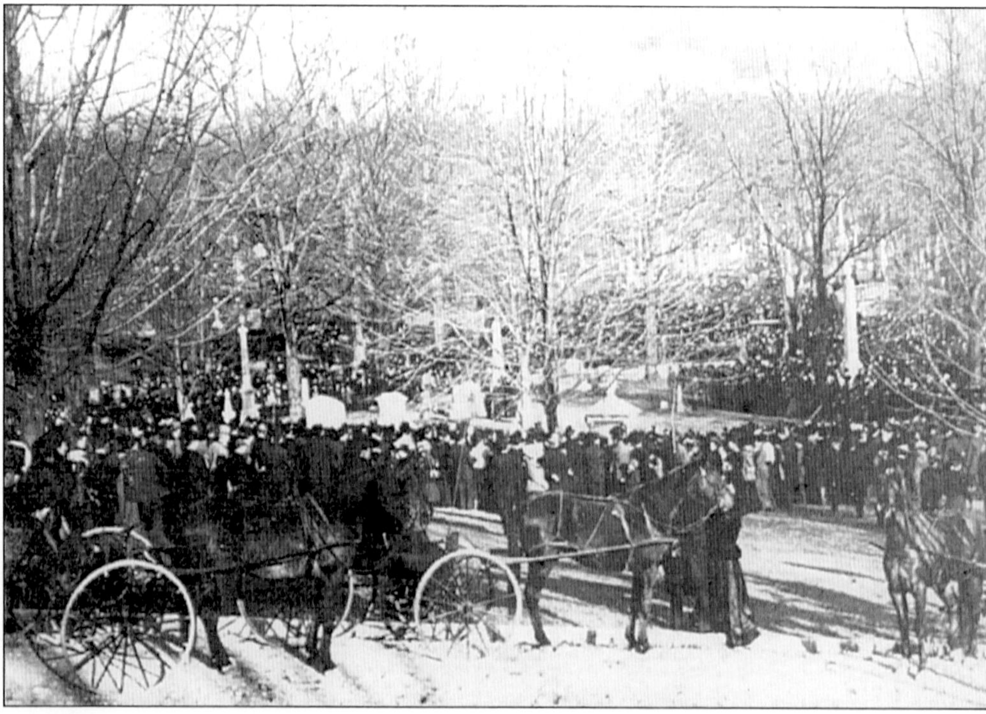

The funeral of President Benjamin Harrison was one of the largest in the history of Crown Hill Cemetery as seen by this photo from 1902. His grave is located in Section 13, Lot 57. (Photo courtesy of Crown Hill Cemetery.)

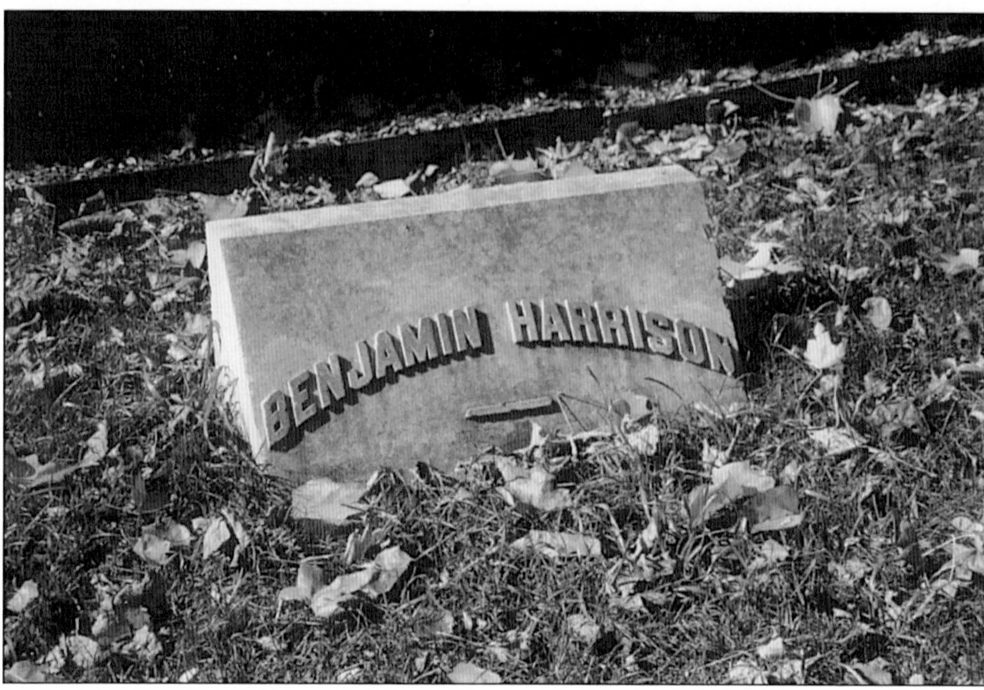

Benjamin Harrison, 1833–1901, was president of the United States, 1889–1893. He served the Union Army as a colonel in the Civil War for 17th Indiana Volunteers then became a brevetted Brigadier General. He served in the U.S. Senate for a term before becoming president. The country experienced a period of prosperity during his term as president, but he was defeated by Grover Cleveland. His father was William Henry Harrison, the ninth president of the U.S. He returned to his home in Indianapolis, which is now a museum. Each year, his grave is honored with a military ceremony, below. (Photo courtesy of Marty Davis.)

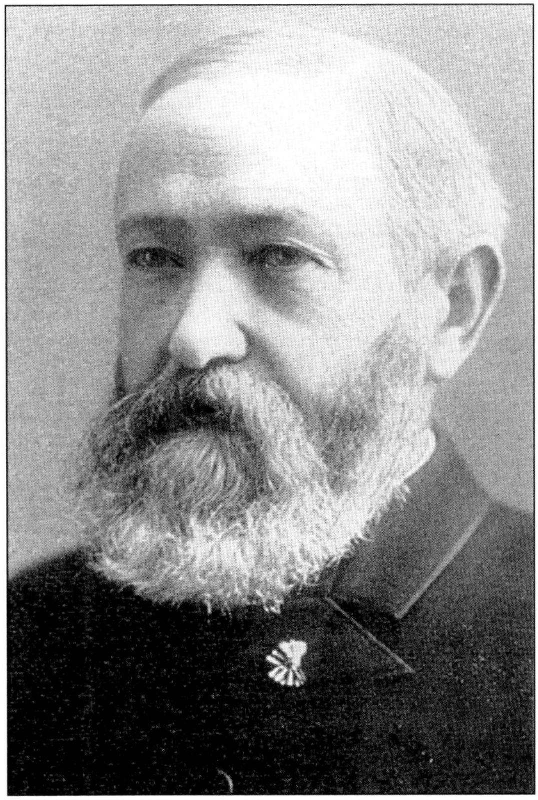

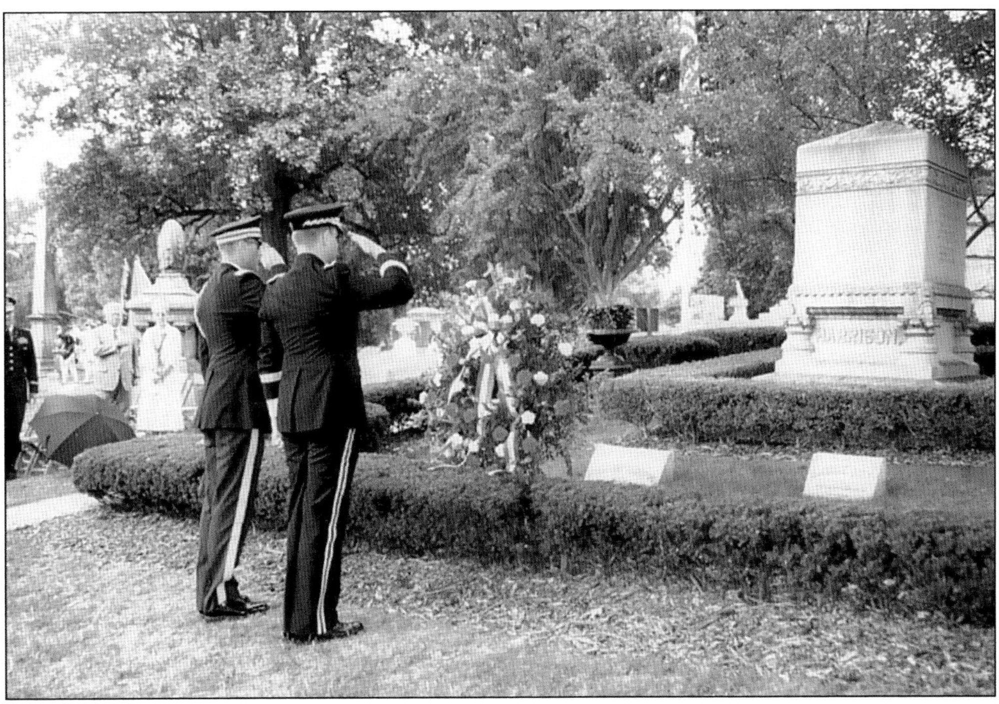

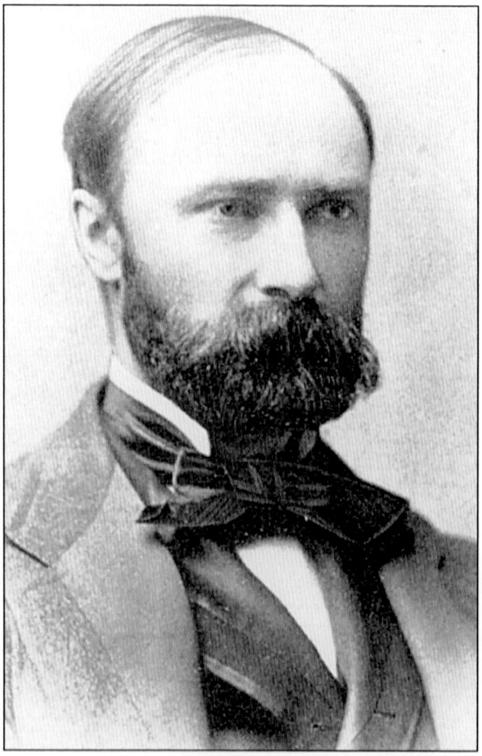

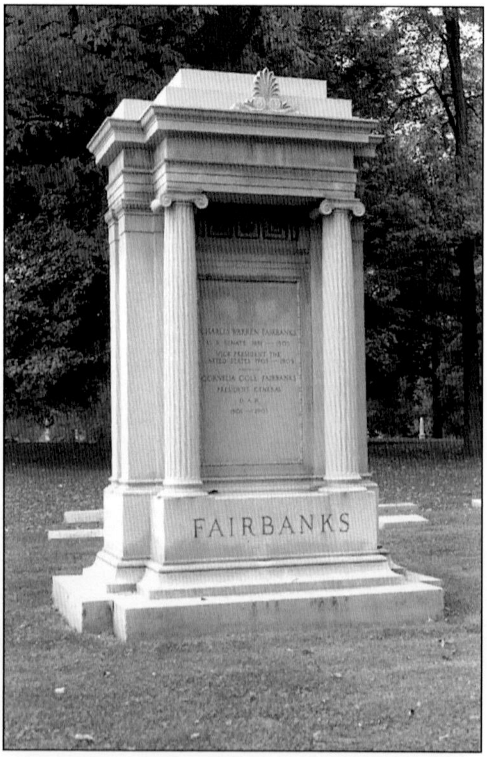

Charles Warren Fairbanks, 1852–1918, served as vice president under Theodore Roosevelt, 1905–1909. Fairbanks, Alaska was named for the lawyer. Born in Ohio, he moved to Indianapolis and became an expert in railroad finance and an astute investor in railroad securities. He was elected to the Senate in 1897 as a Republican. He headed the American delegation to the Joint High Commission that tried to settle all outstanding difficulties with Canada in 1898. The large upright monument with fluted columns is located the southwest part of Section 24.

Albert Gallatin Porter, 1824–1896, was governor of Indiana from 1881–1885 after serving as a controller of the U.S. Treasury. Born in Lawrenceburg, Indiana, he also served in Congress, 1858–1861. He was named as U.S. minister to Italy by President Benjamin Harrison and helped settle a dispute with Italy over outrages of the Mafia in New Orleans. His remains are located in Section 14, Lot 92.

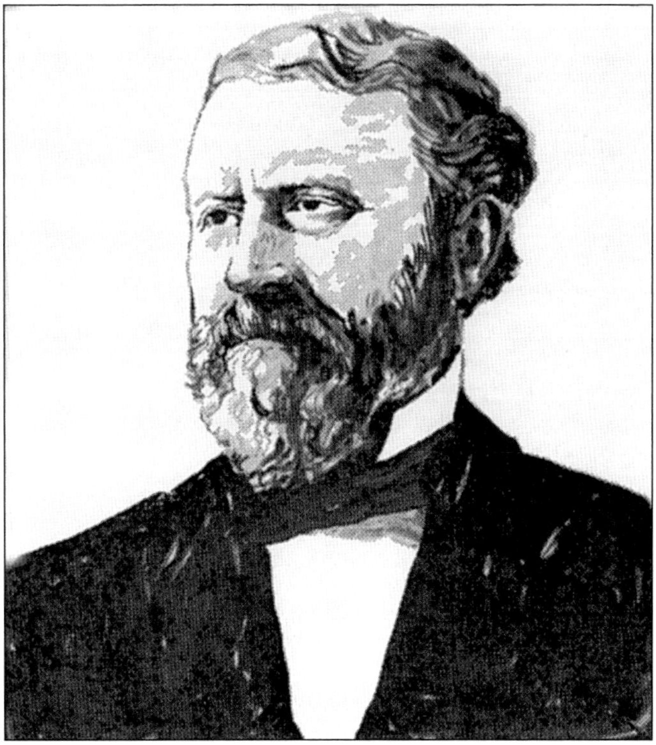

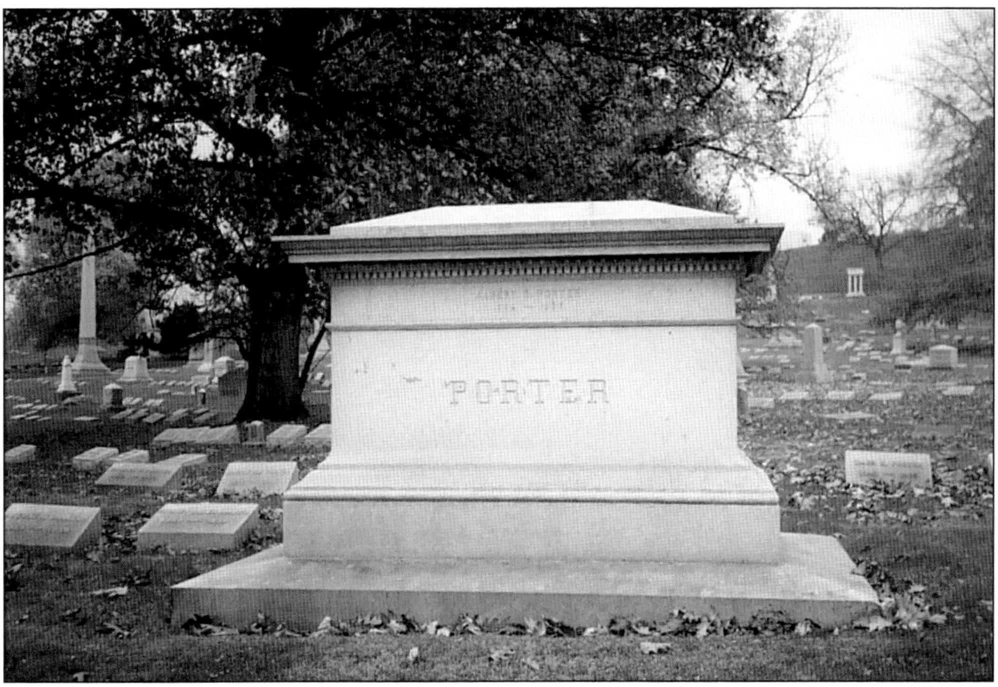

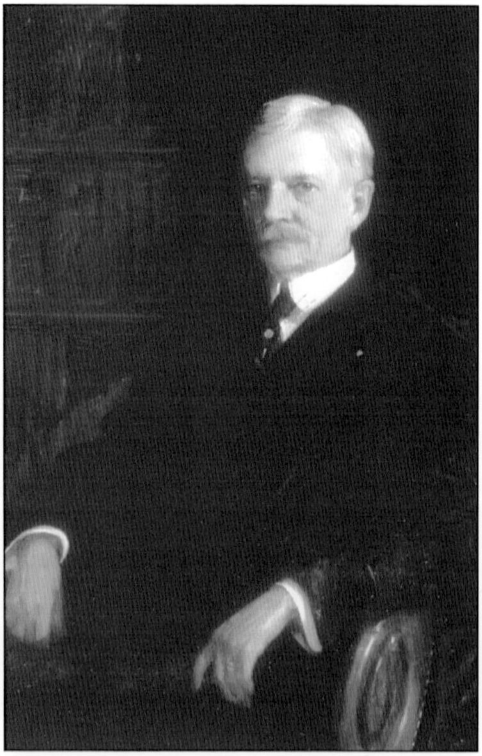 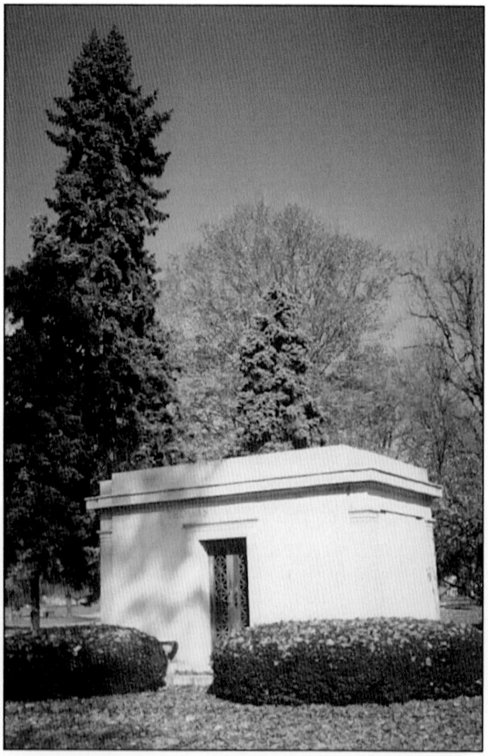

Thomas Riley Marshall, 1854–1925, was elected as vice president of the U.S. while serving as governor of Indiana, 1909–1913. He served as vice president under Woodrow Wilson for eight years. Born in North Manchester, he practiced law in Columbia City for 30 years. He is famous for saying, "What this country needs is a good five-cent cigar!" His remains are located in Section 72, Lot 1. (Photo of Marshall courtesy of Governors' Portraits Collection, Indiana Historical Bureau, State of Indiana.)

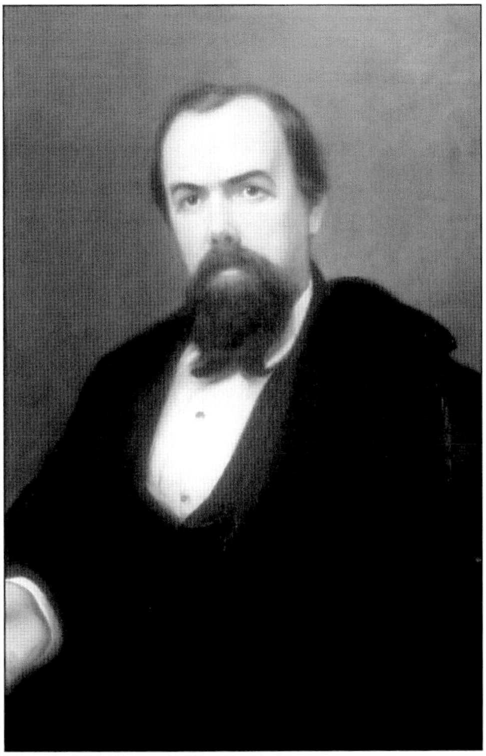

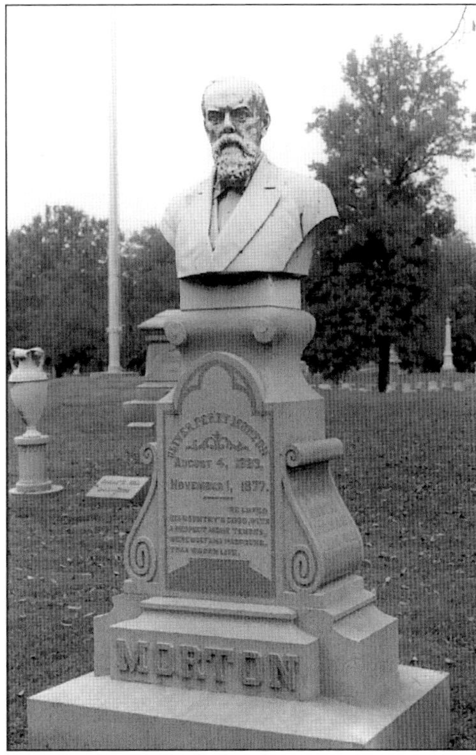

Oliver Perry Morton, 1823–1877, was governor of Indiana, 1861–1867, during the Civil War. He was then elected to two terms in the U.S. Senate, but he died before completing his second term. Born in Wayne County, he became a lawyer before seeking political office. He is buried close to the soldiers who volunteered at his call for troops in 1861. They lie in the national military cemetery within Crown Hill. Morton was a prominent candidate for the presidential nomination by the Republican Party before the Cincinnati Convention. The monument with Morton's bust on top is located in Section 10 near the flagpole. (Photo of Morton courtesy of Governors' Portraits Collection, Indiana Historical Bureau, State of Indiana.)

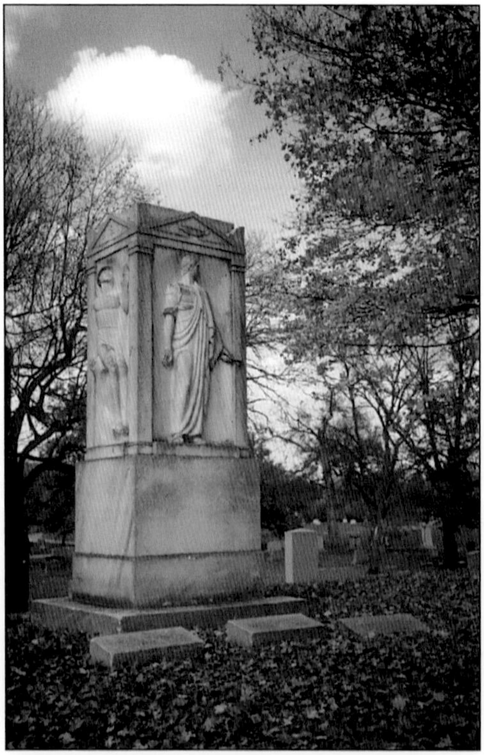
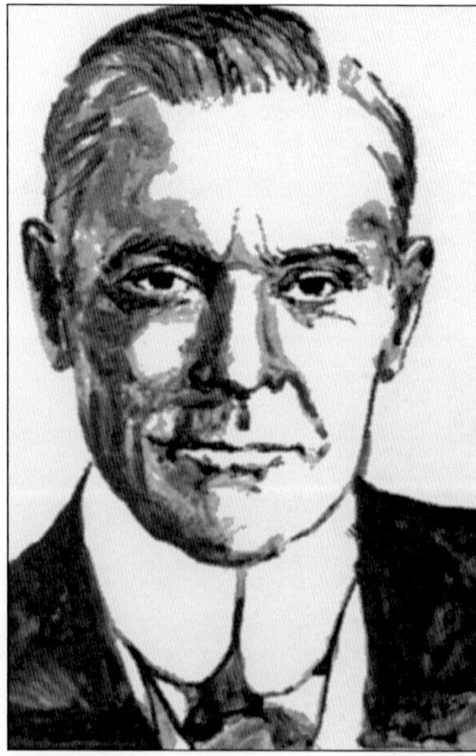

Albert Jeremiah Beveridge, 1862–1927, was an author, orator, and statesman. He was a U.S. senator from Indiana, 1899–1911. The senator opposed America getting out of the Philippines following the Spanish American War. He contended that the U.S. should remain to help that country develop a self-governing capability. He wrote two monumental works: *The Life of John Marshall* and *Abraham Lincoln*. His large white monument with a Greek figure carved on each side is located in Section 45, Lot 22.

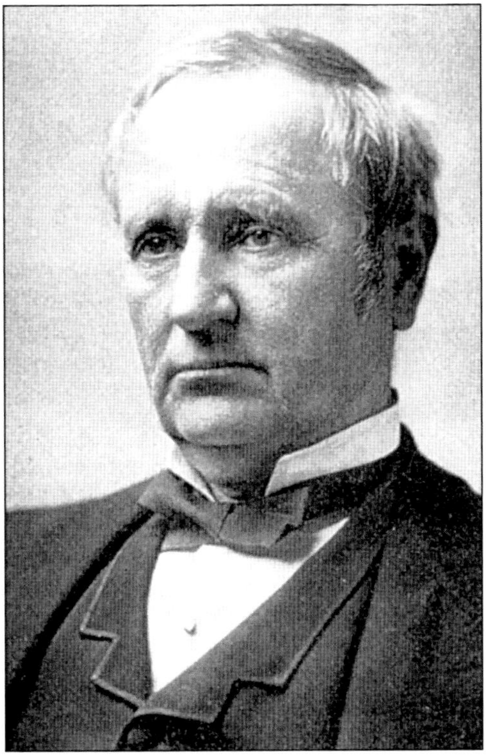

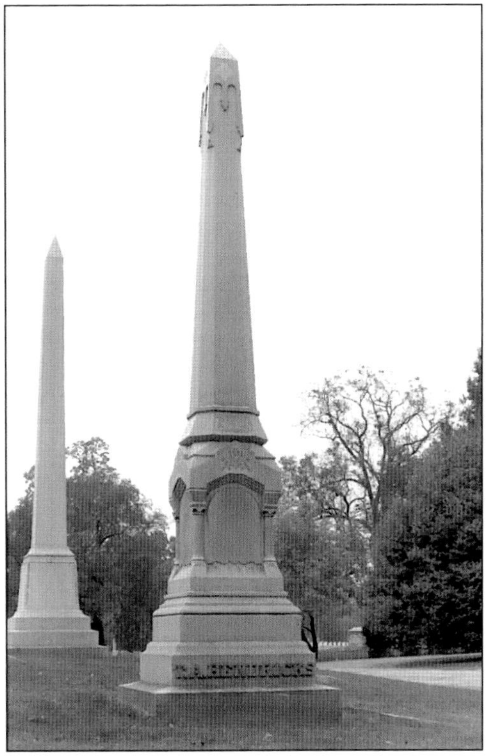

Thomas A. Hendricks, 1819–1885, was vice president under Grover Cleveland, but he died after eight months in office. Born near Zanesville, Ohio, he served as a state legislator, congressman, senator, and governor of Indiana, 1872–1876. The lawyer was elected to the State Legislature in 1848. While serving as senator during the Civil War, he favored the earnest prosecution of the war and opposed conscription. His brother, William, also served as a congressman, governor, and senator. The Hendricks' monument is located across from the Gothic Chapel in Section 29.

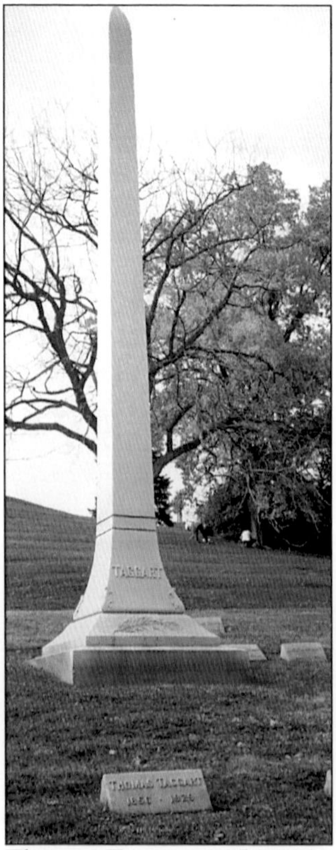

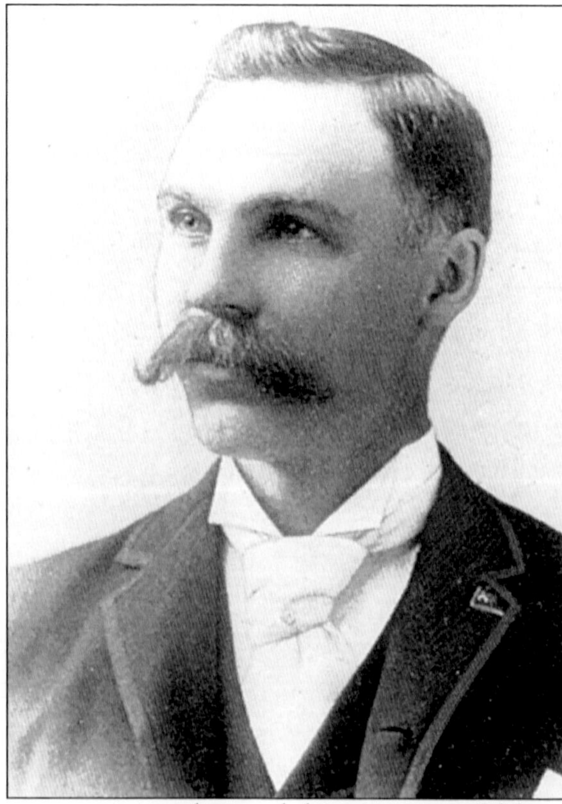

Thomas Taggart, 1856–1929, was a mayor, senator, and one of the most successful hotel operators in the world. He was elected three straight times for mayor of Indianapolis (1895–1901) and during his administration, the city made many public improvements, including the purchase of 900 acres along the White River, which later was turned into parks. He made French Lick Springs Hotel one of the world's finest spas. He was also appointed to the U.S. Senate in 1916 when Senator Shively died in office. Then he was chairman of the board for Fletcher American National Bank and a director for the Indianapolis Light, Heat and Power Company. He is buried in Section 30, Lot 3.

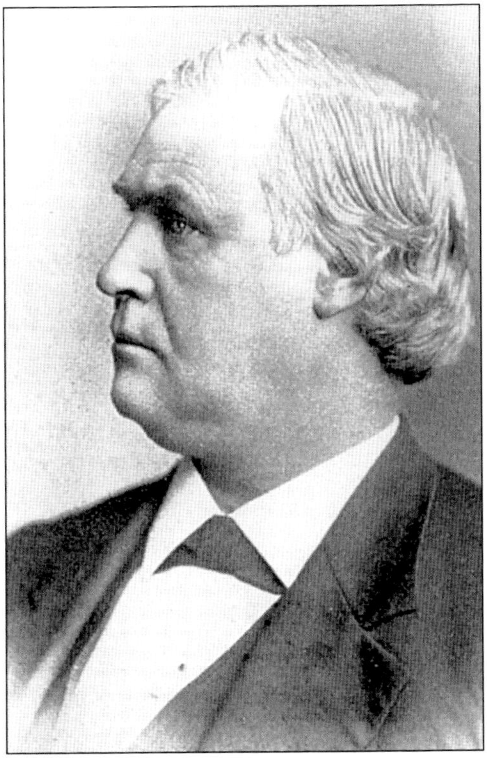

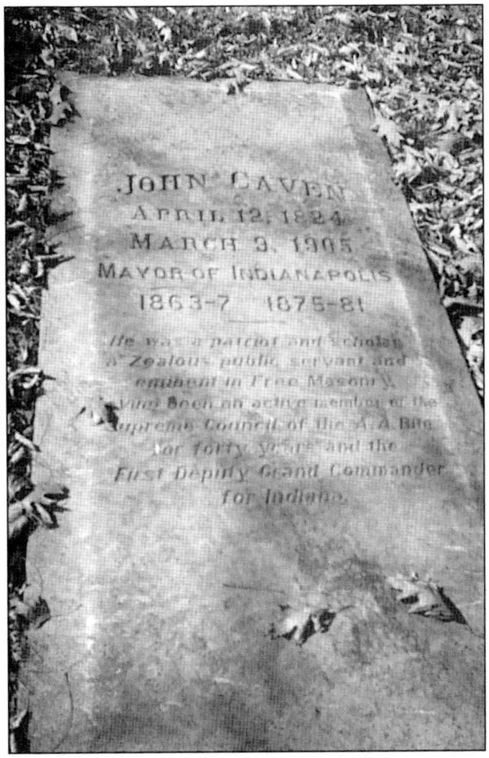

John Caven, 1824–1905, was a state senator and five-time mayor of Indianapolis. He first became the mayor in 1863 during the Civil War. Then he served as a state senator before being elected as mayor again in 1875. He advocated the establishment of schools for colored children and secured the Belt Railroad and stock yards in Indianapolis, which brought hundreds of jobs to the city during a depression. After his political career, he became president of Indianapolis Brush Electric Light and Power Company. He is buried in Section 13, Lot 46.

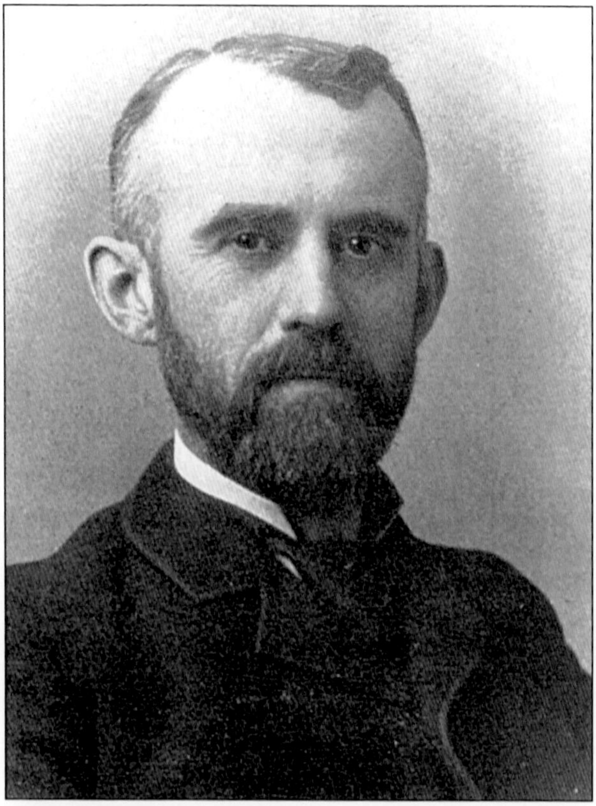

Thomas Lennox Sullivan, 1846–1936, was mayor of Indianapolis, 1890–1893. He was the first mayor who was born in the city. He became an attorney and was appointed as a circuit judge for Marion and Hendricks Counties. The Democratic mayor made vast improvements to the streets in the city during his administration. Later, he became president of the Indianapolis Gas and Coke Company. He is buried in Section 12, Lot 9.

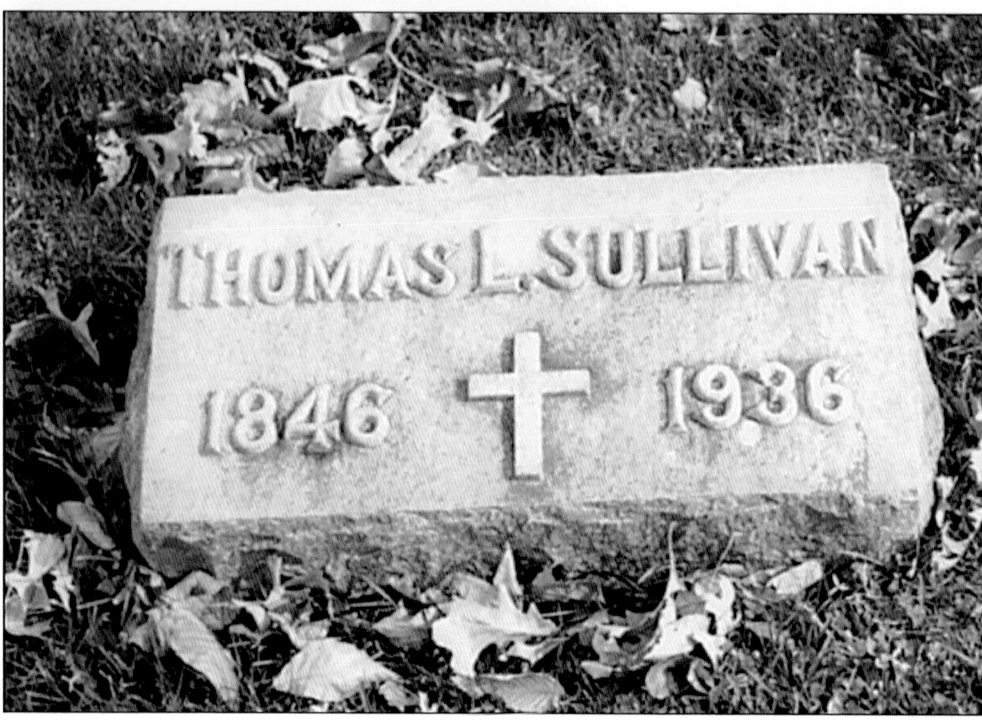

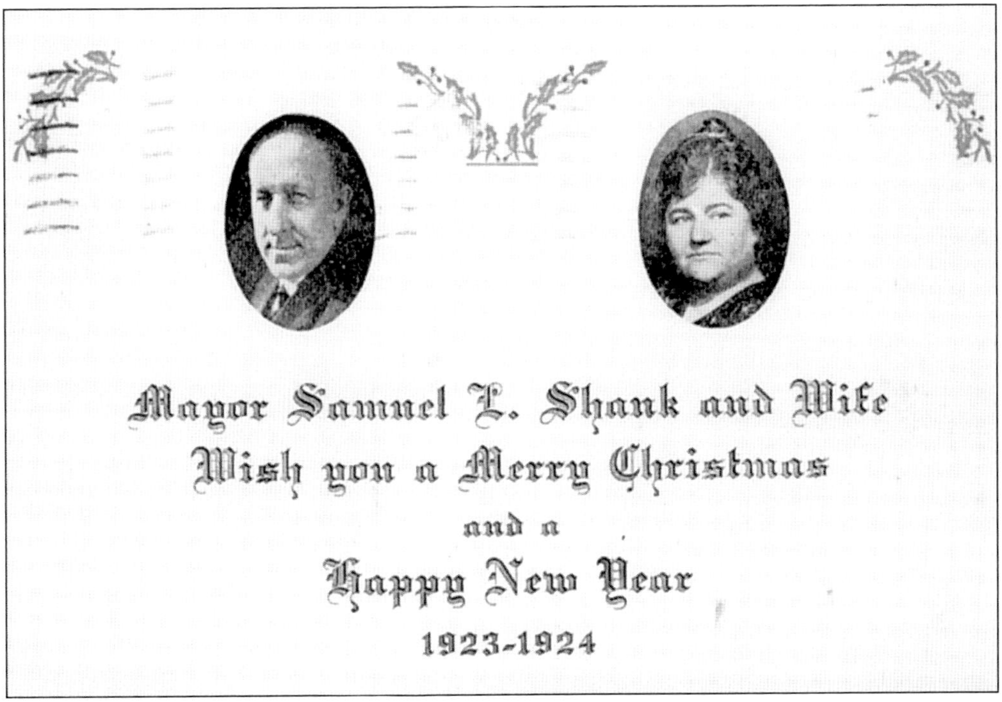

Samuel L. Shank, 1872–1927, served as the Indianapolis mayor twice. The first time was from 1910–1913. He earned the nickname "potato mayor" after auctioning carloads of farmers' vegetables to consumers in his fight over unfair pricing by wholesalers. Then the city went through its worst flood in 1913. That was followed by a violent streetcar strike for eight days, which resulted in the calling up of the National Guard by the Indiana governor. Shank resigned on November 28, 1913, a month before his term ran out in the midst of threatened impeachment proceedings. Then he was mayor 1922–1925. He tried a run at governor, but lost the Republican nomination in 1924. Each Christmas he would send out postcards like this one. He is buried in Section 60, Lot 1125.

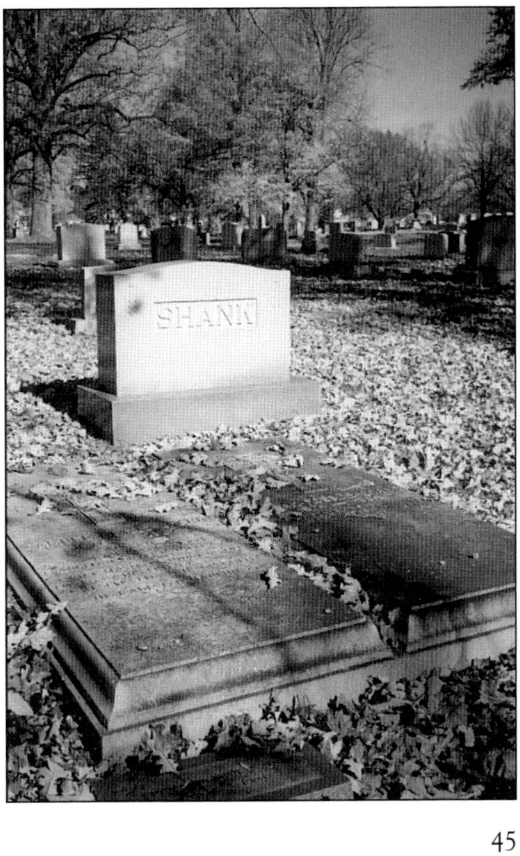

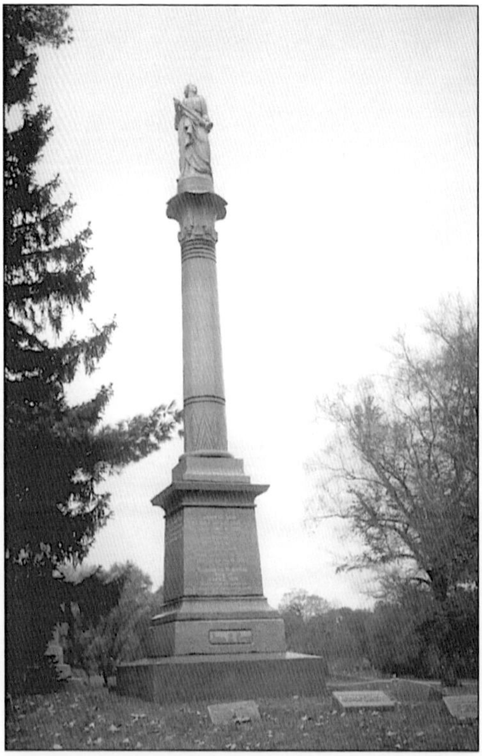 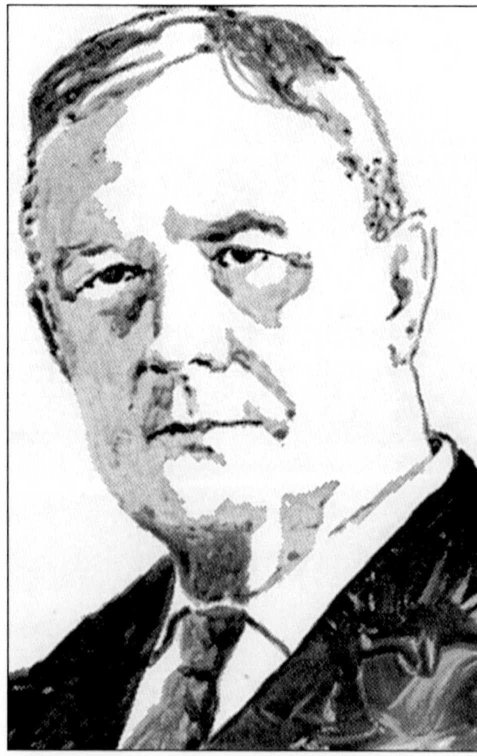

Harry Stewart New, 1858–1937, served as postmaster general under Presidents Harding and Coolidge. Born in Indianapolis, he studied at Butler College and began his career as a journalist. He was elected to the U.S. Senate in 1916. He built the United States' airmail service in 1923 when a flight from New York to San Francisco took 28 hours. His remains are located in an unmarked grave in Section 8, Lot 4.

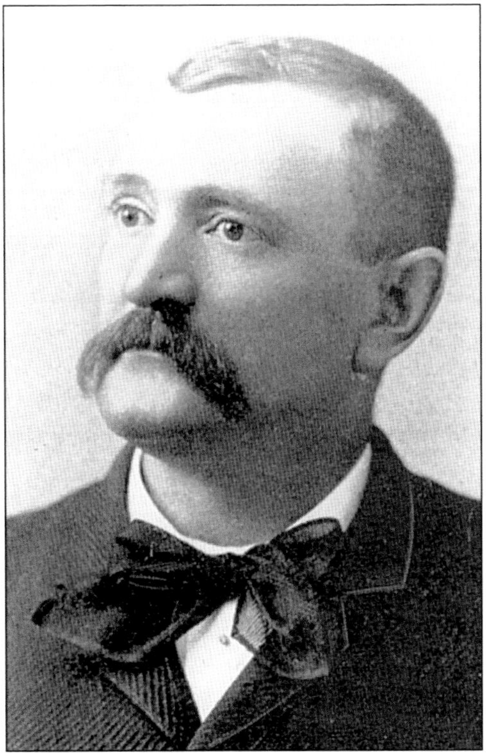

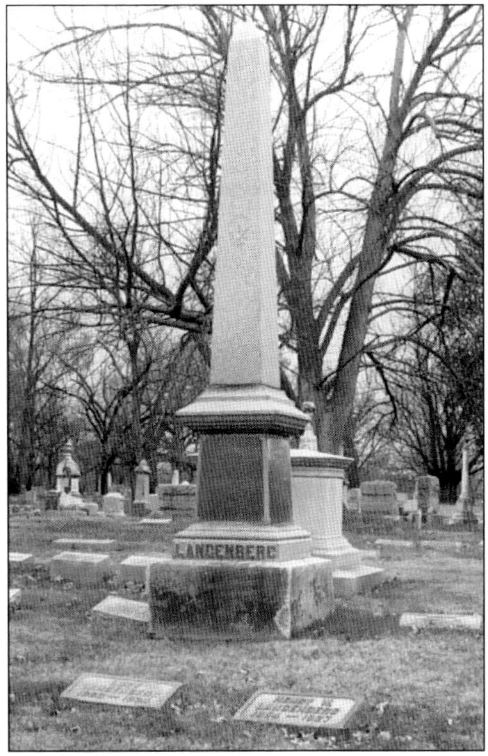

Henry W. Langenberg, 1854–1927, was sheriff of Marion County in the 1890s. Born in Indianapolis, he was one of the youngest sheriffs that ever filled the position. He is buried in Section 27, Lot 174.

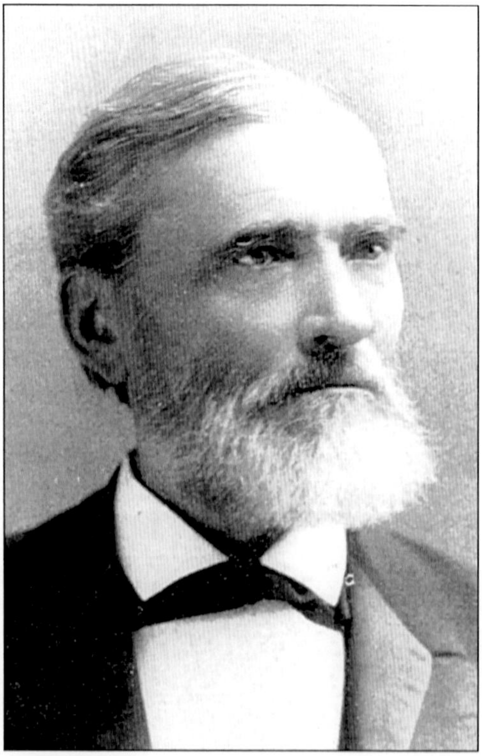

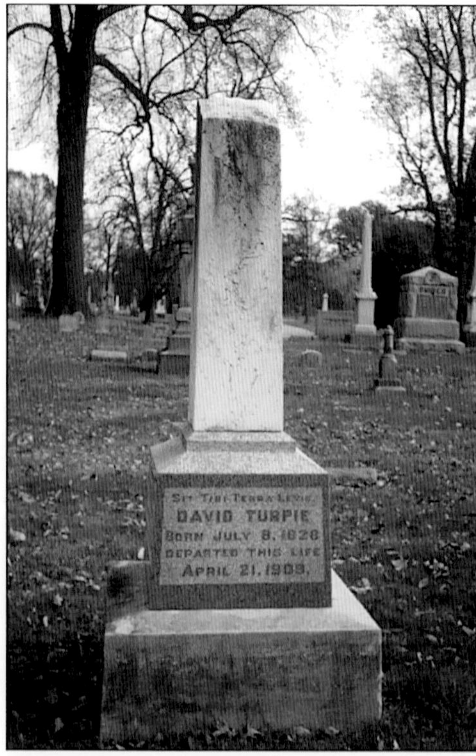

David Turpie, 1828–1909, was twice elected as a U.S. senator from Indiana. Born in Ohio, he became an attorney and moved to Indianapolis, where he became a leading member of the Marion County bar. He was a judge and member of the Indiana House of Representatives before becoming a senator. After retiring, he wrote *In My Own Times*. He is buried in Section 25, Lot 164.

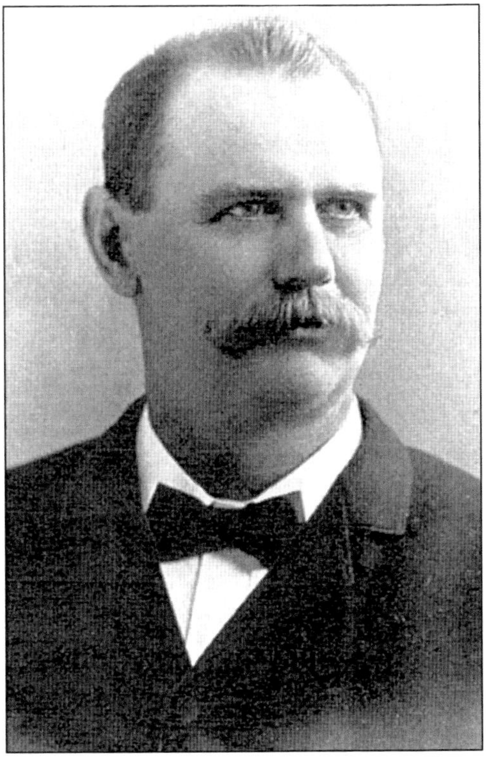

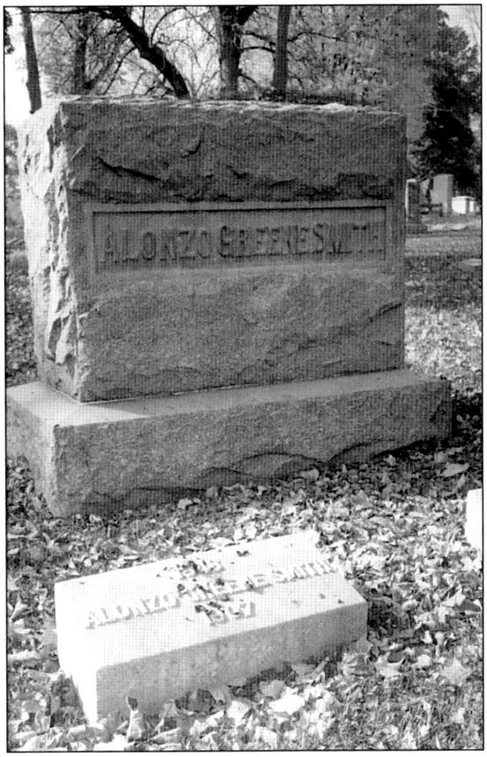

Alonzo Green Smith, 1800–1907, rose to become attorney general of Indiana during his political career. The lawyer was elected to the Indiana State Senate and became the presiding officer in 1887. His grave is located in Section 42, Lot 100.

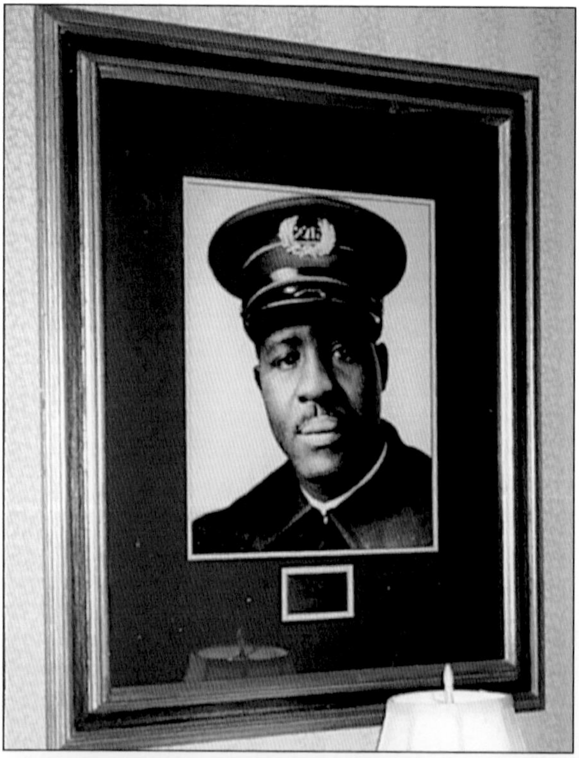

William Whitfield, 1885–1922, was the first black Indianapolis police officer to die in the line of duty. His portrait hangs in the Crown Hill Funeral Home. His unmarked grave is located in Section F, Lot 5906.

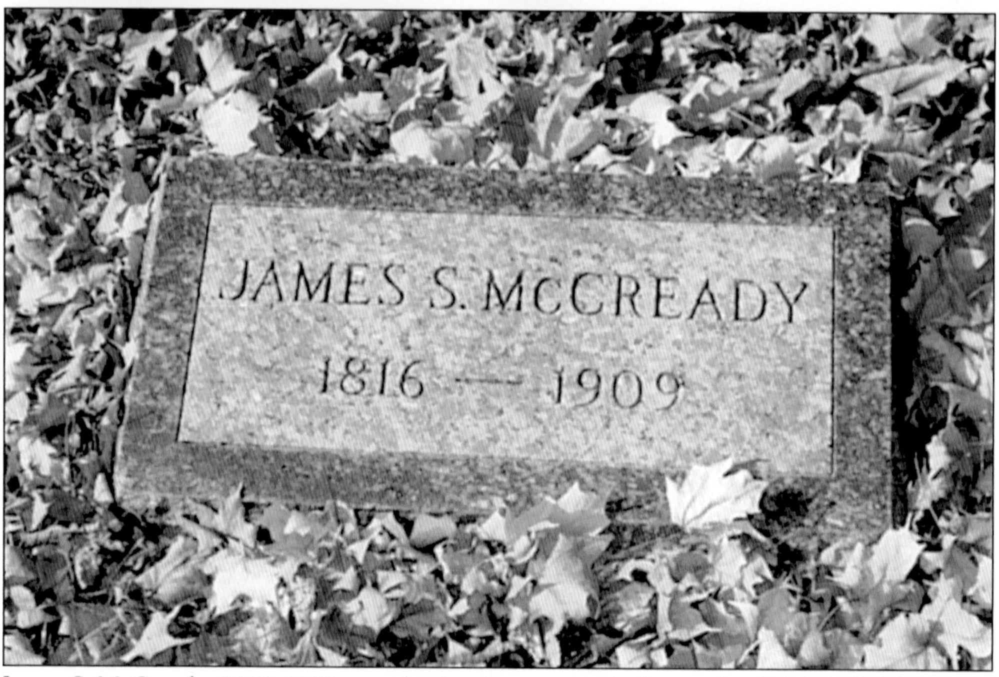

James S. McCready, 1816–1909, was the fourth mayor of Indianapolis, 1854–1856. The tailor became a justice of the peace before defeating incumbent Caleb Scudder for mayor. He was the first Democrat to become mayor. After losing in 1859, became a bookkeeper for Indiana National Bank. He is buried in Section 35.

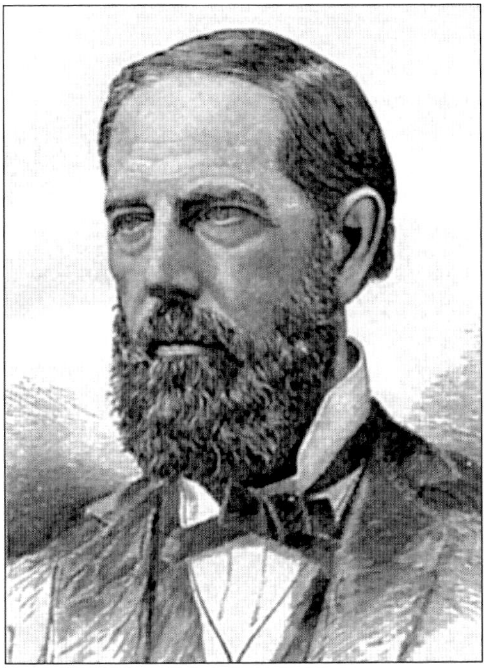
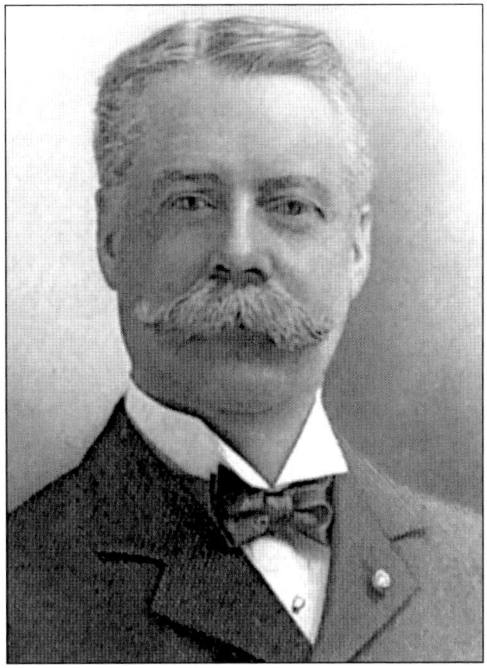

William Hayden English, 1822–1896, (*left*) was a congressman and banker. He was elected to Congress four times. He was author of a compromise measure admitting Kansas as a state, which became known as "the English bill." He helped established the First National Bank of Indianapolis. William Eastin English, 1850–1926, (*right*) was a U.S. congressman from Indiana and managed the English Opera House and Hotel that his father built. "Will" fought in the Spanish American War and was crushed beneath his wounded horse, but he survived. Upon return, he continued in politics and wrote two books about the Masons.

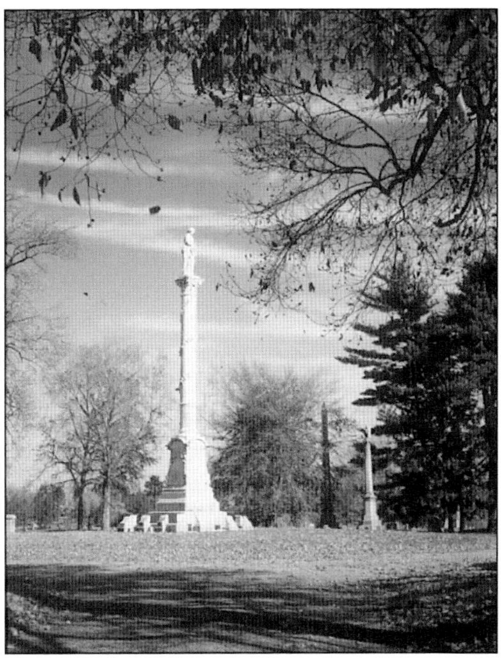

The English brothers were both involved in politics and are buried together in a family plot marked by this large obelisk in Section 1, Lot 72.

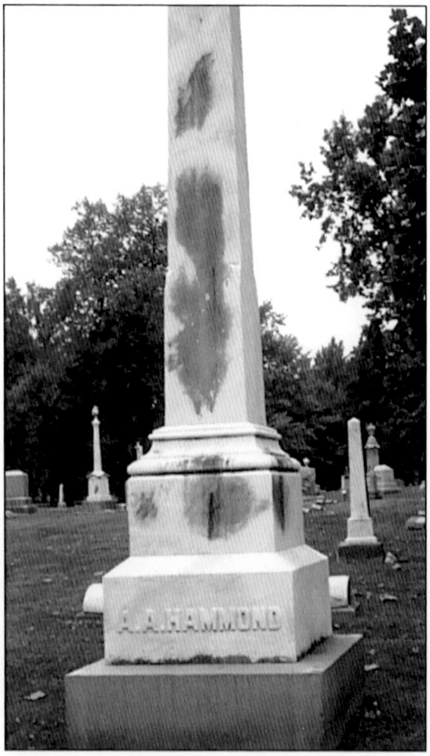

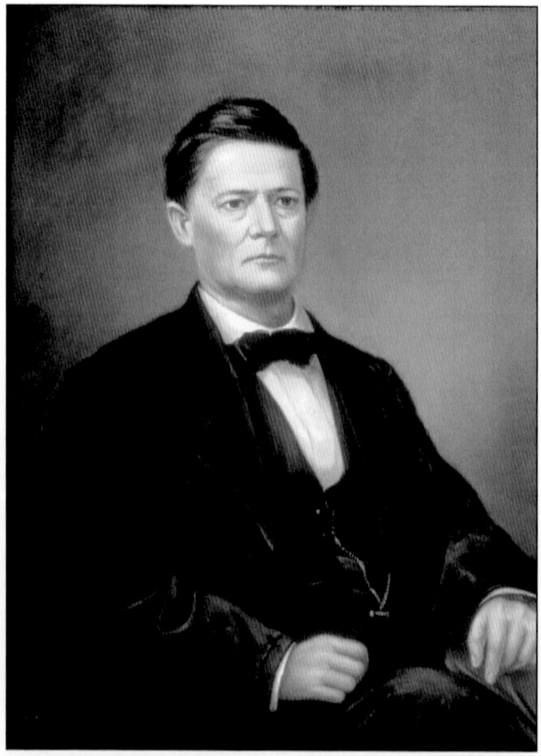

Abram A. Hammond, 1814–1874, was an Indiana governor, 1860–1861. His grave is located in Section 2. Born in Vermont, he came to Brookville, Indiana at age six. He became an attorney then served as judge of the court of common pleas for Marion County. He was elected as the lieutenant governor in 1856 and took over as governor for three months after Ashbel Willard died in office. Soon after his term was over Hammond was severely afflicted with rheumatism and asthma, and he died in Denver, Colorado, in 1874. He is buried in Section 2. (Photo of Hammond courtesy of Governors' Portraits Collection, Indiana Historical Bureau, State of Indiana.)

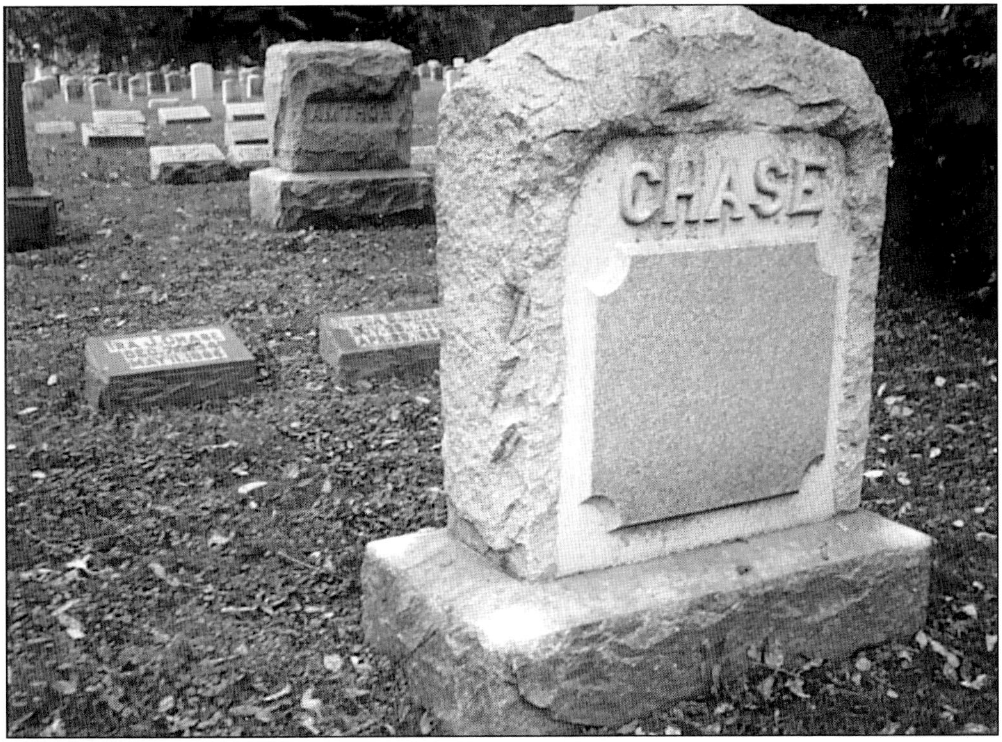

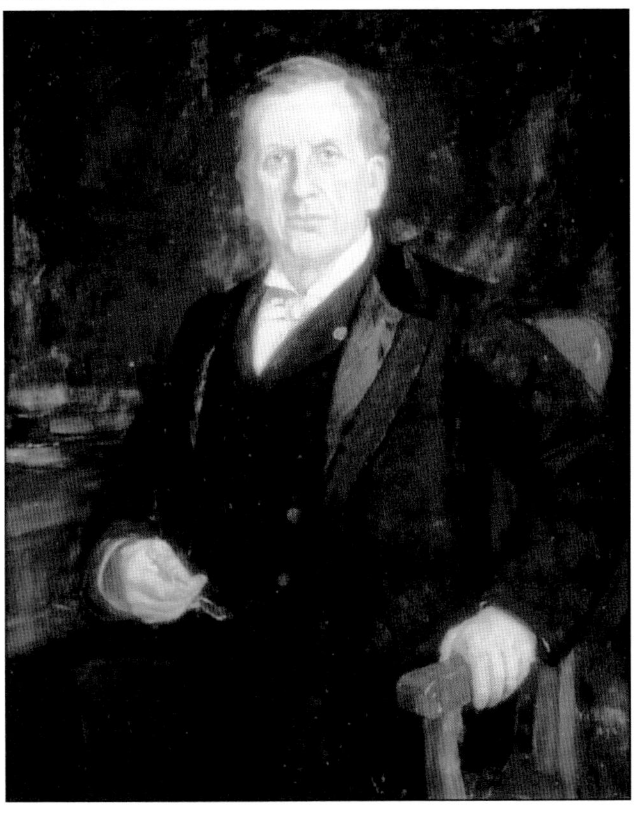

Ira J. Chase, 1823–1895, was Indiana governor from 1891–1893. He was a preacher in the Disciples of Christ Church before being elected to Congress. He was elected as the lieutenant governor in 1888 and took over as governor when Alvin P. Hovey died in office. He served as governor until 1893. He is buried in the Chase family plot located by a walnut tree in Section 10 near the flag pole. (Photo of Chase courtesy of Governors' Portraits Collection, Indiana Historical Bureau, State of Indiana.)

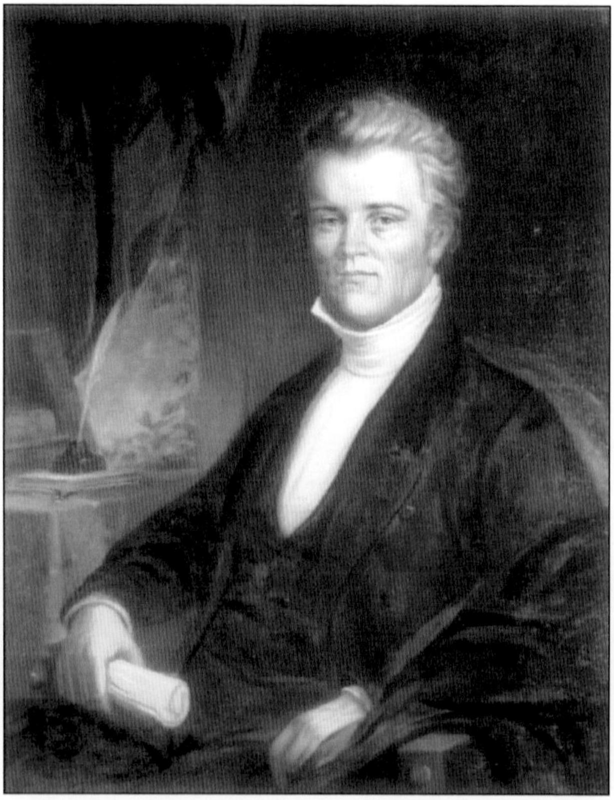

Noah Noble, 1794–1844, was Indiana's fourth governor, 1831–1837. Born in Virginia, he came to Brookville and became a lawyer. He was a sheriff and elected to the Indiana House of Representatives. While he served as governor, a state bank was created and internal improvement legislation was passed, which included the creation of roads and canals. He is buried in Section 1. (Photo of Noble courtesy of Governors' Portraits Collection, Indiana Historical Bureau, State of Indiana.)

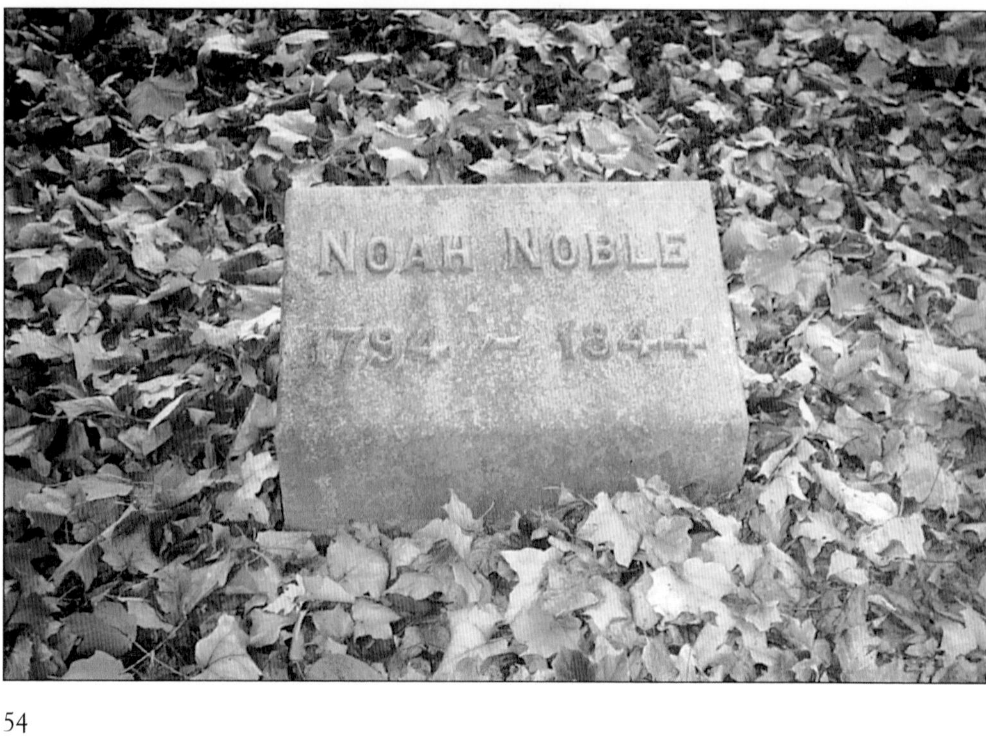

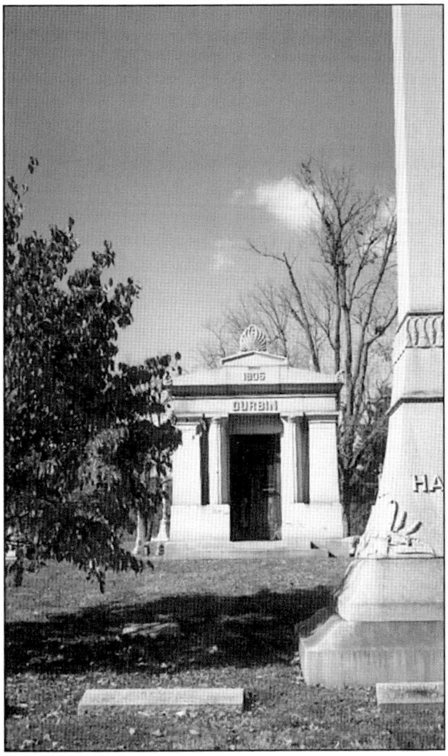

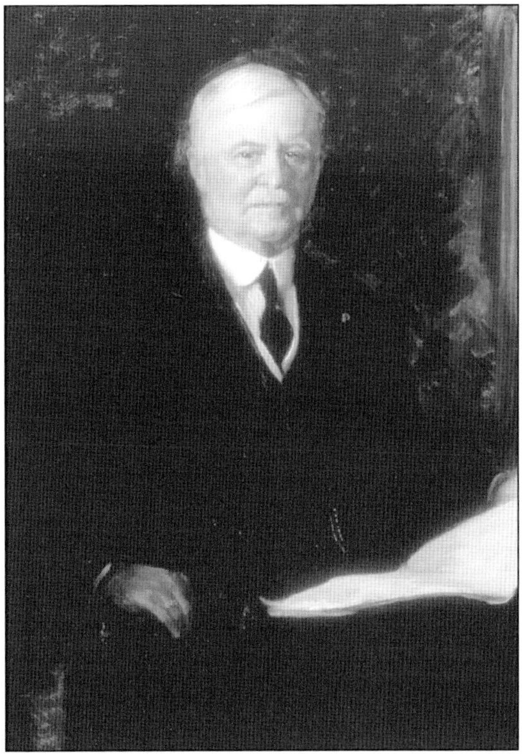

Winfield Durbin, 1847–1928, was a colonel during the Spanish-American War and an Indiana governor. Born in Lawrenceburg, Indiana, he was appointed as a colonel in the 161st Indiana Volunteer Infantry. Upon return from Cuba, he was elected as governor (1901–1905). As governor he took firm action against lynching and advocated both better highways and more state regulation of automobiles. He also ran for governor in 1912, but he lost to Samuel M. Ralston. He died a millionaire in 1928. His mausoleum is located in Section 23. (Photo of Durbin courtesy of Governors' Portraits Collection, Indiana Historical Bureau, State of Indiana.)

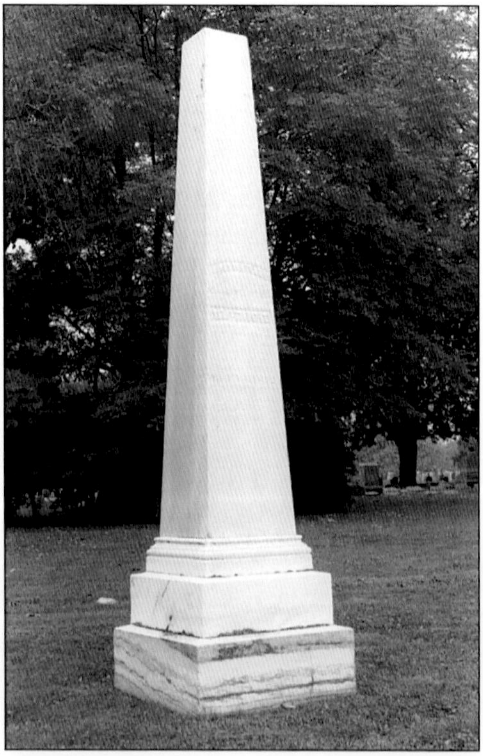 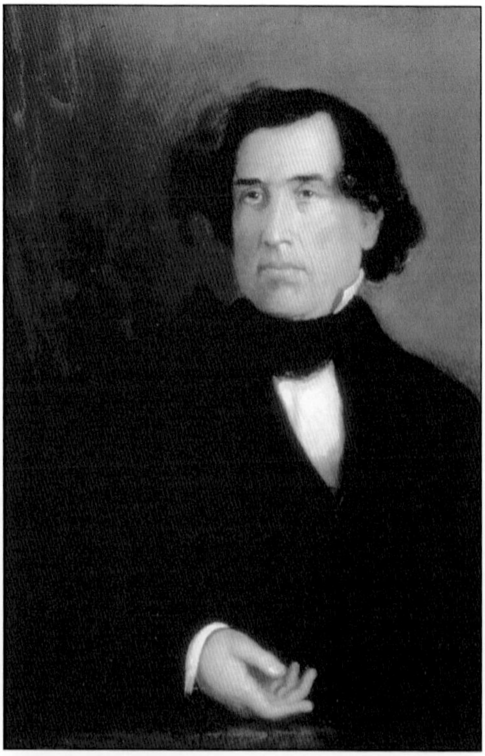

The old obelisk of James Whitcomb is located near the Gothic Chapel in Section 9. Whitcomb, 1795–1852, was governor of Indiana, 1843–1848, during which time the Mexican War was held. He then went on to become a U.S. senator, 1849–1852. He was buried at the City Cemetery for 40 years before his remains were moved to Crown Hill. (Photo of Whitcomb courtesy of Governors' Portraits Collection, Indiana Historical Bureau, State of Indiana.)

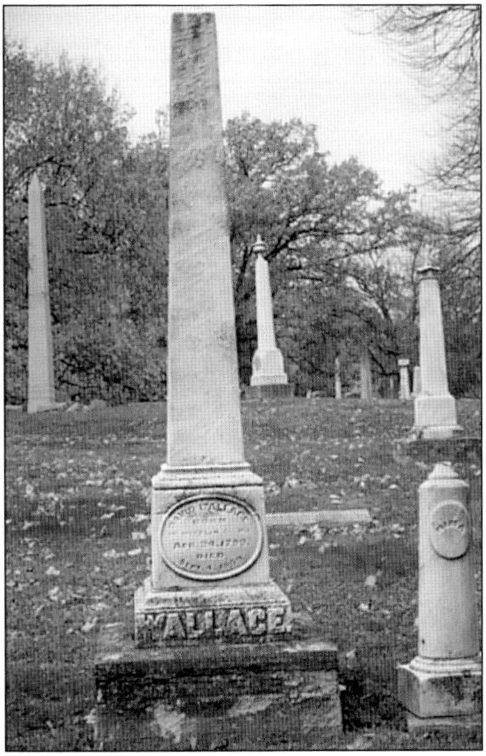

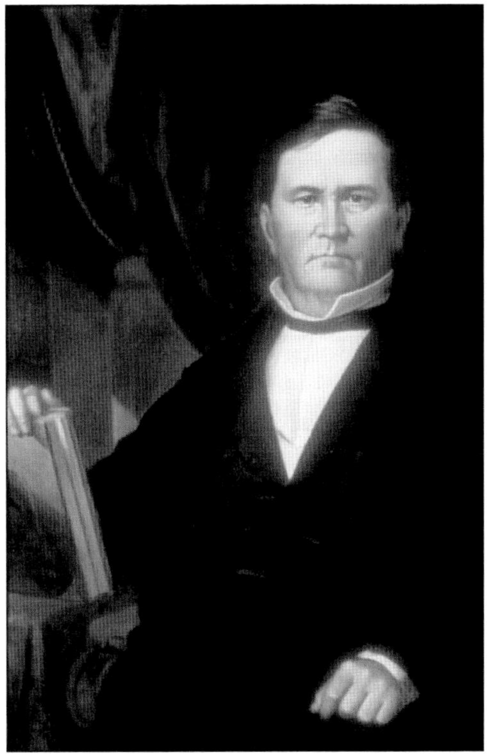

David Wallace, 1799–1859, was the fifth governor of Indiana, 1837–1840. The West Point graduate stayed in the Army only a year after graduation. He became an attorney and was elected to the Indiana House of Representatives before being elected as the lieutenant governor and governor from the Whig Party. After that he was elected to the U.S. House of Representatives. His son was Gen. Lew Wallace, the author of *Ben Hur*. His grave is located in Section 3. (Photo of Wallace courtesy of Governors' Portraits Collection, Indiana Historical Bureau, State of Indiana.)

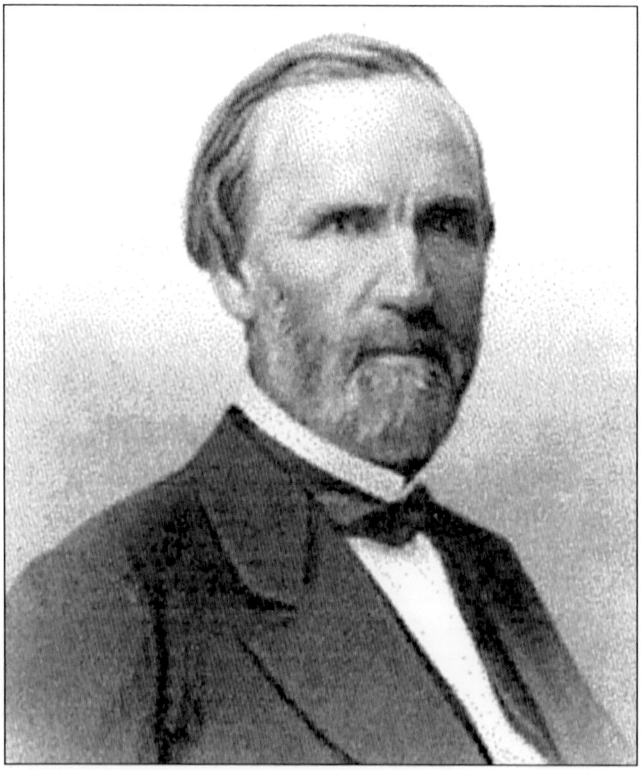

George Washington Julian, 1817–1899, was a congressman, 1860–1871. Born in Centerville, he became a lawyer in 1840. He was elected to Congress in 1860 with the Republican Party. For eight years, he was the chairman of the Committee on Public Lands and was heavily involved in the passage of the Homestead Act. He moved to Irvington in 1873 and served President Cleveland as the Surveyor General of New Mexico. He is buried in Section 27.

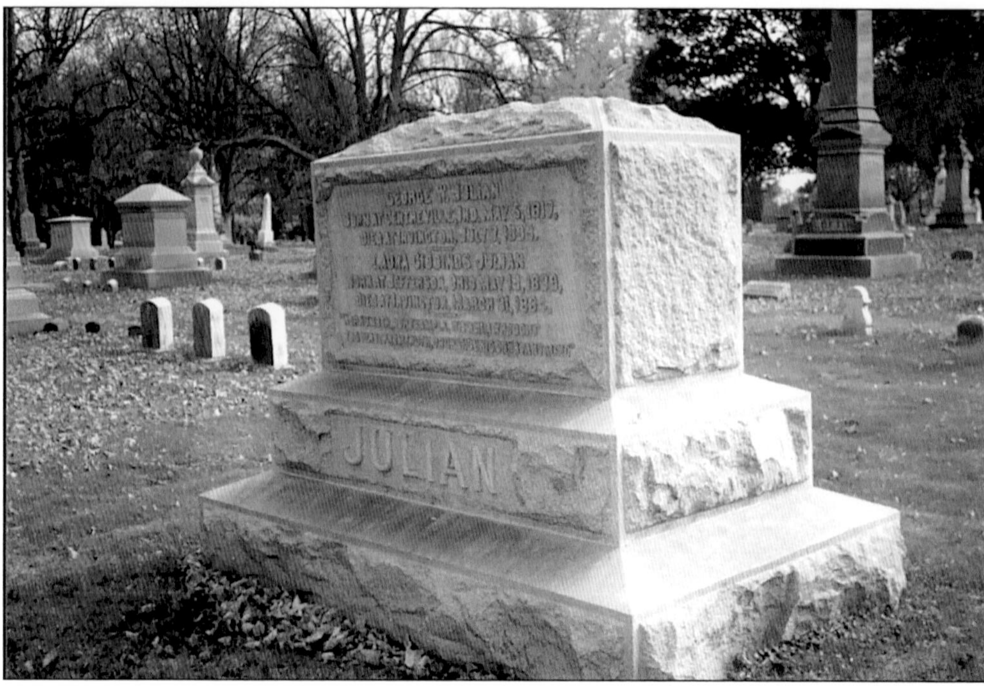

Three

Military Figures

The Crown Hill National Military Cemetery, which lies south of the Gothic Chapel within the cemetery, was purchased by the United States government in 1866 for the purpose of reburying 707 Union soldiers from the City Cemetery.

In late 1866, William W. Weaver, a local undertaker, was commissioned to rebury the Union dead in this section. With the opening of the northern addition came more veterans of many other American conflicts.

Two of the last three military personnel to be buried in the National Cemetery were volunteers of the Spanish-American War who died in 1898. A final internment was made in this area in 1969 when Maj. Robert W. Hayes, an Air Force pilot killed in Vietnam, was buried there. In all, 2,135 soldiers and sailors are buried in the area representing all the services.

Across the roadway to the southeast is another veterans' area dedicated on Memorial Day in 1988. A large black granite monument has been erected there to the memory of all five services.

Another area for war veterans in Crown Hill is the Confederate Burial Mound. The area in Section 32 is the final burial place for 1,616 Confederate prisoners of war confined to Camp Morton (the old Fair Grounds) during the Civil War.

Other graves of former military men are scattered around the cemetery like trees in a forest standing tall and proud. They represent every service and every war since the Civil War.

Crown Hill is now in the process of constructing a new military section and mausoleum on the north portion of the cemetery for veterans. The Field of Valor was dedicated on Veteran's Day.

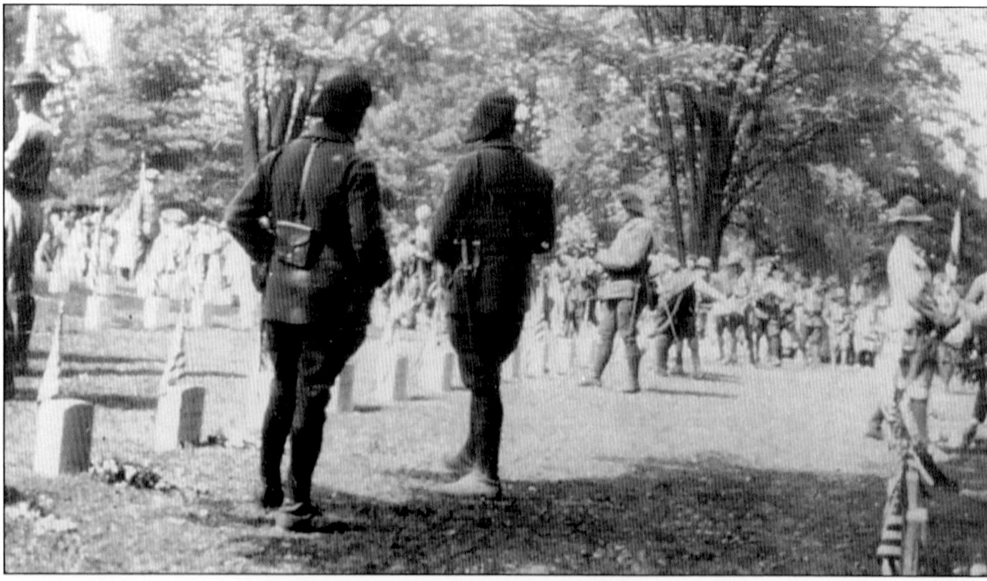

Many military veterans are buried throughout Crown Hill. This photo was taken at a burial during World War I. (Photo courtesy of Crown Hill Cemetery.)

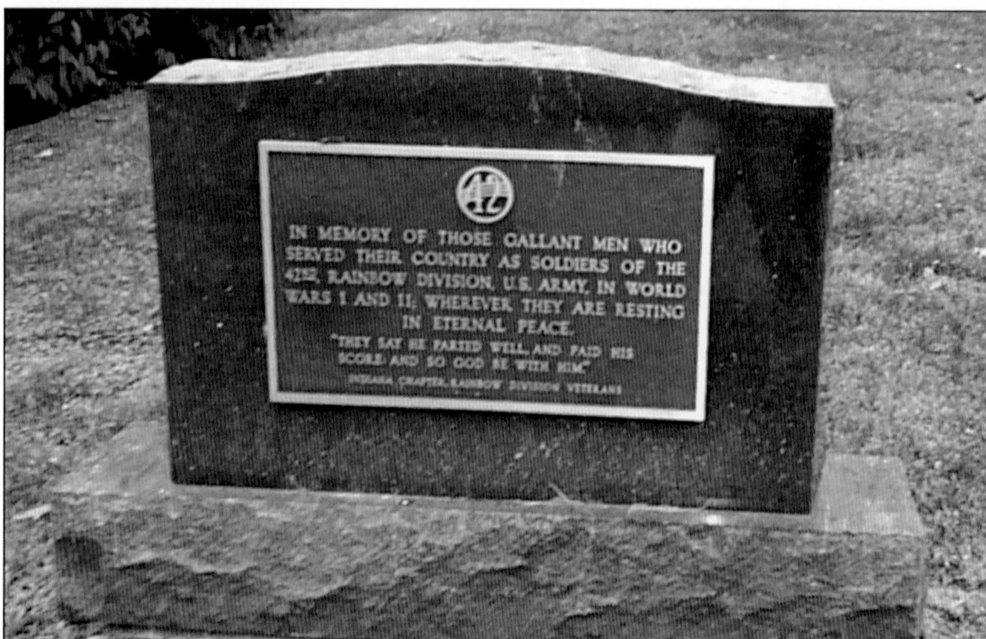

This plaque in the National Military Cemetery reads: "In memory of those gallant men who served their country as soldiers of the 42nd Rainbow Division, U.S. Army, in World Wars I and II, wherever they are resting in eternal peace. 'They say he parted well, and paid his score and so God be with him.' "

A plaque in the National Military Cemetery reads:

The muffled drum's sad roll has beat
The soldier's last tattoo.
No more on life's parade shall meet
That brave and fallen few.

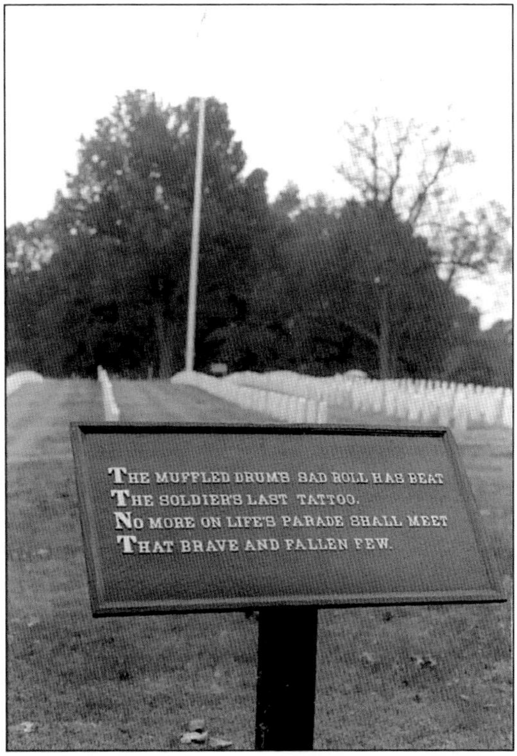

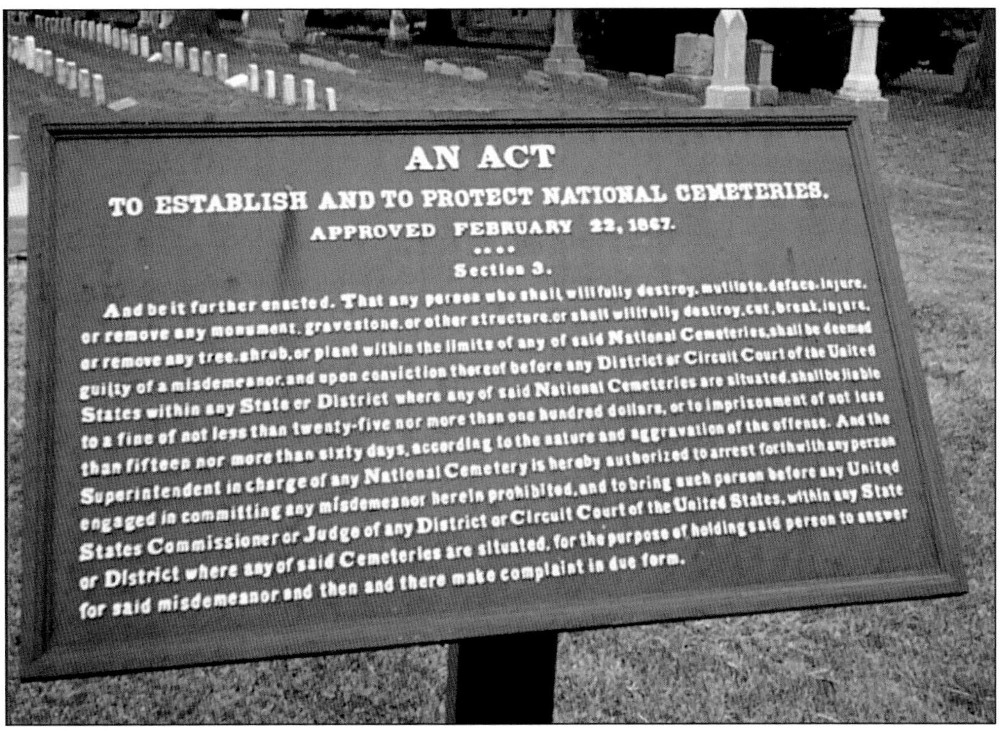

The act which established Section 3 of Crown Hill Cemetery as a National Military Cemetery was approved on February 22, 1867. The act is printed on this plaque.

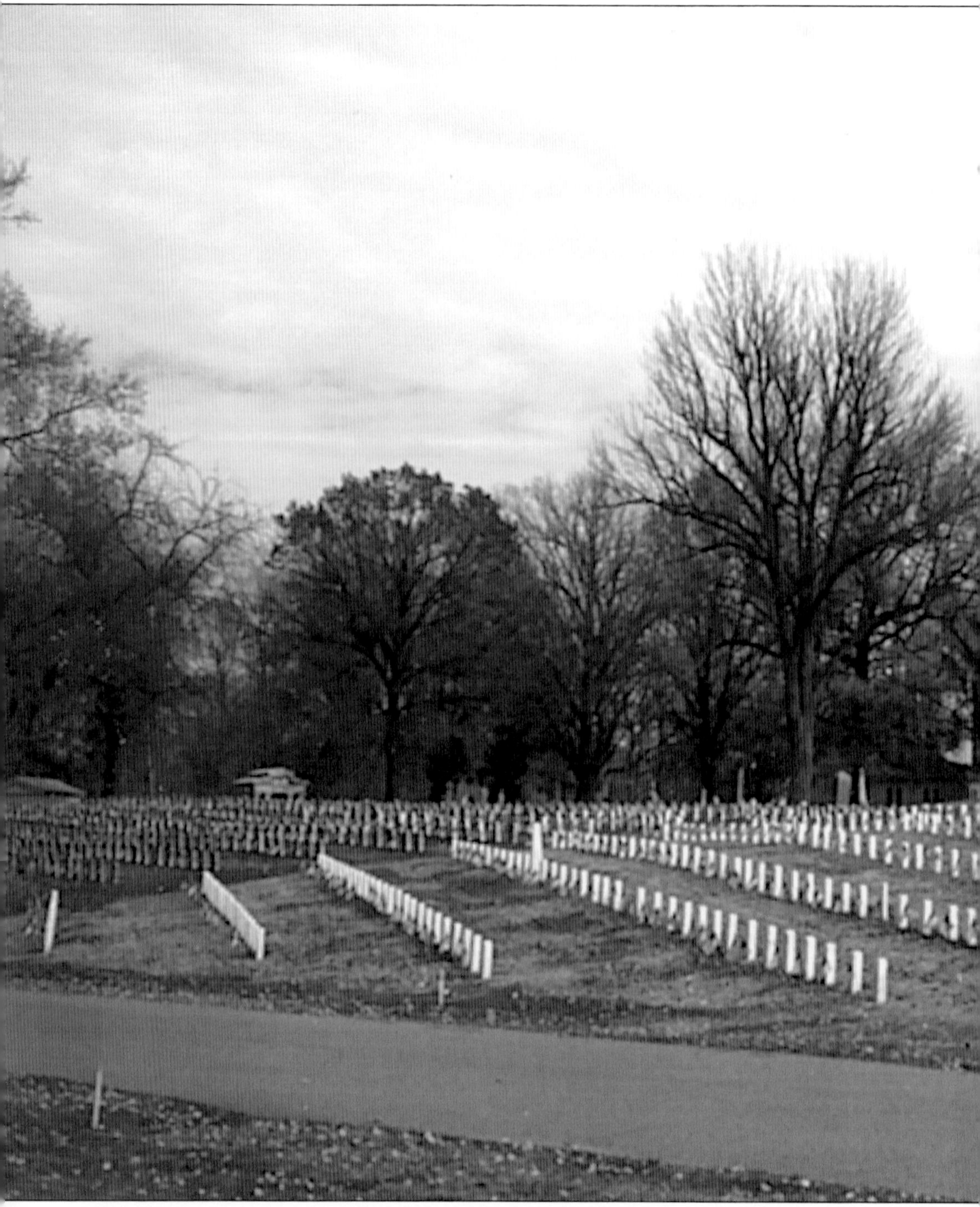

Flags are put at each grave in the National Military Cemetery during special days honoring the

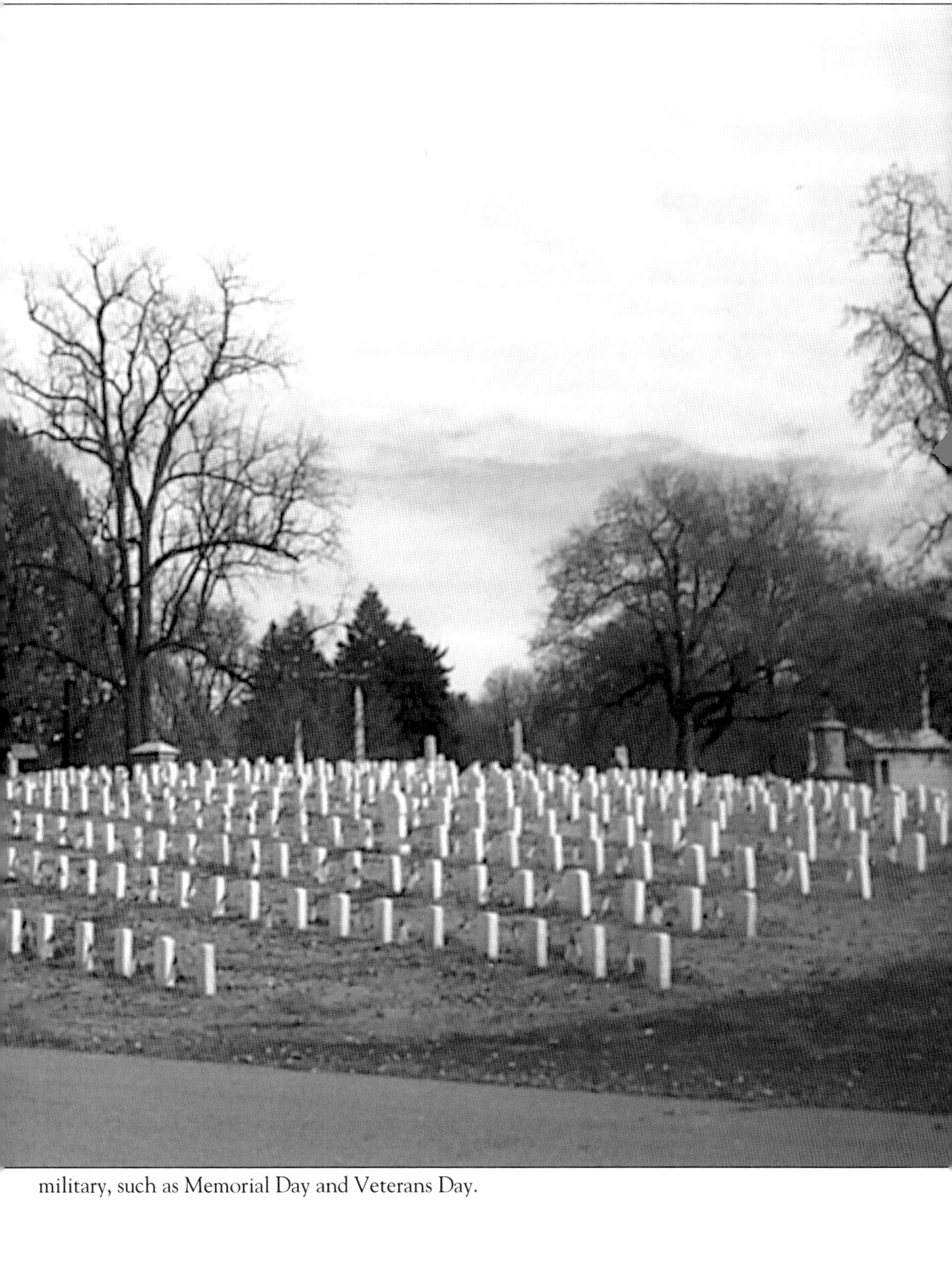

military, such as Memorial Day and Veterans Day.

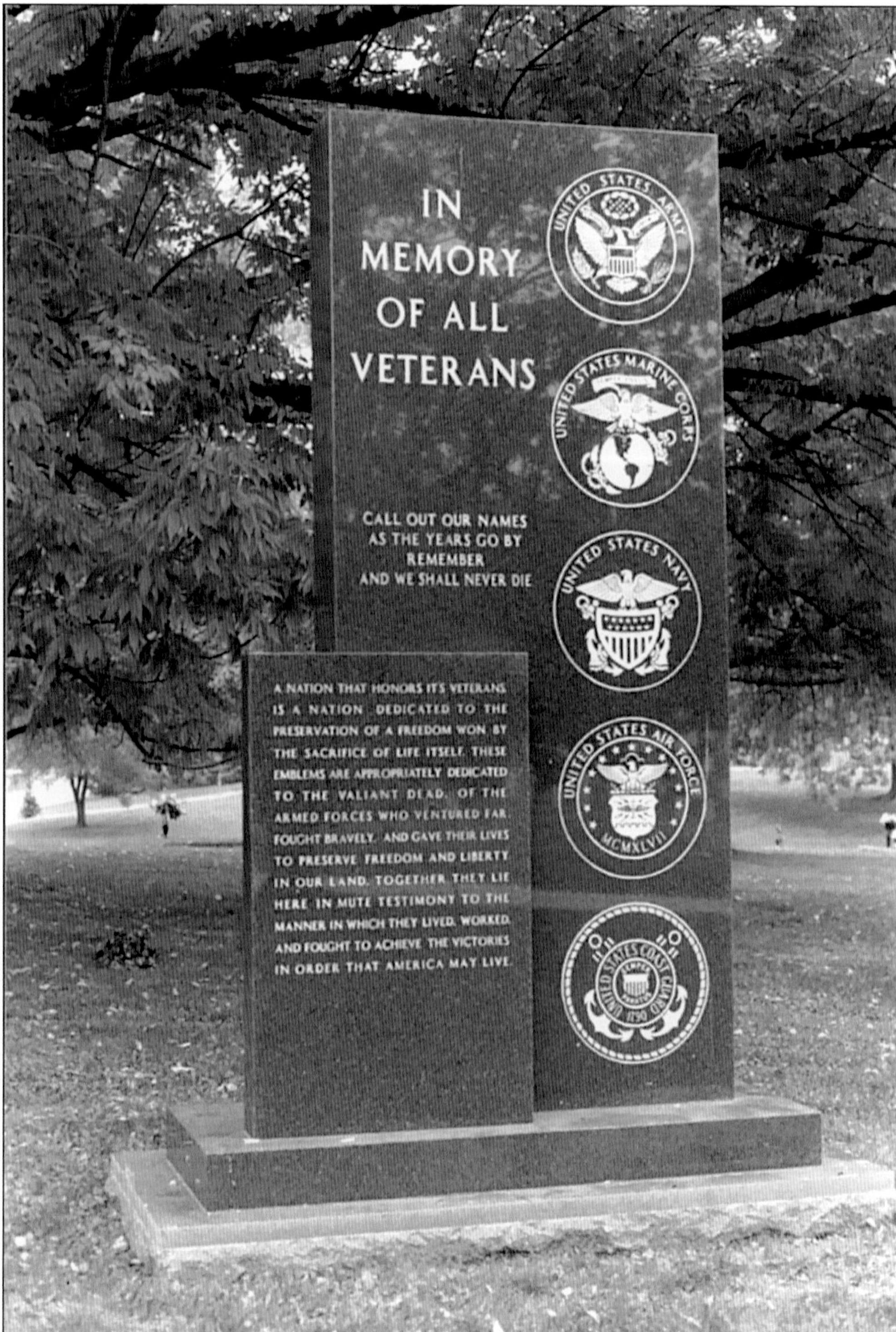

This plaque honors the members of the five military services who are buried in the National Military Cemetery.

The Confederate Burial Mound is the final burial place for 1,616 Confederate prisoners of war confined to Camp Morton, 1862–1865. Most of these prisoners died at the City Hospital and were originally buried in the City Cemetery. All were removed to Crown Hill in 1931. A two-year project to identify these veterans was completed by Stephen Staletovich, an Indianapolis police officer, and the Crown Hill Society. As a result of their work, ten bronze plaques mounted on granite bases were placed at the site. Each bears the names of all Southerners who died at Camp Morton. The monument and plaques were rededicated on October 3, 1993.

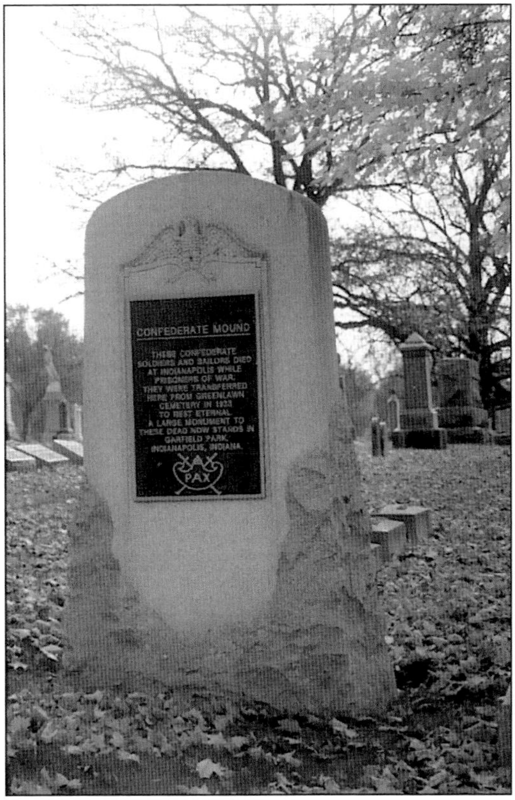

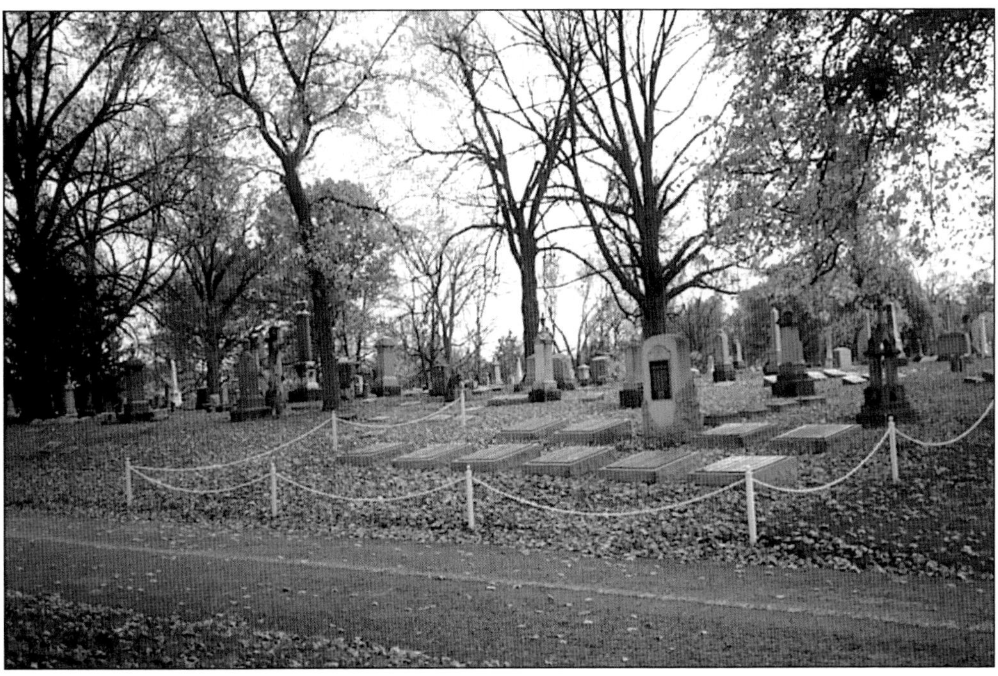

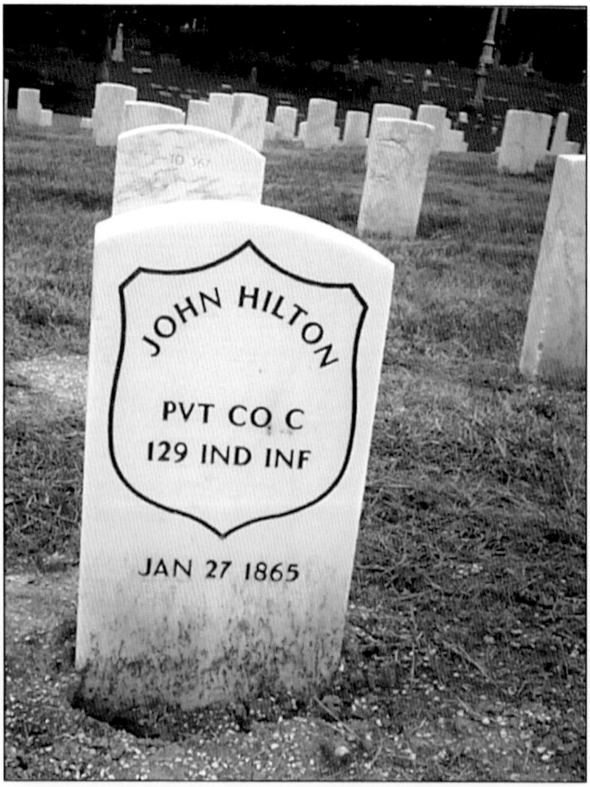

Some of the headstones in the National Military Cemetery have been refurbished like this one.

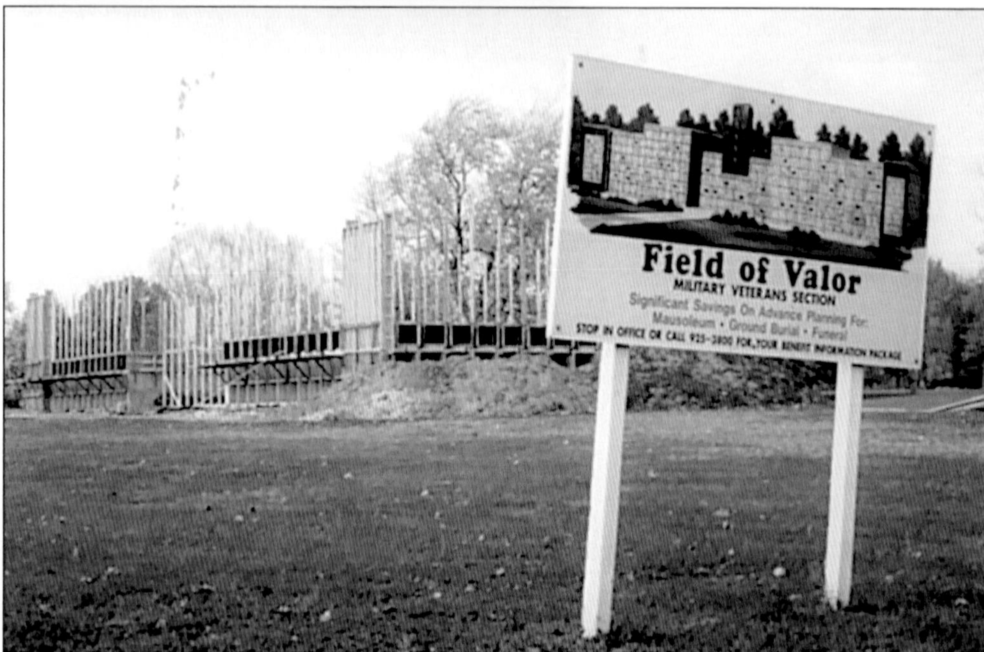

Crown Hill is building a mausoleum that will be called the "Field of Valor." The military veterans section offers significant savings to veterans for burials there. The new mausoleum will be completed in 2004.

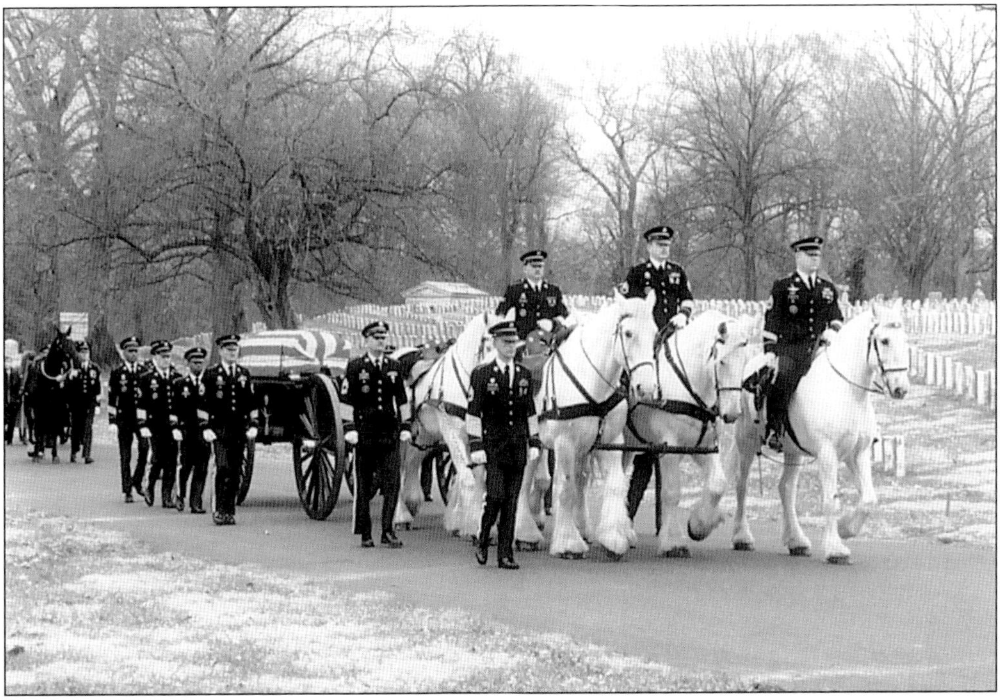

Col. William A. Scott was laid to rest by the Army with full military honors. This was the procession on December 8, 1995. (Photo courtesy of Marty Davis.)

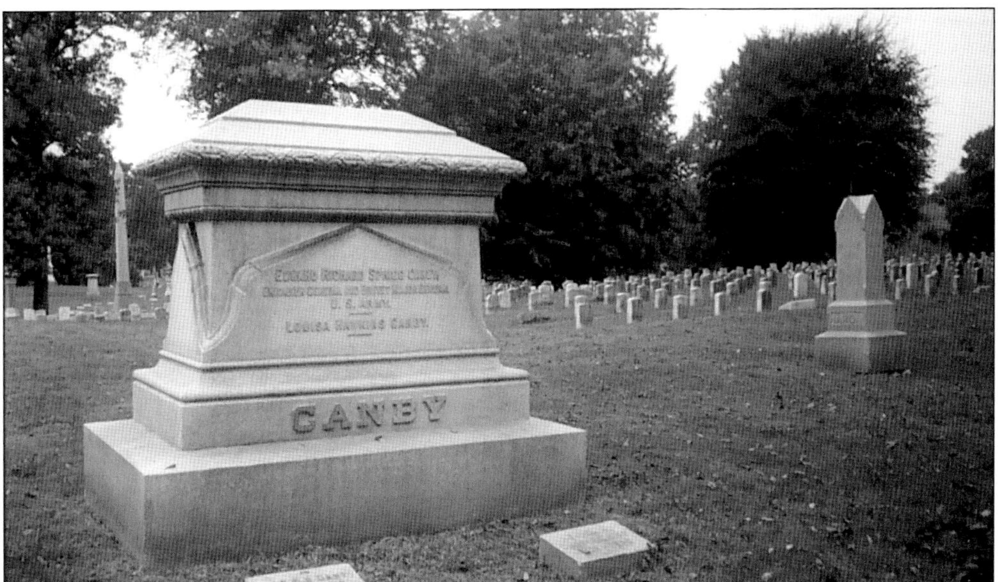

The Canby family plot is located in Section 10 near the flagpole. Edward R.S. Canby, 1817–1873, was a West Point graduate who served as a general during the Civil War. After the war, he commanded troop in California and was killed while attempting to negotiate a peace treaty with a renegade chief of the Modoc Indians.

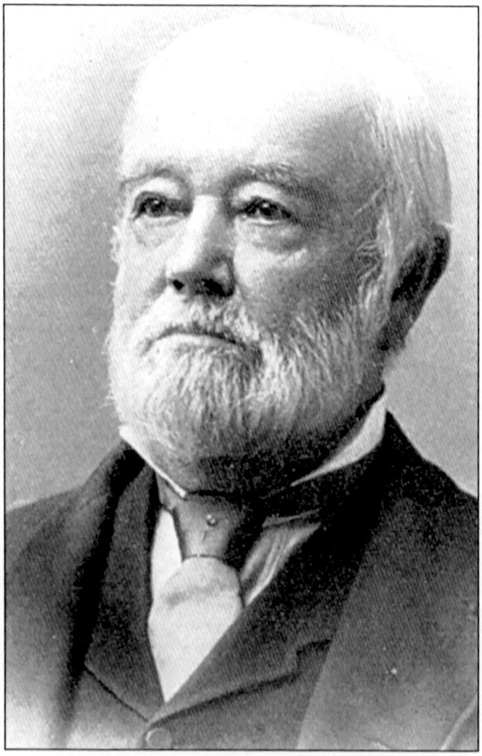

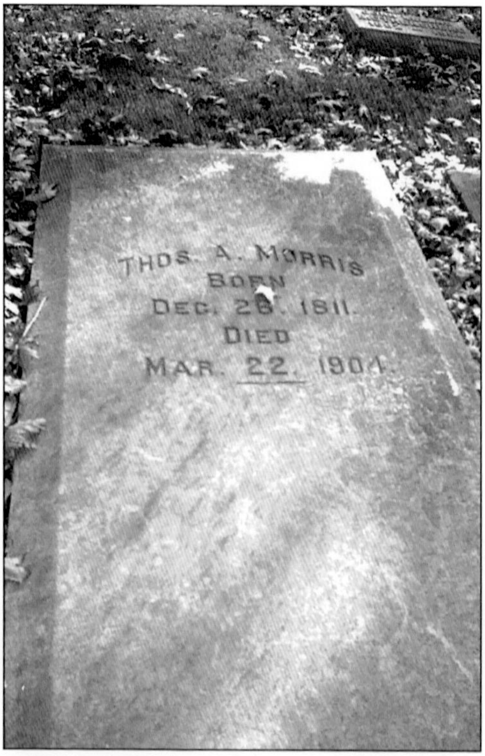

Gen. Thomas A. Morris, 1811–1904, was a brigadier general during the Civil War and an Indianapolis businessman. The West Point graduate was an assistant engineer on the National Road, which ran through Indianapolis on its way to Illinois. He was a militia commander during the first three months of the war. Later, he was the superintendent of the Madison & Indianapolis Railroad, president of the Indianapolis Water Company and a founding corporator of Crown Hill Cemetery. A sepulchral slab marks his grave on the north side of Section 6.

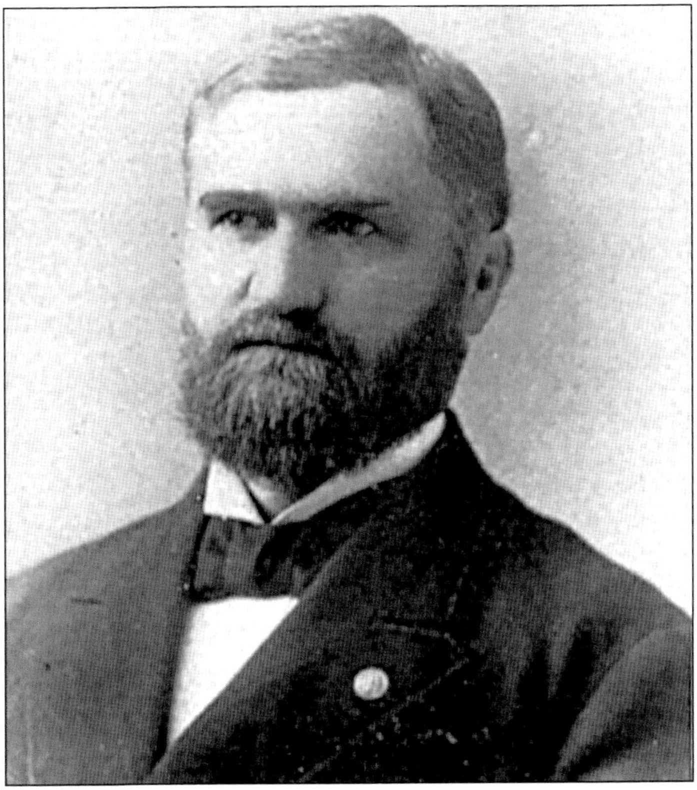

Smiley Newton Chambers, 1845–1907, was a United States attorney in Indianapolis in the late 1800s. He fought in the Civil War for the 150th Indiana Regiment before becoming a lawyer. Then President Benjamin Harrison appointed him as U.S. attorney in 1889.

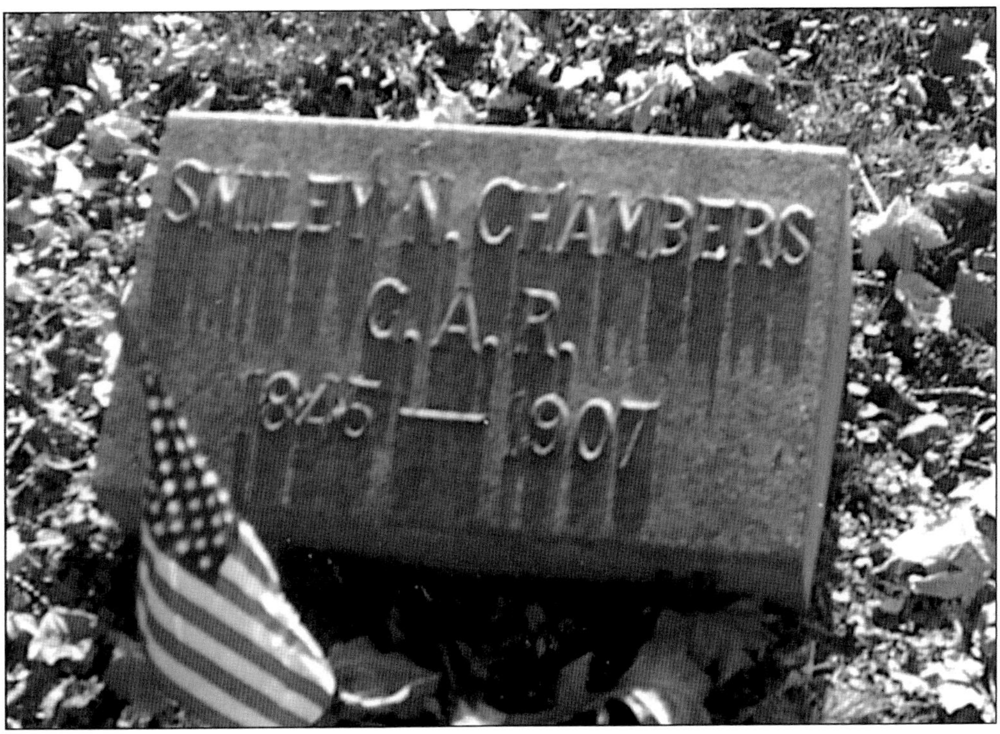

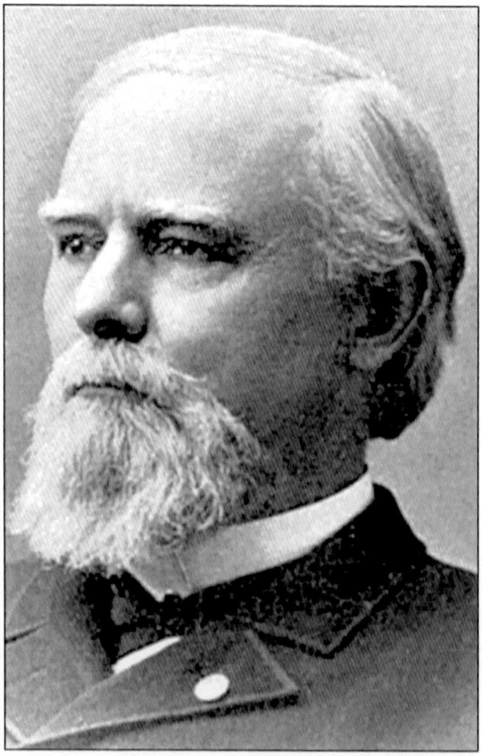

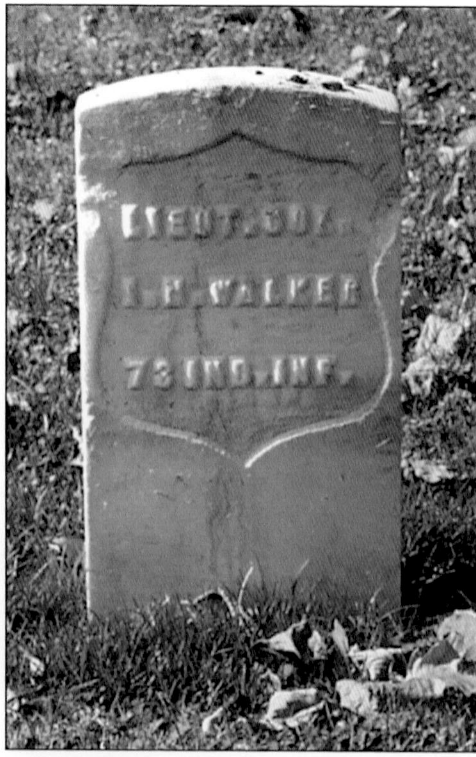

Col. I.N. Walker, 1839–1905, commanded the 73rd Indiana Volunteers during the Civil War. He was captured by the Confederates and spent more than a year in Libby Prison before escaping. His grave is located in Section 13, Lot 31.

James L. Mitchell, 1827–1905, was a Civil War veteran, mayor, and prosecuting attorney. He served as a major during the Civil War with the 17th Indiana Volunteers and took part in the Atlanta campaign. The graduate of Indiana University practiced law until being elected mayor of Indianapolis in 1873. He was the first Democrat to be elected to that position. Mitchell's grave is located in Section 44, Lot 334.

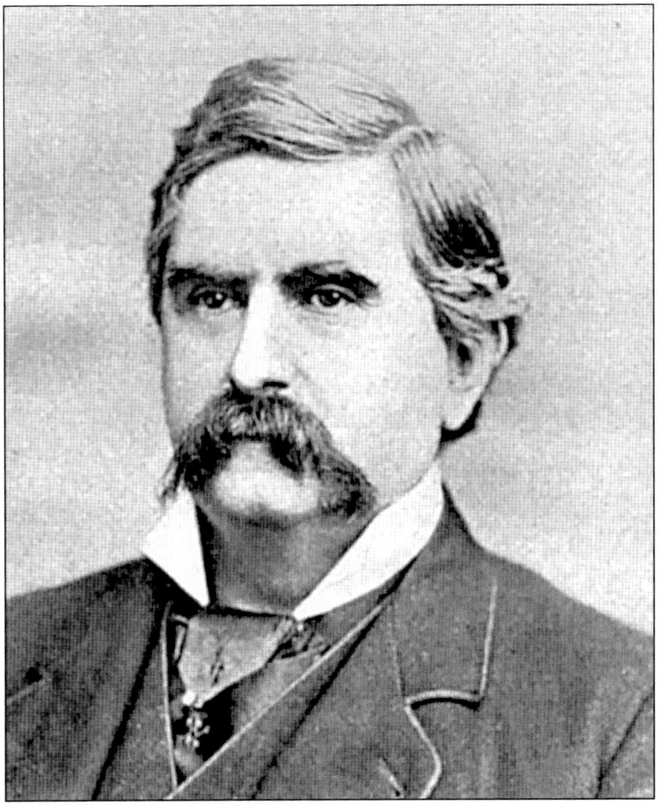

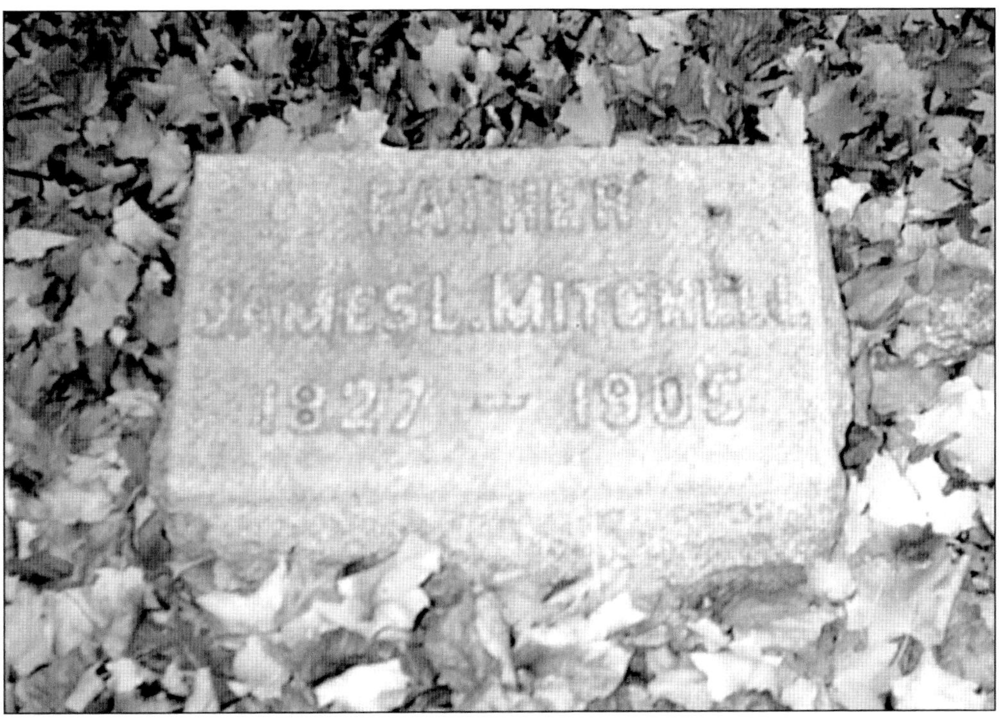

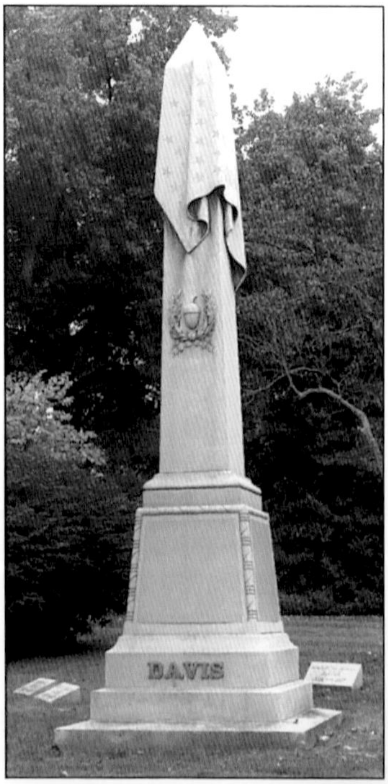

Jefferson C. Davis, 1828–1879, was at Fort Sumter during the Confederate attack in April 1861. The colonel led the 22nd Indiana Volunteer Infantry during the Civil War and was promoted to brigadier general and brevet major general. He commanded troops in California and put an end to the Modoc War. The tall obelisk of Davis is located at the southwest corner of Section 29 directly across from the National Cemetery.

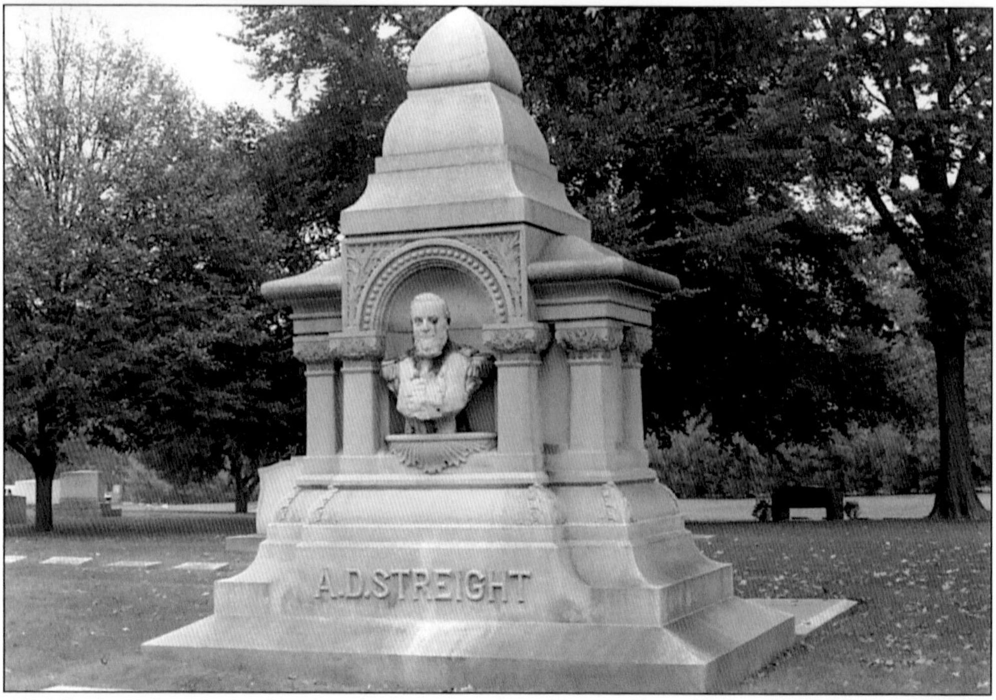

Abel D. Streight was a colonel with the 51st Indiana Volunteer Infantry during the Civil War. He planned and executed an escape from Libby Prison that freed himself and one hundred other Union officers. He also led a famous raid into Alabama. He became a brevet brigadier general. After the war, he was a book publisher. The large monument of Steight with his bronze bust is located in Section 29 near the Chapel.

Four

BUSINESS LEADERS

Because of its central location, Indianapolis has become the "Crossroads of America," which has helped it in securing businesses to the Circle City. Several businesses have also decided to locate their headquarters here. As a result, some business leaders have decided to put their remains at Crown Hill Cemetery. Many local business men and women are buried there as well.

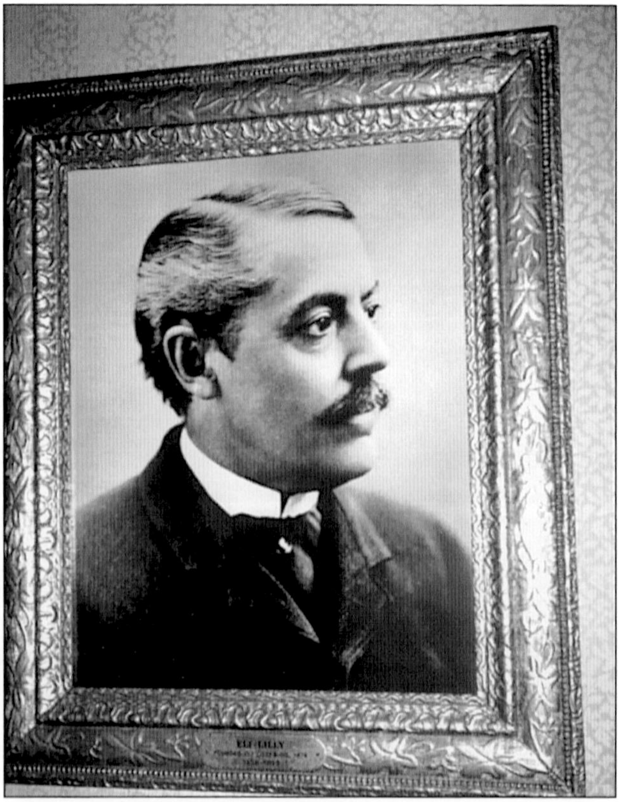

Colonel Eli Lilly, 1838–1898, founded a small laboratory in 1876 that has turned into a huge corporation in Indianapolis. After fighting for the Union Army, the colonel became a leader in civic and charitable affairs. Eli Lilly & Company now employs 43,000 worldwide and sells drugs used throughout the world. The Colonel Eli Lilly Civil War Museum was established in the Soldiers and Sailors Museum. This portrait of Lilly hangs in the Crown Hill Funeral Home. He is buried in a mausoleum in Section 13, Lot 19.

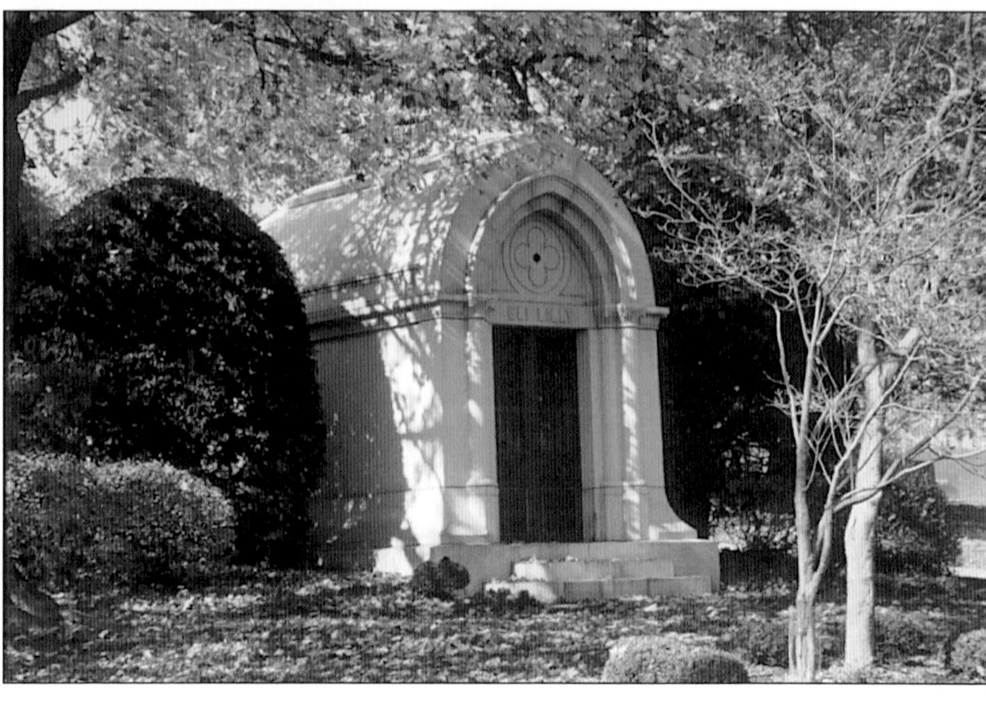

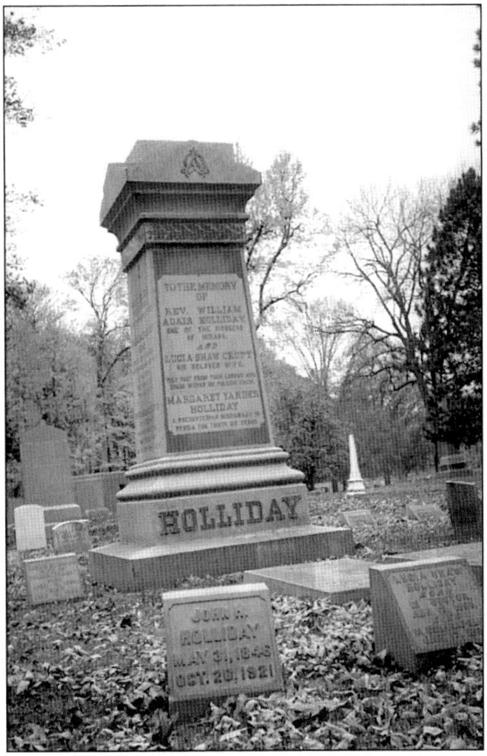

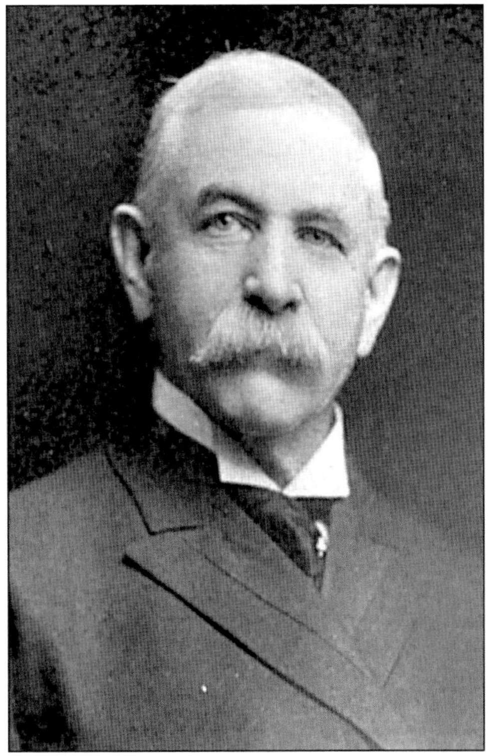

John Hampden Holliday, 1846–1921, founded the *Indianapolis News* at age 23. The Civil War veteran began the paper on December 6, 1869. His editorship spanned more than 25 years. After leaving the newspaper, he organized the Union Trust Company and became its president. He founded the *Indianapolis Press* in 1899 to compete with his old newspaper but it failed to do so and it was consolidated with the *Indianapolis News* a few years later. Holliday Park is named for him. His grave is located in Section 7, Lot 39 in the family plot.

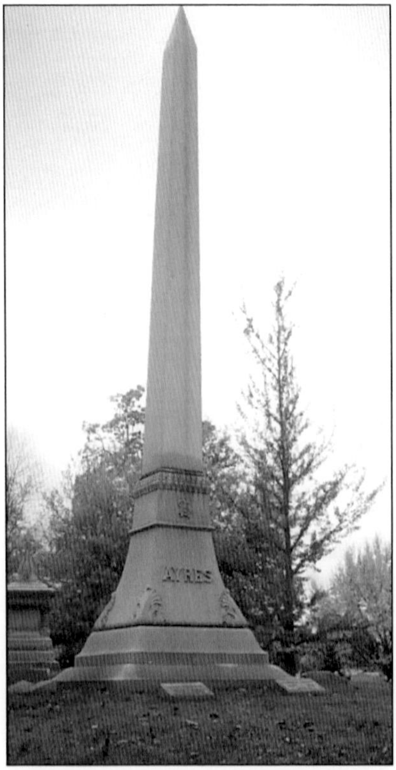

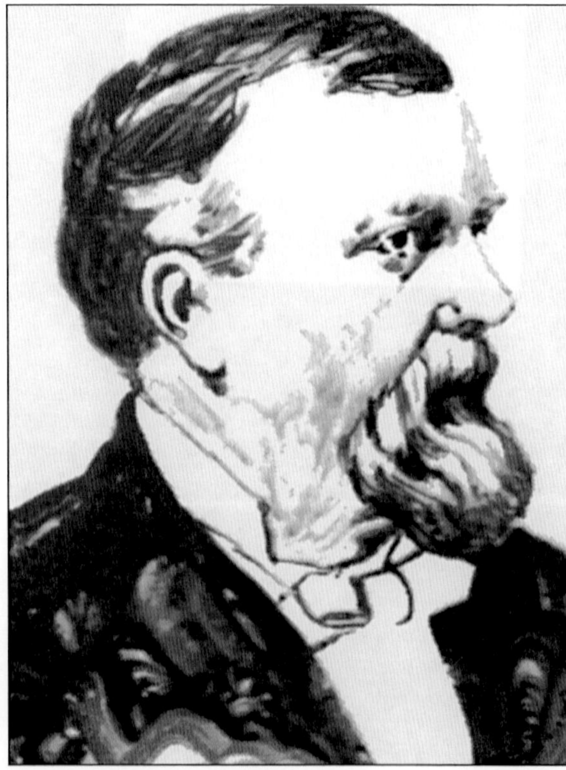

Lyman S. Ayres, 1824-1896, got into the dry goods business in 1872 then opened his own store, L.S. Ayres, two years later. The store became a favorite shopping stop for Indianapolis residents for years to come. He is buried in Section 11, Lot 19 in a family plot.

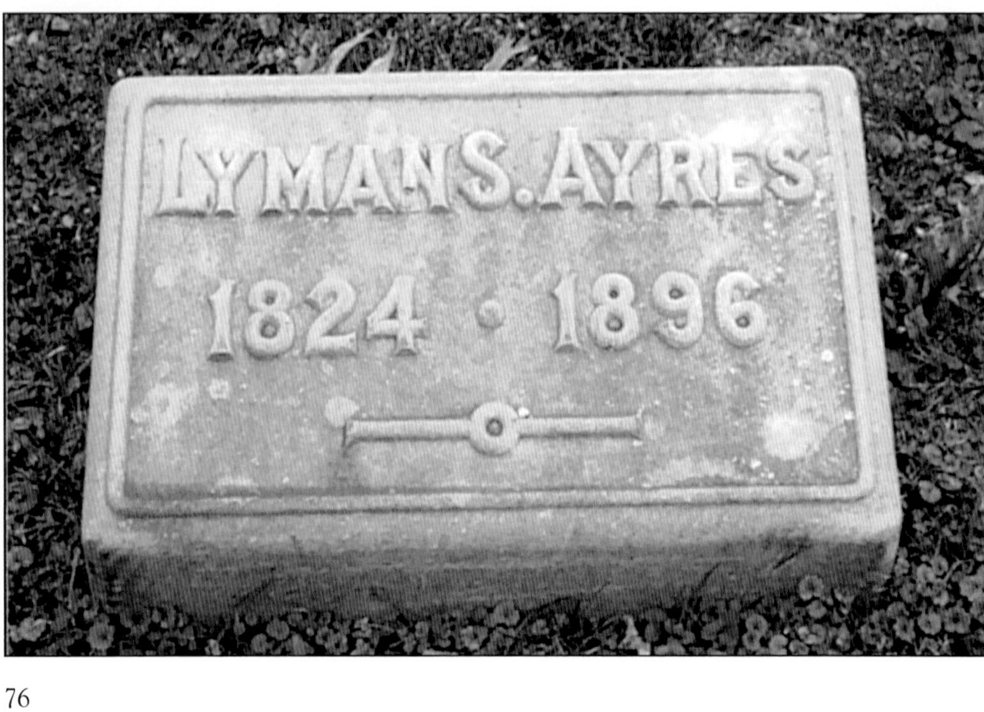

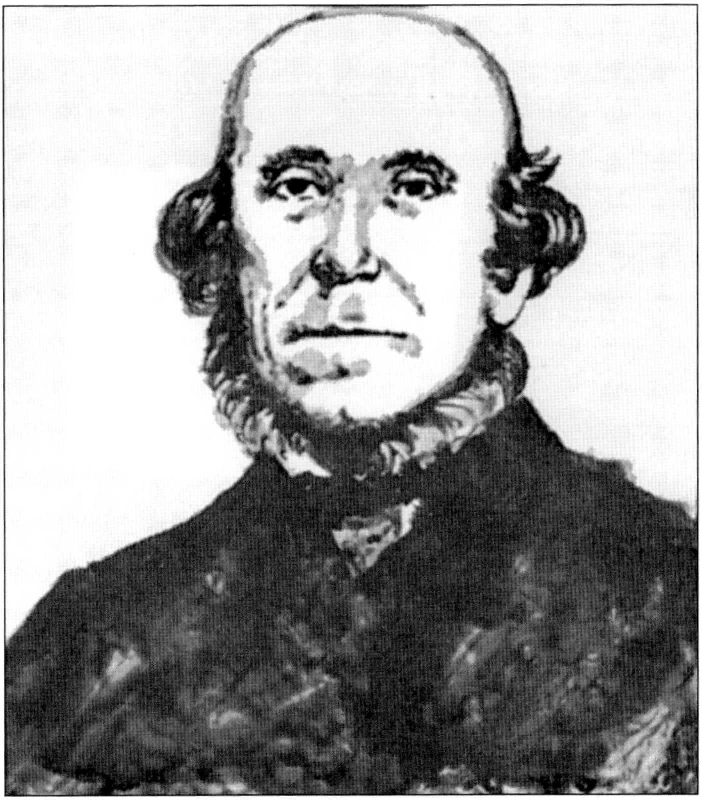

William Tinsley, 1804–1885, designed the beautiful Christ Church Cathedral on Monument Circle in 1858. He was born in Ireland and died in Cincinnati where he helped to design the open plaza there. His relatives placed this marker next to his sarcophagus on December 25, 1982. His remains are located in Section 7, Lot 43.

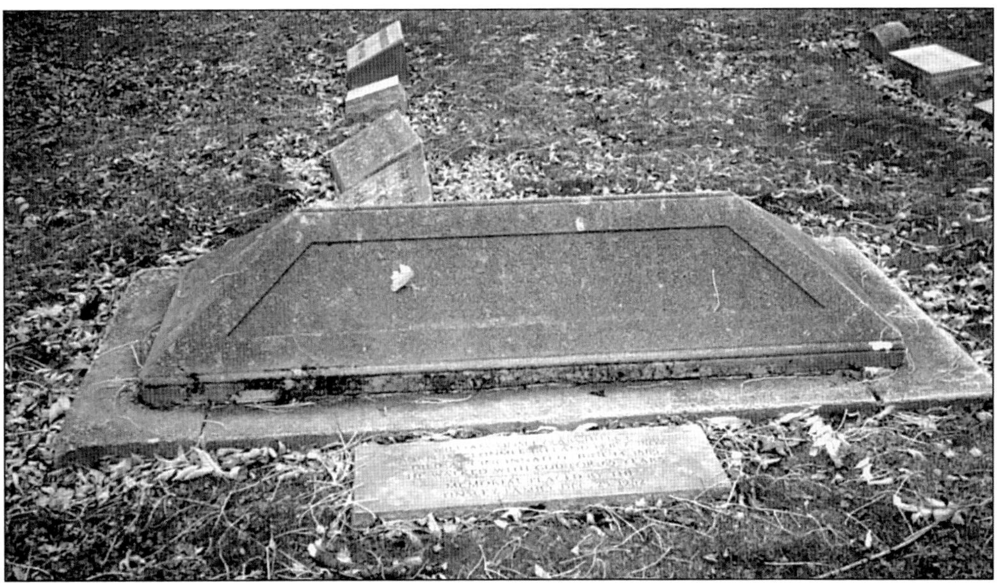

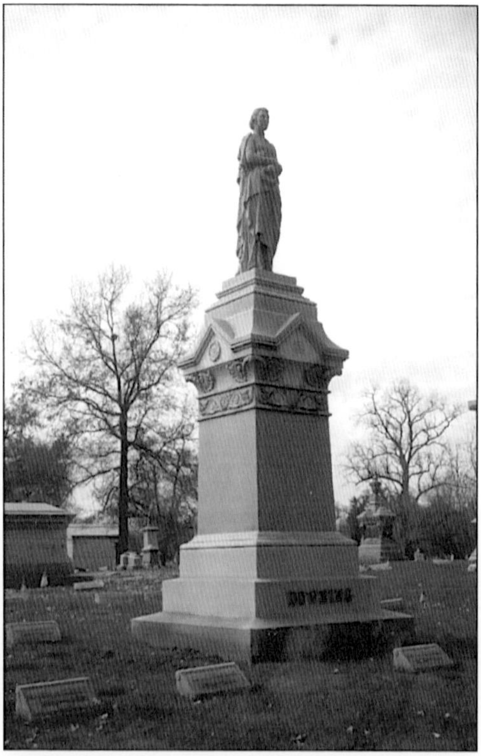

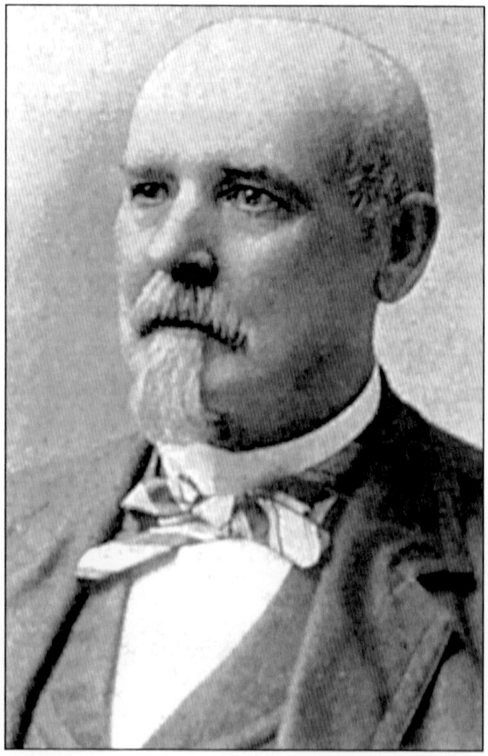

Michael A. Downing, 1835–1910, was the general manager during the construction of the stockyards, which brought the Belt Railway to Indianapolis in the 1880s. He is buried in Section 29, Lot 9.

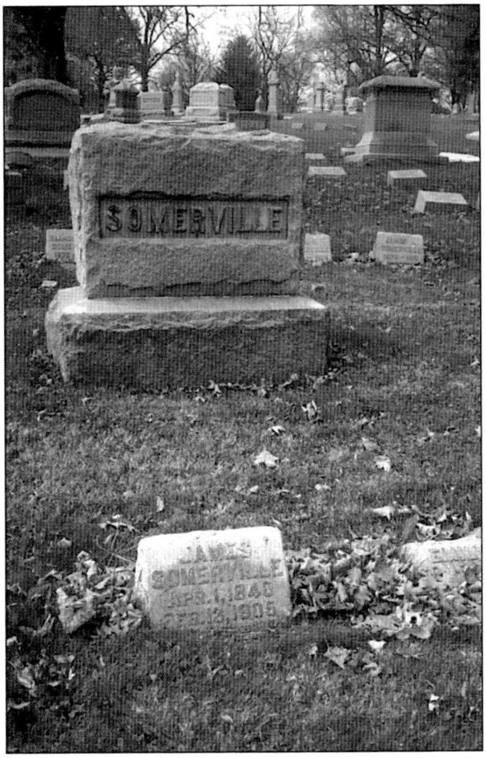

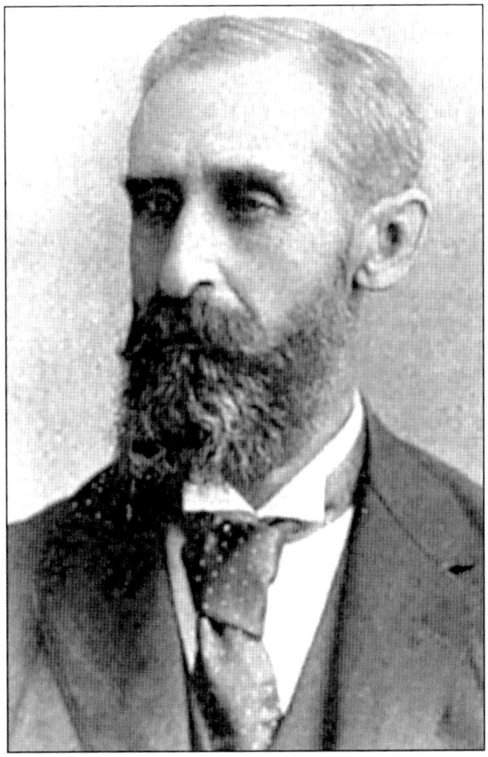

James Somerville, 1841–1905, was involved in the early gas business in Indianapolis. Born in Scotland, Somerville began working in gas in London at age 17. He came to Indianapolis in 1879 and became the superintendent of the Indianapolis Gas Company. His grave is located in Section 36, Lot 136.

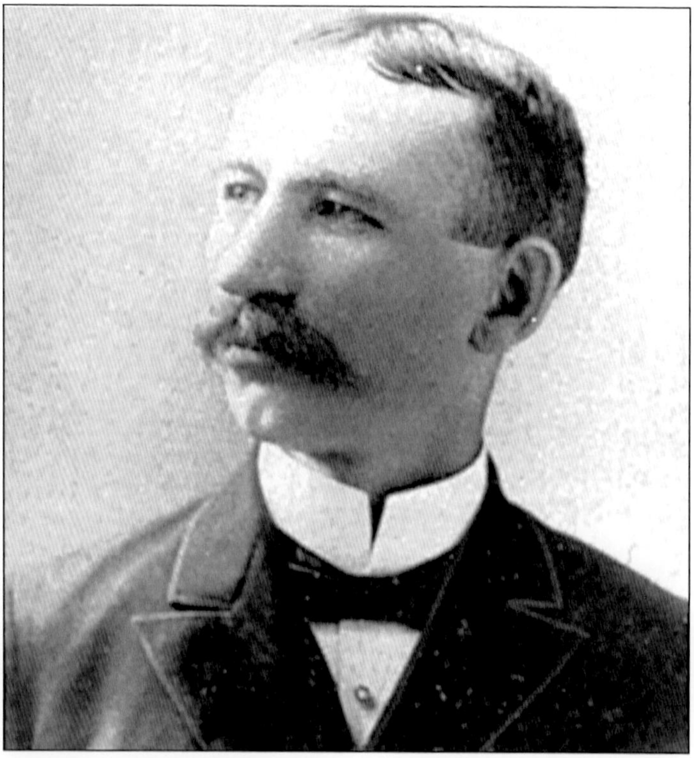

Charles E. Coffin, 1849–1934, was president of the Indiana Savings and Investment Company and State Life Insurance Company. He is buried in Section 29, Lot 37 in the shadow of the Gothic Chapel.

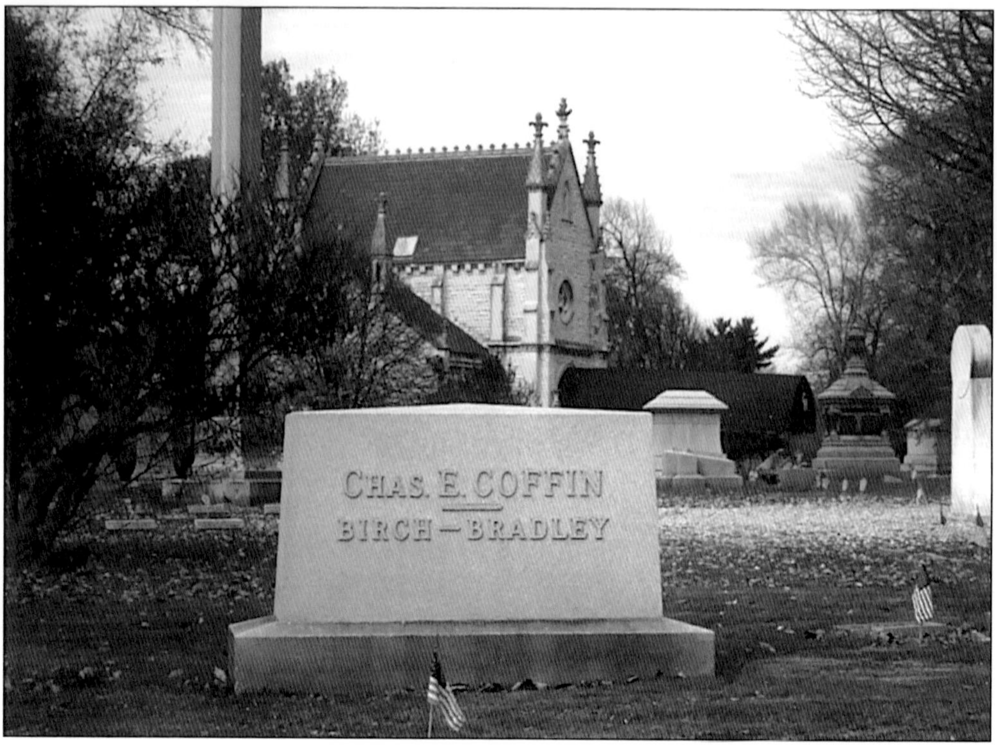

Edna Balz Lacy, 1906–1991, was a business leader in Indianapolis. She was thrown into the business world after her husband unexpectedly died in 1959. She became the president and chairman of the board of U.S. Corrugated-Fibre Box Company. She was involved in many business projects in Indianapolis and paved the way for many women into business. Three governors named her a "Sagamore of the Wabash" for her efforts. In 1995, the Edna Balz Lacy Family Park was completed at 700 Greer Street. This portrait of Lacy hangs in the Crown Hill Funeral Home.

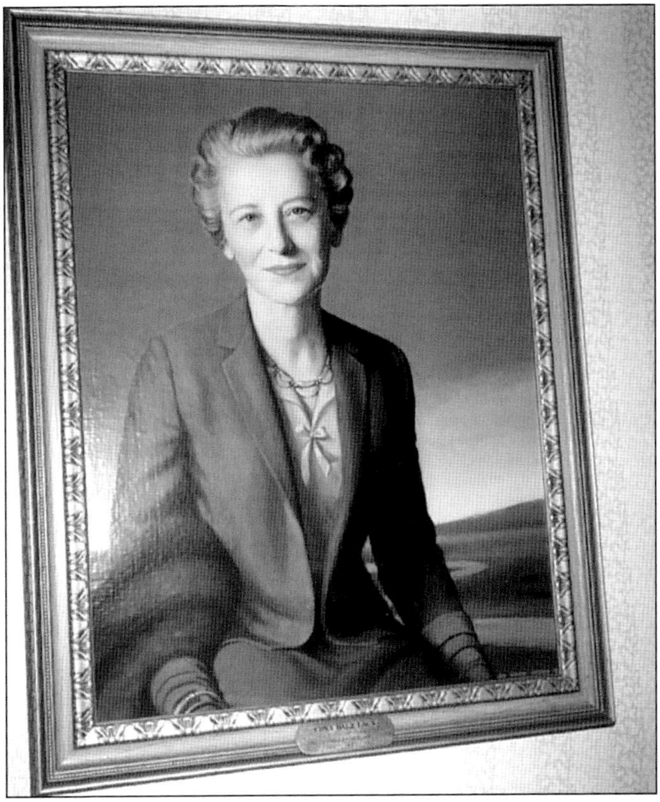

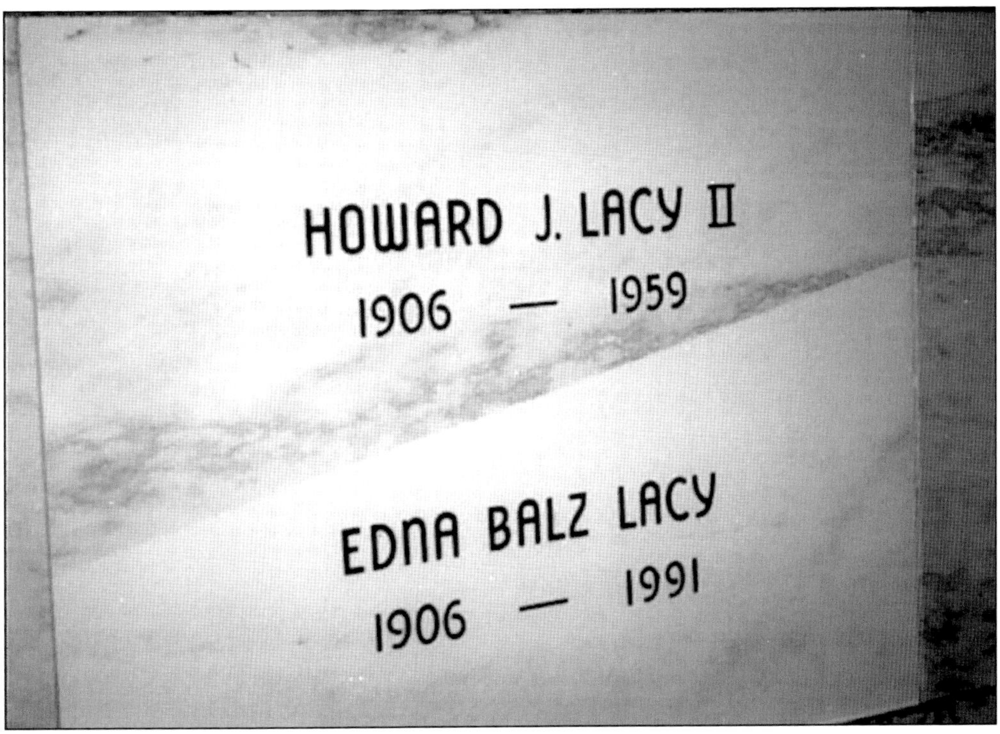

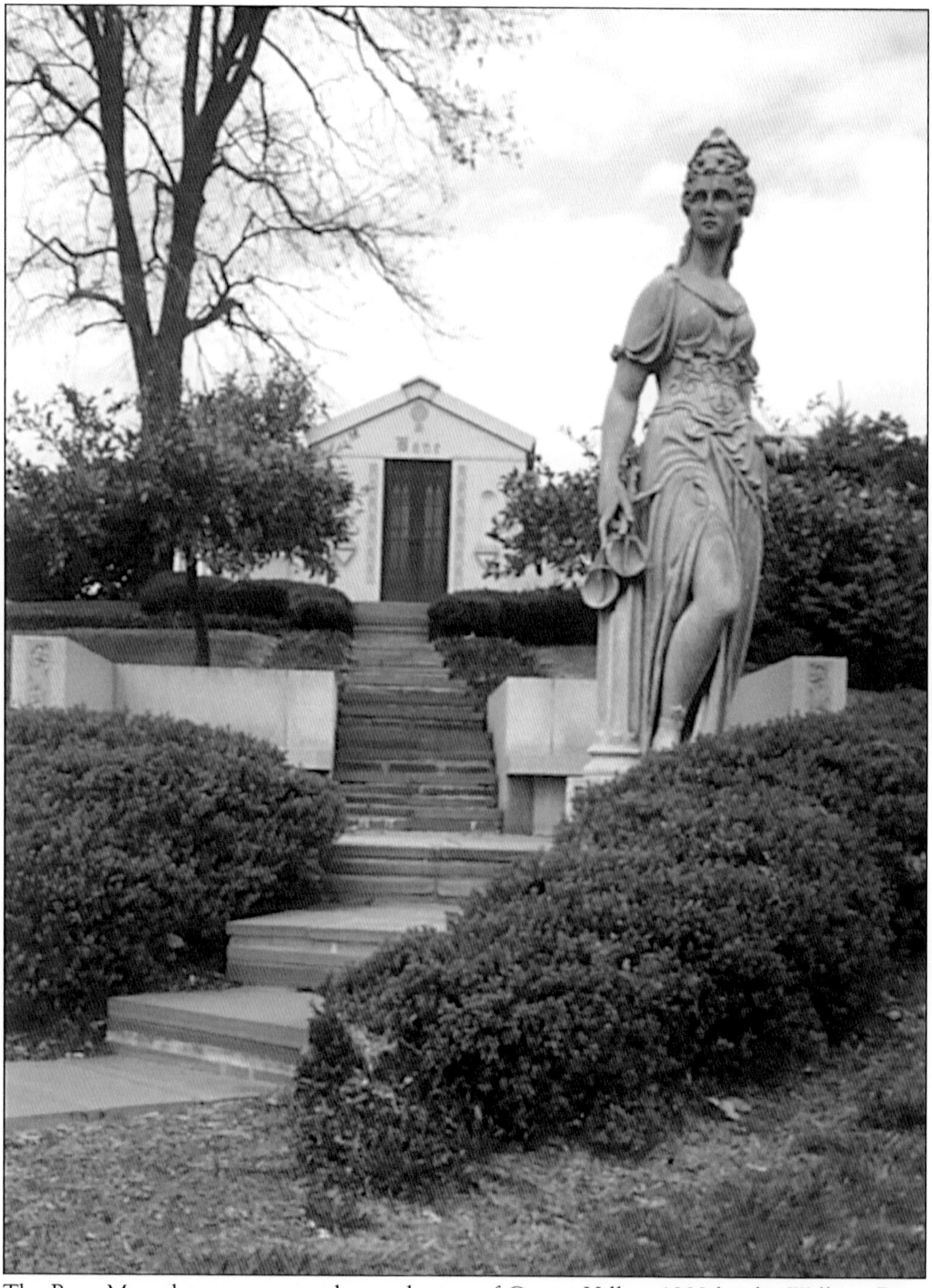

The Bane Mausoleum was erected near the top of Crown Hill in 1988 by the William Bane family, but no member of the family is buried there yet. "It was my mom's original thought," explained William Bane Jr. "She thought a mausoleum was the way to go. She didn't want to be buried in the ground." Its stained glass window inside contains a leprechaun with animals of the forest. The Bane family owns an international carpet cleaning business and an advertising agency in Indianapolis.

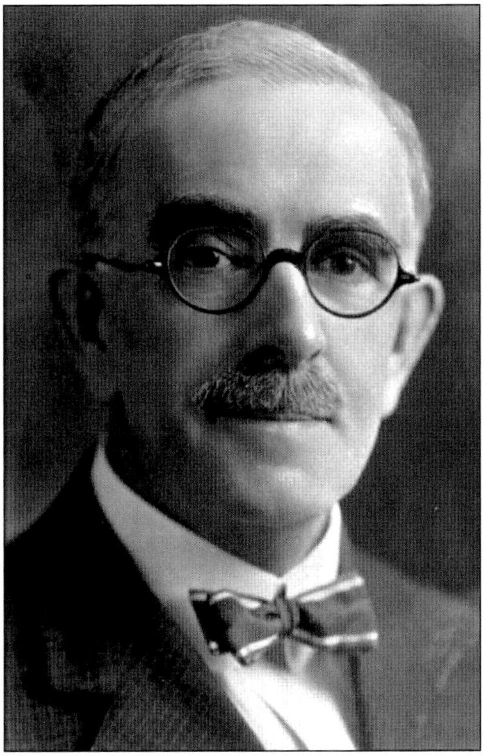

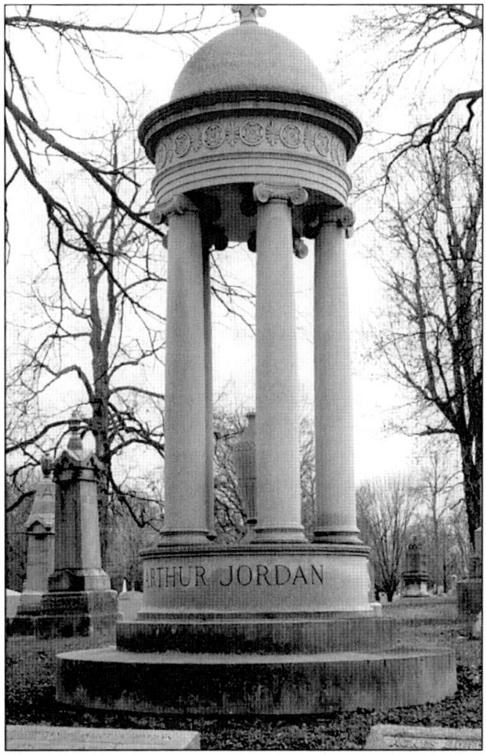

Arthur Jordan, 1855–1934, was a businessman and philanthropist. He donated Jordan Hall to Butler University. The music department and Arthur Jordan Foundation also bear his name. He is buried in Section 25, which is marked by this ornate circular columned canopy.

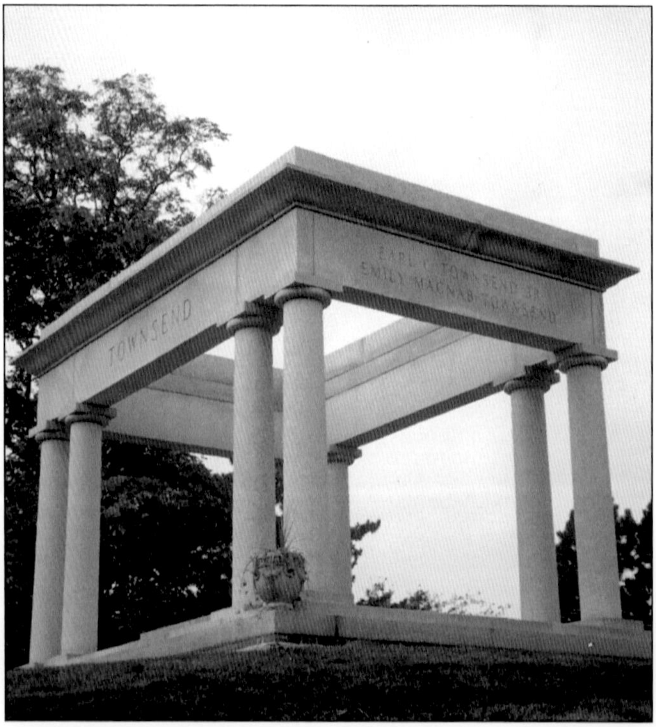

Near the top of Crown Hill lies the Townsend monument, which will someday house the remains of Earl C. Townsend Jr. and other Townsends. The lawyer, who is still alive, today, was one of the broadcasters of the first Indy 500 to be aired on television in 1949 on WFBM. He also has the largest collection of birdstones in the world and wrote *Birdstones of the North American Indians* in 1959. He's also a member of the Indiana Basketball Hall of Fame. (Photo courtesy of Marty Davis.)

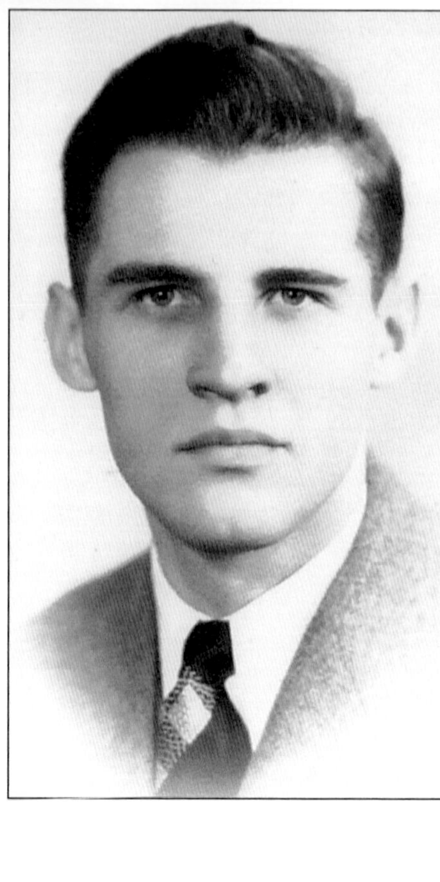

Five

The Arts

Many writers, artists, sculptors, and others involved in the arts have called Indianapolis home and several are buried in Crown Hill. The most famous of them all is James Whitcomb Riley, who is buried at the highest spot in the cemetery. He wrote the following poem about the cemetery:

At Crown Hill

Leave him here in the fresh greening grasses and trees
And the symbols of love, and the solace of these—
The saintly white lilies and blossoms he keeps
In endless caress as he breathlessly sleeps.
The tears of our eyes wrong the scene of his rest,
For the sky's at its clearest—the sun's at its best—
The earth at its greenest—its wild bud and bloom
At its sweetest—and sweetest its honey'd perfume.
Home! Home!—Leave him here in his lordly estate,
And with never a tear as we turn from the gate!

Turn back to the home that will know him no more,—
The vines at the window—the sun through the door,—
Nor sound of his voice, nor the light of his face! . . .
But the birds will sing on, and the rose, in his place,
Will tenderly smile til we daringly feign
He is home with us still, though the tremulous rain
Of our tears reappear, and again all is bloom,
And all prayerless we sob in the long-darkened room.
Heaven portions it thus—the old mystery dim,—
It is midnight to us—it is morning to him.

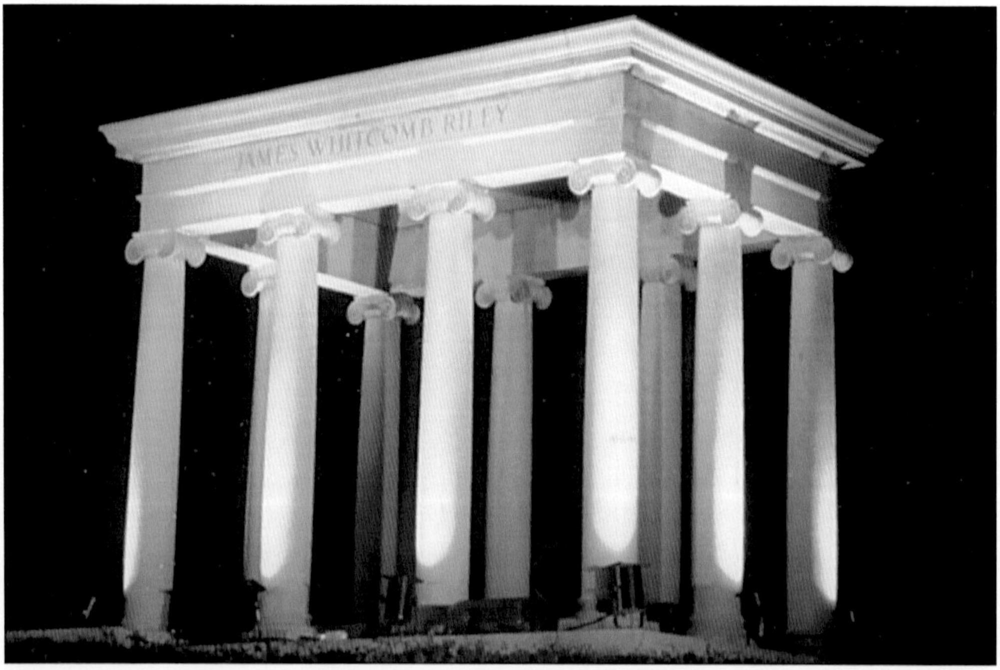

The top of the summit, the highest point in Indianapolis, belongs to James Whitcomb Riley, 1849–1916. Known as the "Hoosier Poet," Riley's poetry became famous and he penned many poems and books. His best-known poems include "Little Orphan Annie," "The Raggedy Man," and "When the Frost Is on the Pumpkin." Born in nearby Greenfield, Riley's home in Indianapolis is now a museum. When he died, some 35,000 people filed past his casket as it lay in state under the dome of the Indiana State Capitol. After he died, the Crown Hill Board of Incorporators offered to bury his remains at the peak of Crown Hill, but his family was buried in Greenfield. The family decided to go along with Crown Hill and his remains sat in the Gothic Chapel for more than a year before he was put in his final resting place. His open canopy monument overlooks the city and is a favorite spot for visitors to the cemetery. At Greenfield, the view would have been that of a sewage plant. The photo of Riley comes from a postcard. (Photo of monument at night courtesy of Marty Davis.)

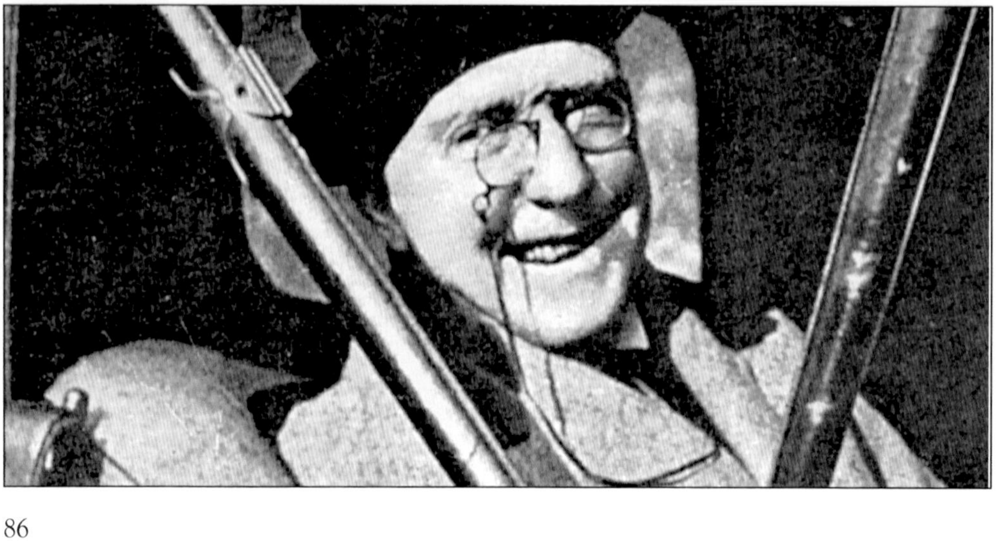

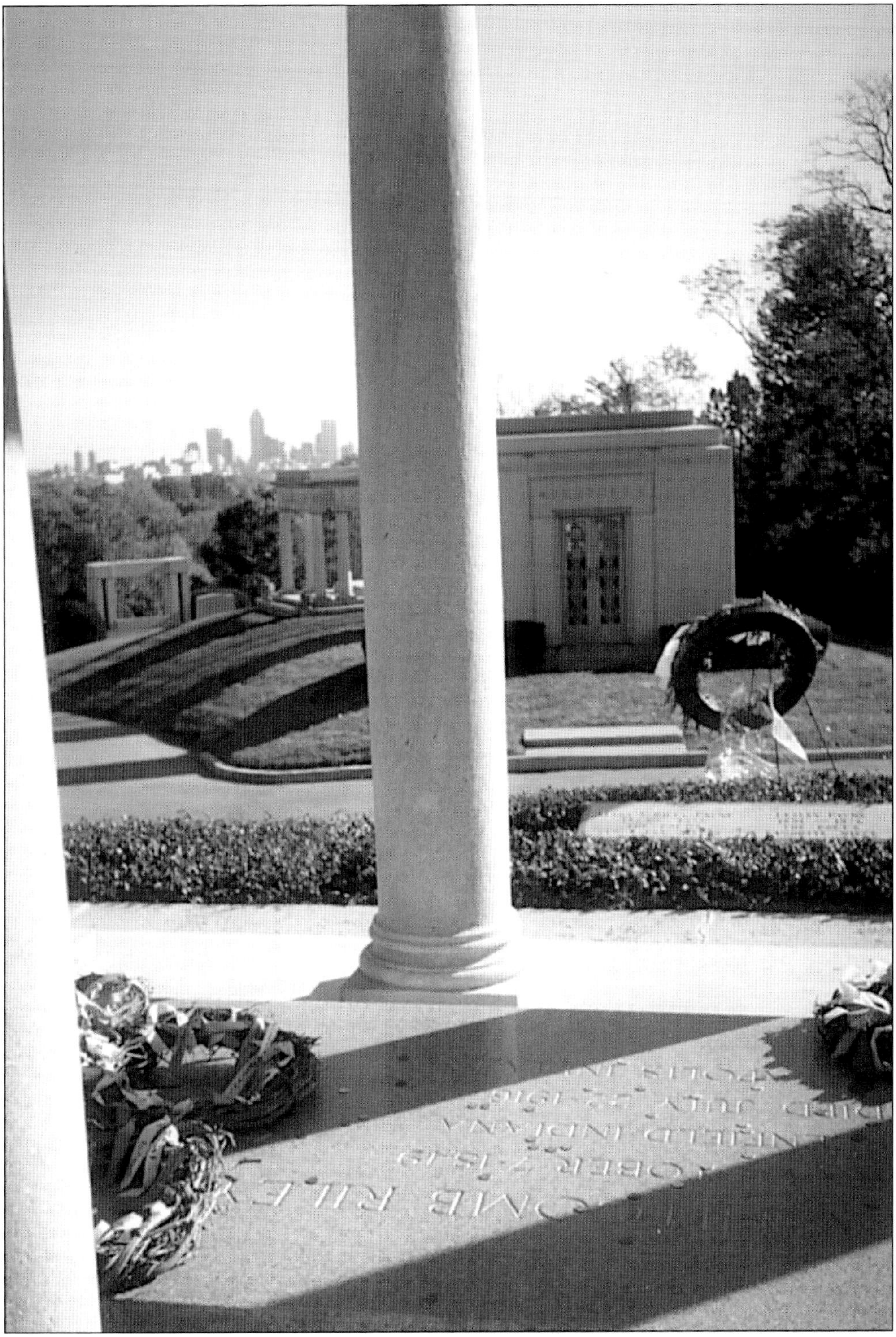

Visitors to Riley's monument on top sometimes leave coins, flowers, and other mementos. The monument provides a fantastic view of downtown Indianapolis.

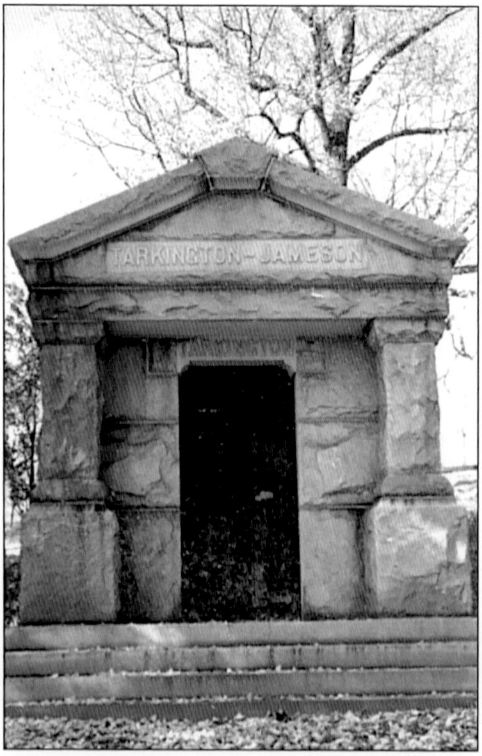

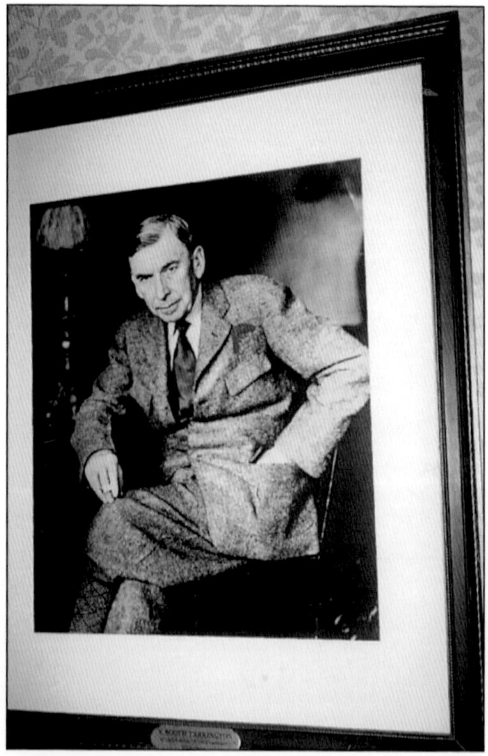

Newton Booth Tarkington, 1869–1946, was a novelist and dramatist. His first successful novel, *The Gentleman from Indiana*, was published in 1899. Other successful works included *Penrod*, *Penrod and Sam* and *Seventeen*. His many plays included *Clarence*, *The Man From Home*, and *Monsieur Beaucaire*. His remains are located in the Tarkington-Jameson mausoleum in Section 13, Lot 56. This picture of Tarkington hangs in the Crown Hill Funeral Home.

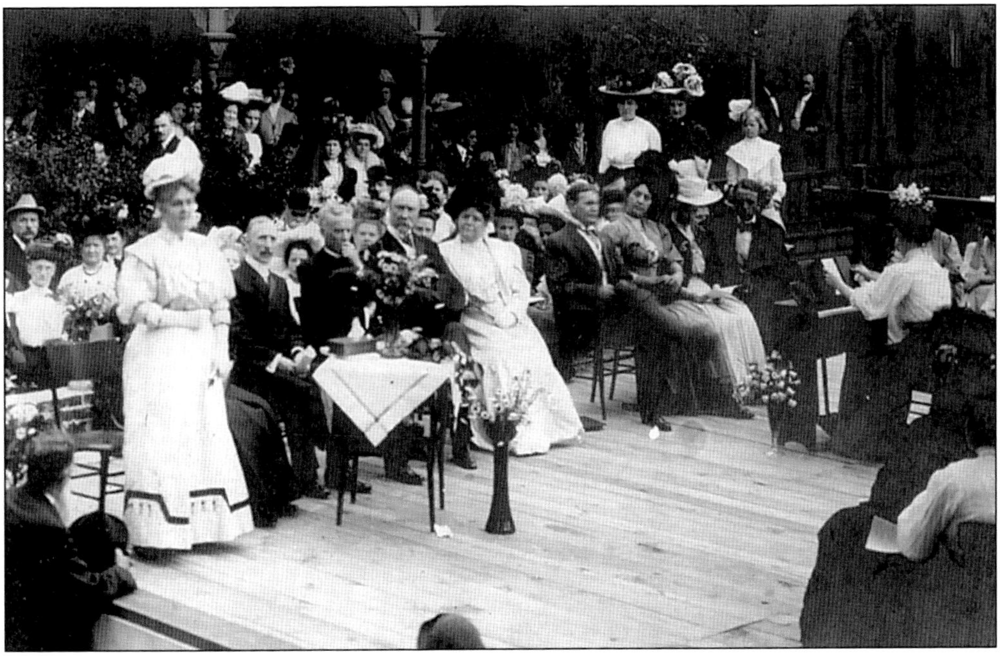

May Wright (Mary Eliza) Sewall, 1844–1920, was an educator and leader in art and other cultural interests in Indianapolis. Born in Greenfield, Wisconsin, Sewall first came to Indianapolis and taught at the first high school. She campaigned for women's suffrage and helped found the Equal Suffrage Society of Indianapolis. Then she founded the Propylaeum and the Contemporary Club, and was president of the International Council of Women, 1899–1904. After she moved from Indianapolis, she wrote *Neither Dead Nor Sleeping* (1920) before her death. Her remains are located in Section 13, Lot 24.

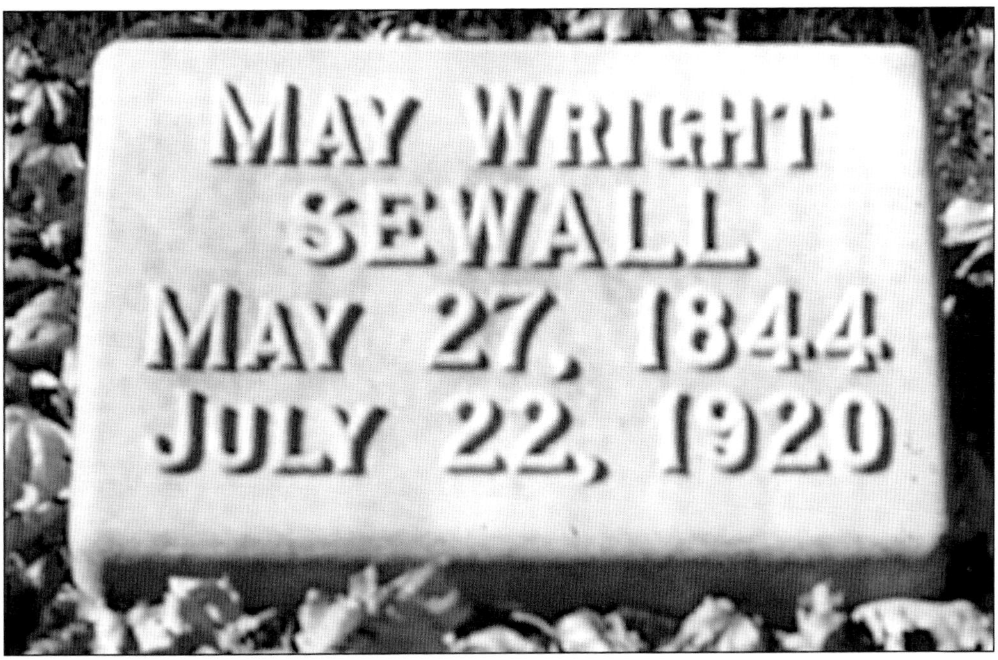

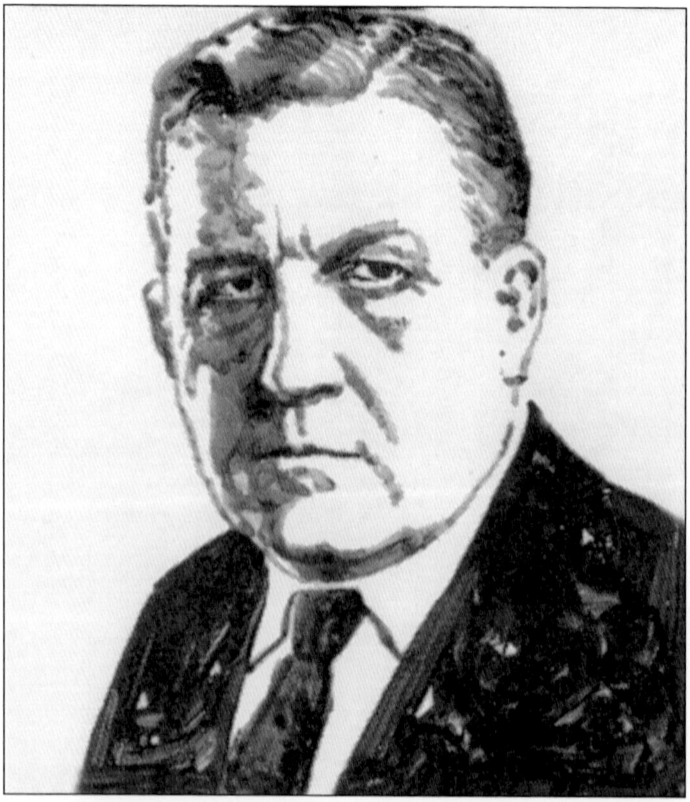

Meredith Nicholson, 1866–1947, was a writer and diplomat. He rose to national literary fame in 1905 with the publication of *The House of a Thousand Candles*. He wrote many works in which his love of Indiana was reflected. He worked a dozen years on the *Indianapolis News*. Later in life he turned to politics and became the U.S. minister to Uruguay, Venezuela, and Nicaragua. The small raised headstone of Nicholson is located in the northeast corner of Section 4.

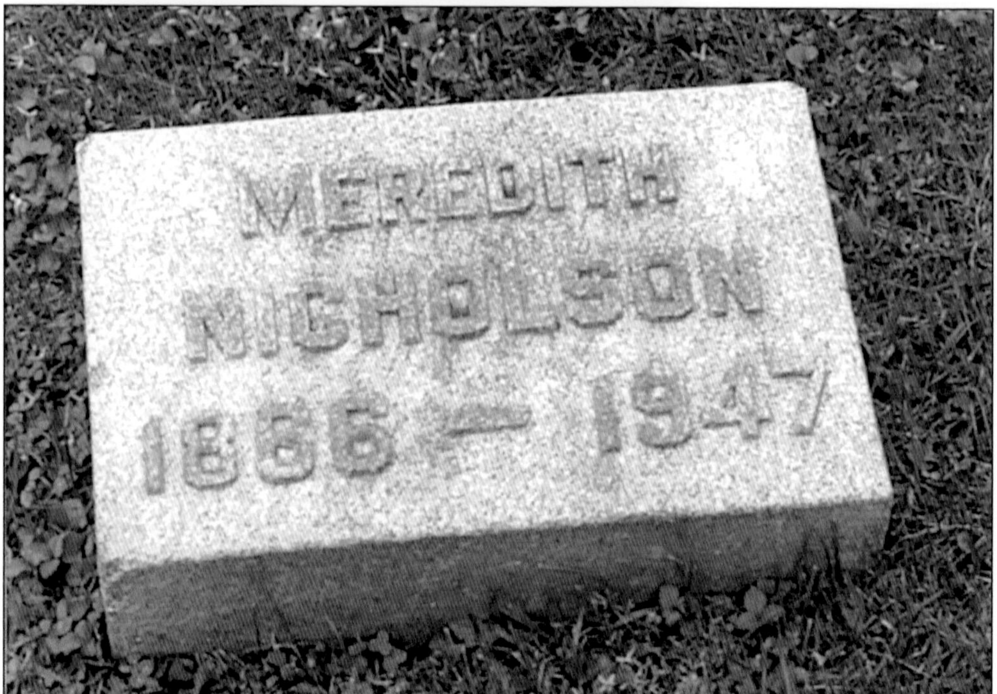

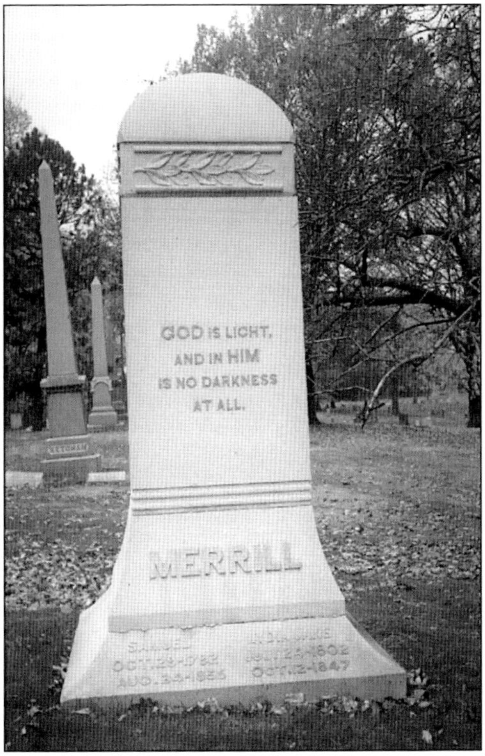

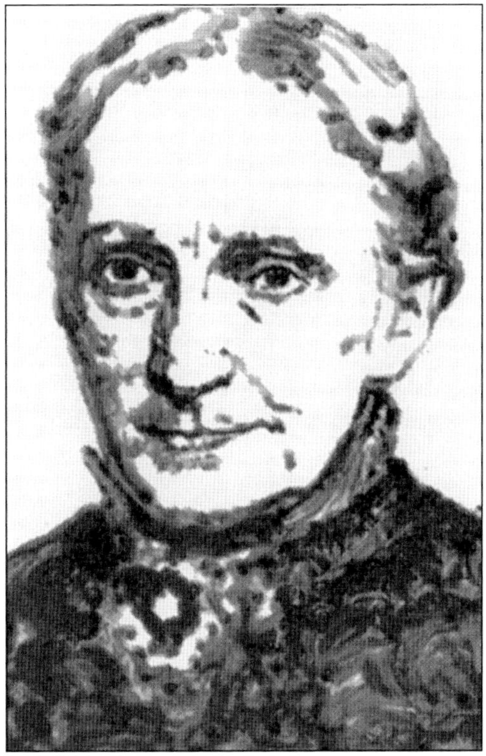

Catharine Merrill, 1824–1900, was an educator and literary authority. She volunteered as a nurse during the Civil War and wrote about it in *The Soldier of Indiana in the War for the Union.* She became the second woman in the United States to hold a full college professorship when she taught at Northwestern Christian University, which later became Butler College. Her remains are located in an unmarked grave in the family plot in Section 7, Lot 16.

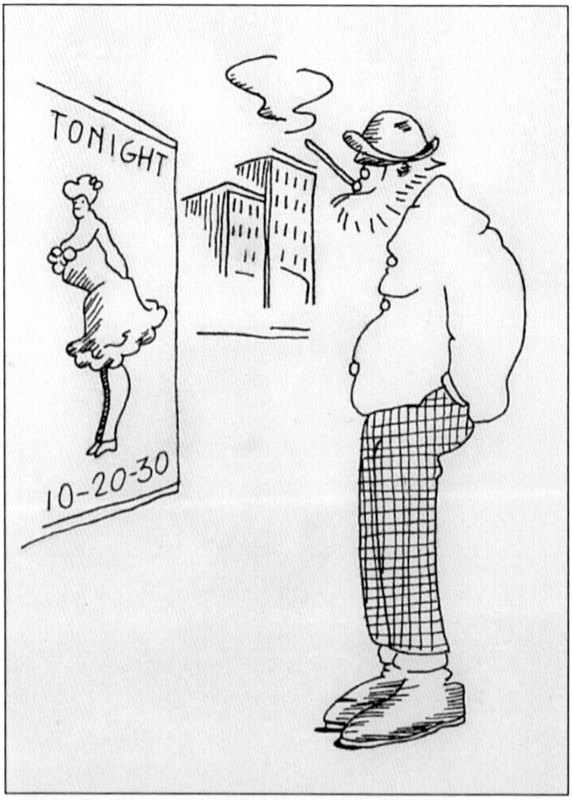

Frank McKinney "Kin" Hubbard, 1868–1930, created Abe Martin, a rustic Hoosier character that began in the *Indianapolis News* and was syndicated in more than 300 newspapers. Hubbard's first cartoon of Abe Martin appeared in the *Indianapolis News* on December 17, 1904. It was captioned: "If I thought that blamed troupe done everything it has pictures fer, I'd stay over this evening and go home on the interurban." He worked for 30 years at the *Indianapolis News*. He also wrote *Abe Martin's Almanack* and other books that are now collectors' items. The lodge at Brown County State Park is named for Abe Martin. His grave is located in the Community Mausoleum, GG-C-6.

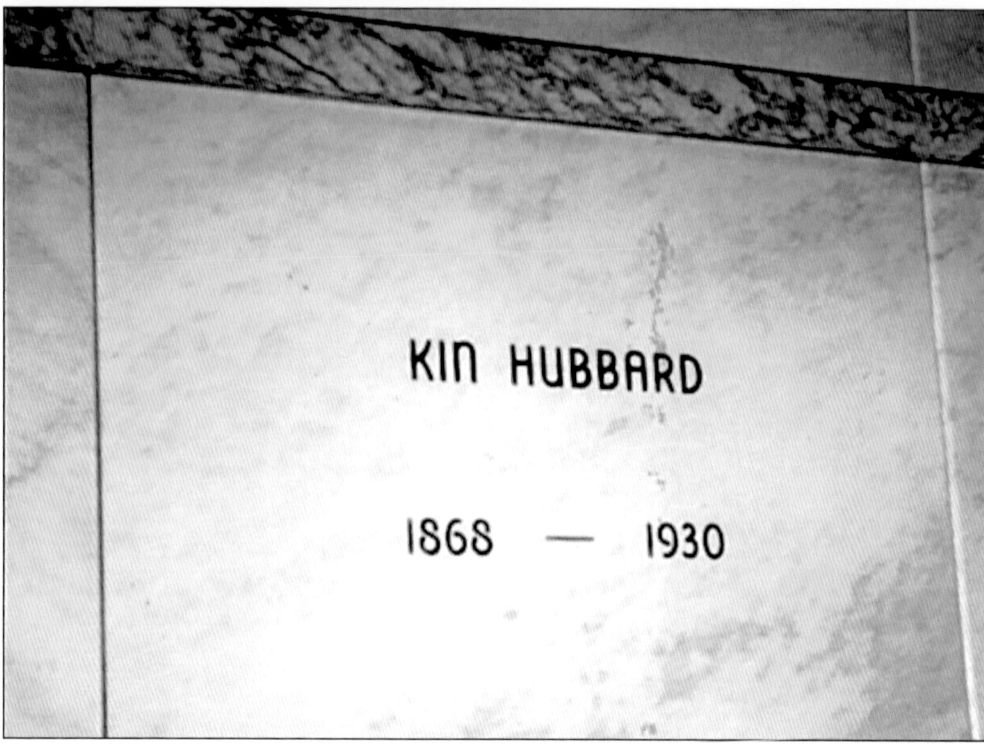

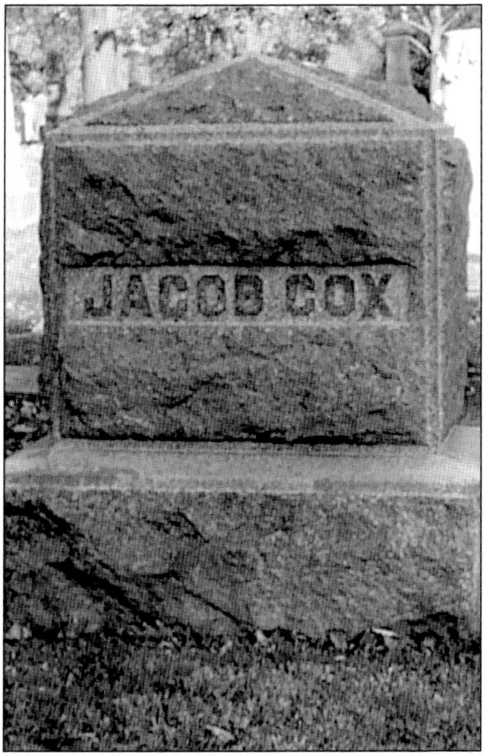

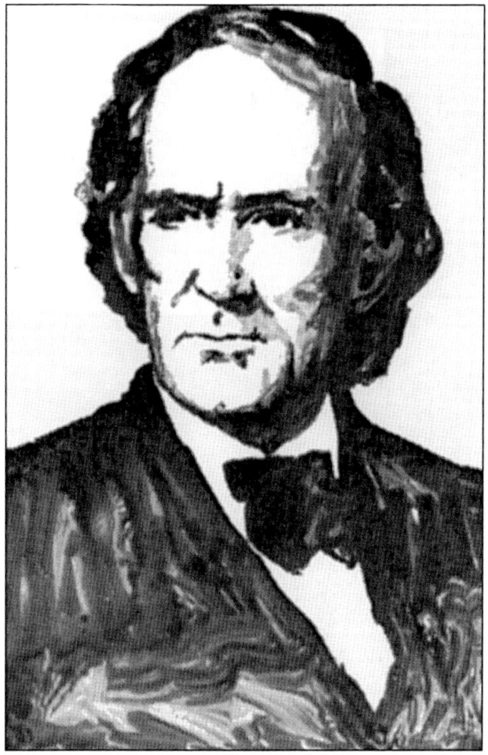

Jacob Cox, 1810–1892, was the first professional portrait and landscape painter in Indianapolis. His oils of six early Indiana governors hang in the Statehouse. Cox's paintings can be found at the Indianapolis Museum of Art, the Indiana State Museum, the Indiana State House, and the Morris-Butler House. His grave is located in Section 54, Lot 1870, but there is no marker.

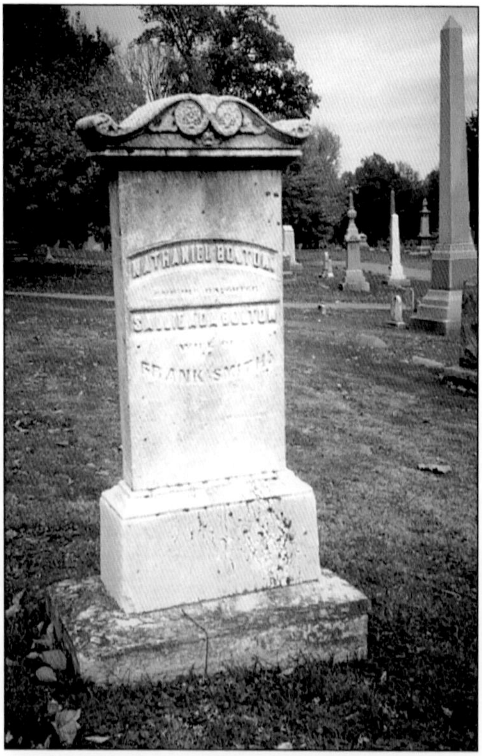

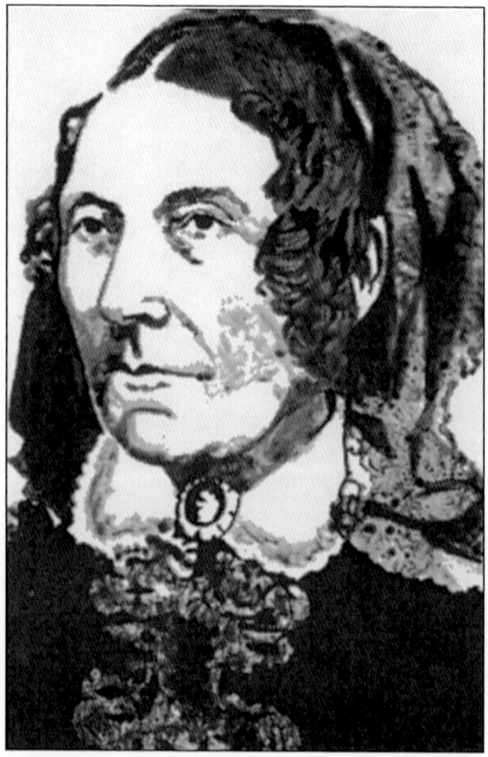

Sarah T. Bolton, 1814-1893, was the first Hoosier poet laureate. The poem that gained her widest national recognition was *Paddle Your Own Canoe*. She also was an advocate for women's property rights. The Sarah Bolton Society Poetry Group still meets today at the Beech Grove Public Library. She was married to Nathaniel Bolton, the publisher of the *Indianapolis Gazette*, the first newspaper published in the capital city. After he died, she married Judge Addison Reese. Both Boltons are buried in Section 5.

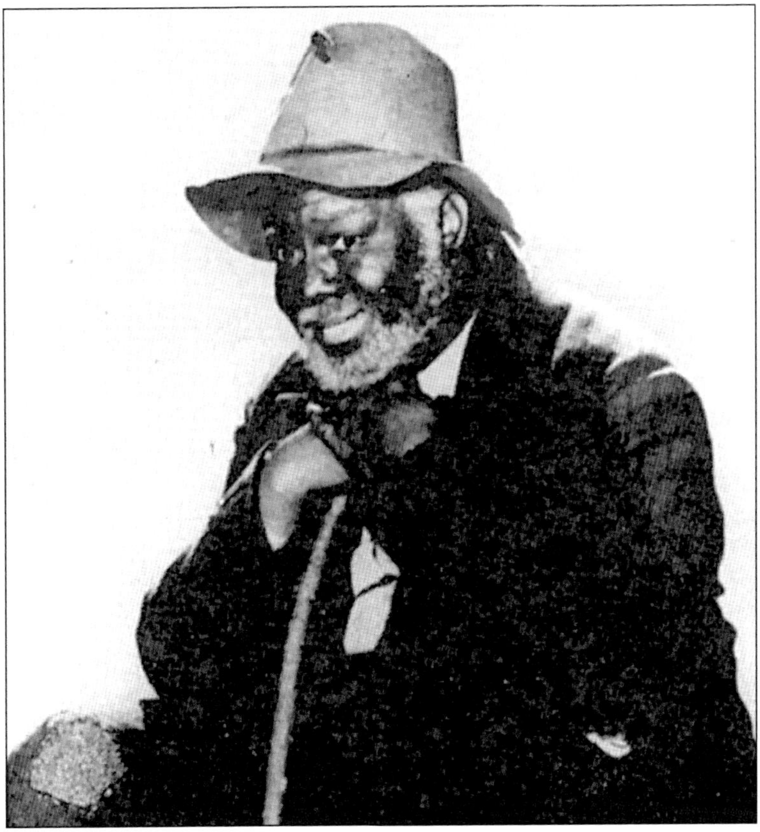

James Baskett, 1904–1948, was a black actor who portrayed Uncle Remus in the 1946 Walt Disney movie Song of the South. Baskett was awarded a special Academy Award for his role. He is buried in Section 37.

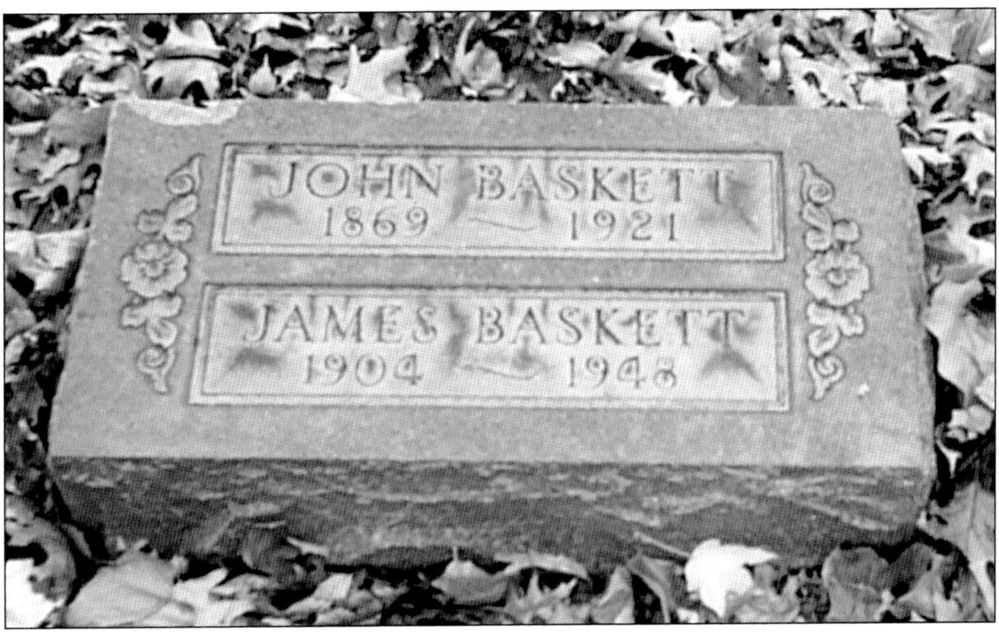

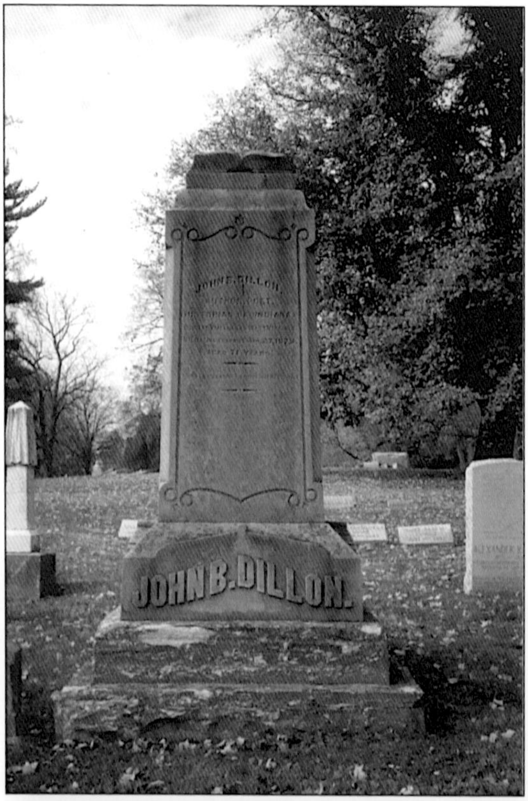

John B. Dillon, 1808–1879, was a historian and author. He penned the first history of Indiana in 1843 and served as the state librarian. He also wrote several volumes including a history of the Northwest Territory. Dillon is buried in a charity lot reserved for "Destitute Instructors of Public Schools" in 1874. A total of eight persons are buried in this lot in Section 3.

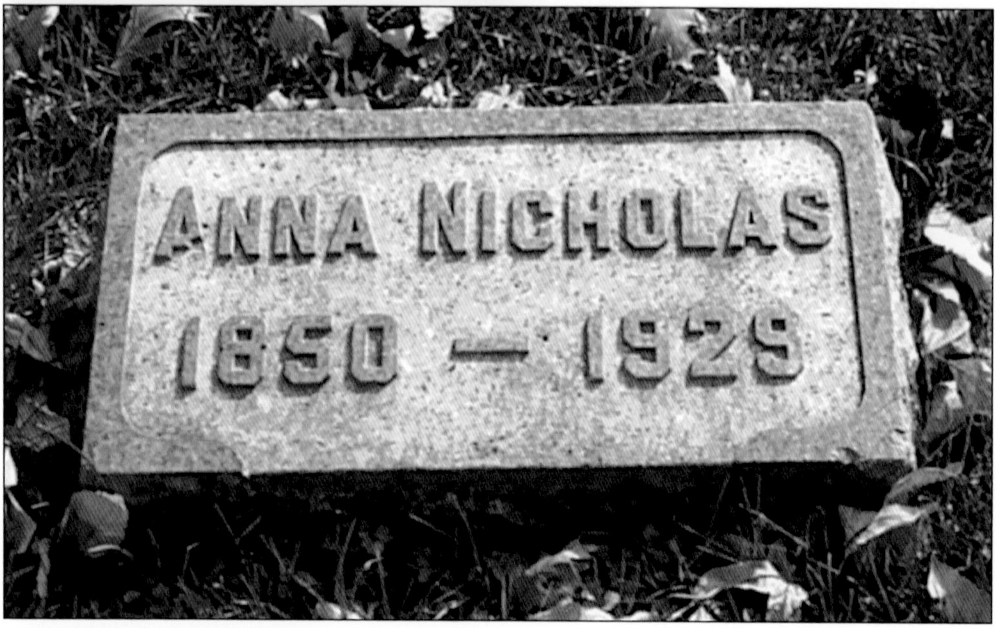

Anna Nicholas, 1850–1929, was a newspaper writer and wrote *The Story of Crown Hill*, published a year before her death. Her book was used for some of the research that went into this book. Her brother, John D. Nicholas, 1842–1893, was a well-known newspaper columnist and is buried next to her in Section 15.

Six

SPORTS FIGURES

Since Indianapolis is host to the "Greatest Spectacle in Racing," many automotive racing greats are buried in Crown Hill. The Indianapolis Motor Speedway was founded in 1906 by Carl Fisher, James Allison, Arthur Newby, and Frank Wheeler, who are all buried at Crown Hill. In 1911, the Speedway held the first Indy 500 race and two of the drivers were Frank Fox and Charles Merz, who are buried in Crown Hill. Two winners of the Indy 500 are buried at Crown Hill: Louis Schneider in 1931 and Howdy Wilcox in 1919. Other veteran drivers who are buried in Crown Hill include George Amick, Erwin "Cannonball" Baker, Tony Bettenhausen Jr., Floyd Davis, Jimmy Daywalt, Ronnie Duman, Jerry Hoyt, Jim Hurtubise, Herbert Jones, Chet Miller, and Paul Russo.

Several other racing officials involved in the 500 are interned at Crown Hill, including Thomas Binford, chief steward; Robert Bowes, car sponsor; Frankie Del Roy, riding mechanic and USAC official; "Eddie" Waldo Edenburn, chief steward; Gaylord "Snappy" Ford, riding mechanic and track official; Harry "Cotton" Henning, chief mechanic on Wilbur Shaw's racing team; Karl Kizer, mechanic and curator; Arthur B. Lathrop, car owner; Theodore "Pop" Myers, Speedway general manager; George M. Ober, co-founder of USAC; Herb Porter, mechanic for several drivers; Jack Rodgers, co-owner of Tony Bettenhausen Jr.'s racing team; Louis Schwitzer, automotive engineer; Pat Vidan, chief starter; Charles Wiggins, mechanic; and Charles Wyatt, promoter.

The cemetery is also home to some of the automotive makers who put cars in the great race. Local automotive builders who entered cars in the 500 included the Marmon family, Harry Stutz, and the Duesenberg family.

While many racing greats are buried at Crown Hill, some of the other professional sports figures have found their way to the cemetery. The owner of the Indianapolis Colts, Robert Irsay, is buried at Crown Hill as well as professional player Stacey Toran of the Los Angles Raiders.

Professional baseball is represented by a couple of figures. C.I. Taylor was part of the Indianapolis ABCs, a black professional team which played in the early 1900s. Also, Hod Eller played in the major leagues.

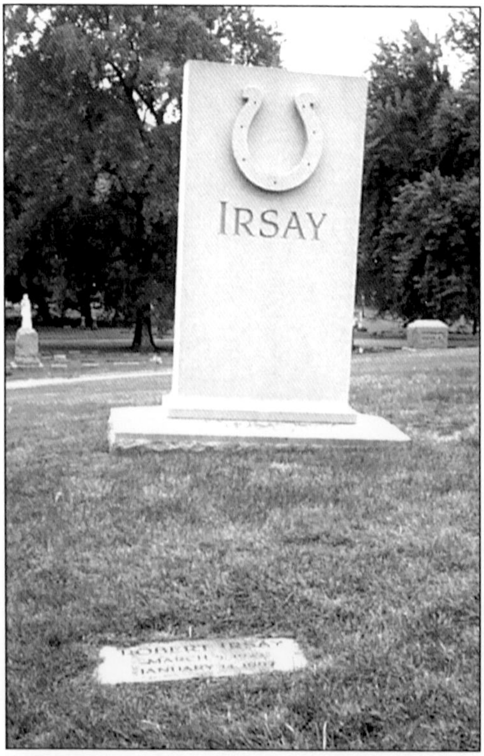

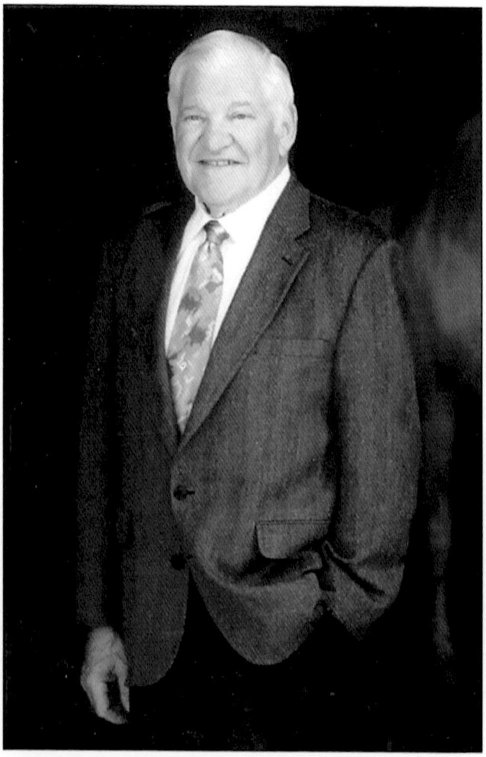

Robert Irsay, 1923–1997, was the former owner of the Indianapolis Colts. He has a plot at the base of Crown Hill. Born in Chicago, he bought the Baltimore Colts in 1972 and moved the team to Indianapolis in 1984. A graduate of the University of Illinois, Irsay built one of the largest heating, ventilating, and air conditioning companies in the world. "It is my intention for the Colts to be a vital contributing member of the greater Indianapolis community," he once said. His son, James, took control over the team after his passing. (Photo courtesy of the Indianapolis Colts.)

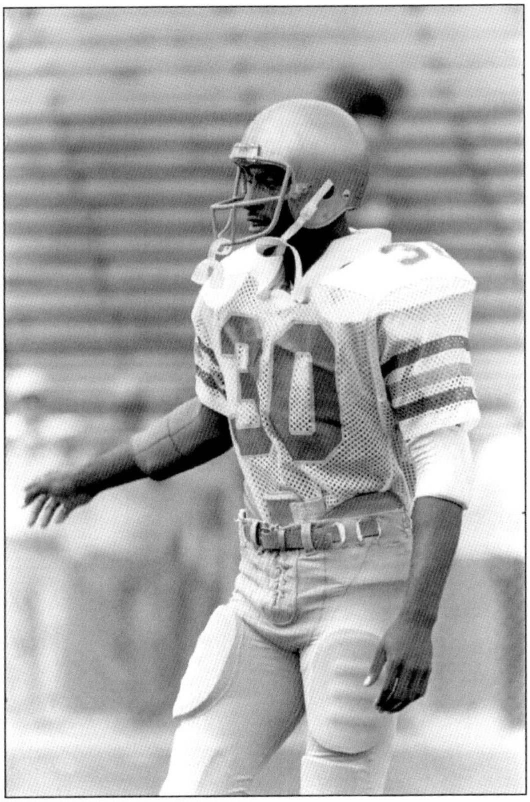

Stacey J. Toran, 1961–1989, played in the National Football League for five seasons. The Broad Ripple High School graduate was a co-captain on the Notre Dame football team before being drafted by the NFL, where he played for the Los Angeles Raiders, 1984–1988. He was named to the All (John) Madden Team. He died on August 5, 1989 in alcohol-related auto accident. After his death, the Stacey Toran Foundation was established. His remains are located in Section 225.

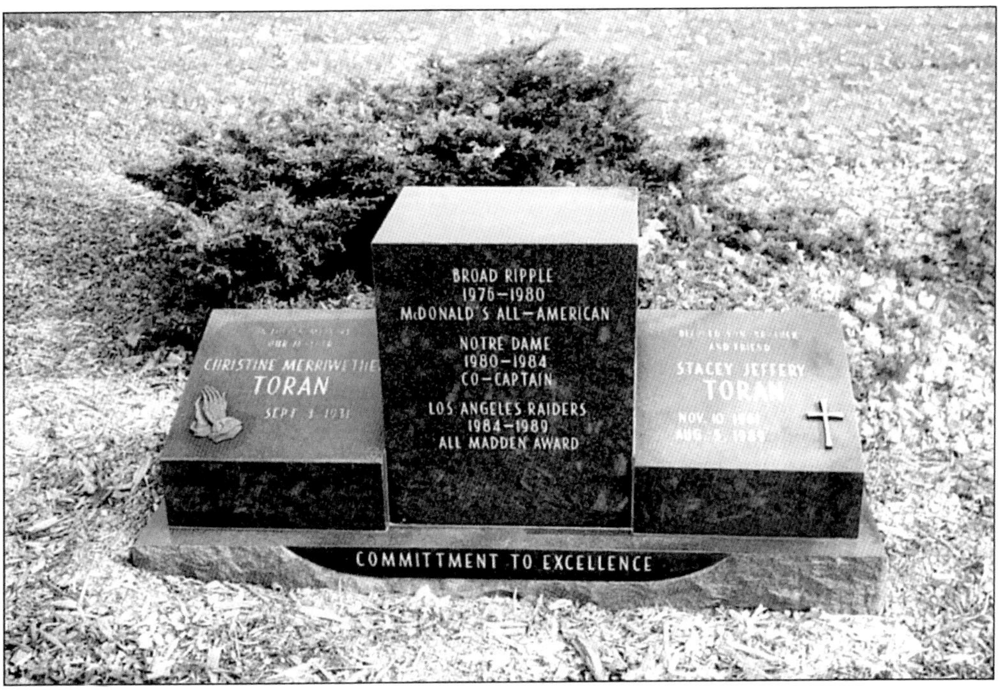

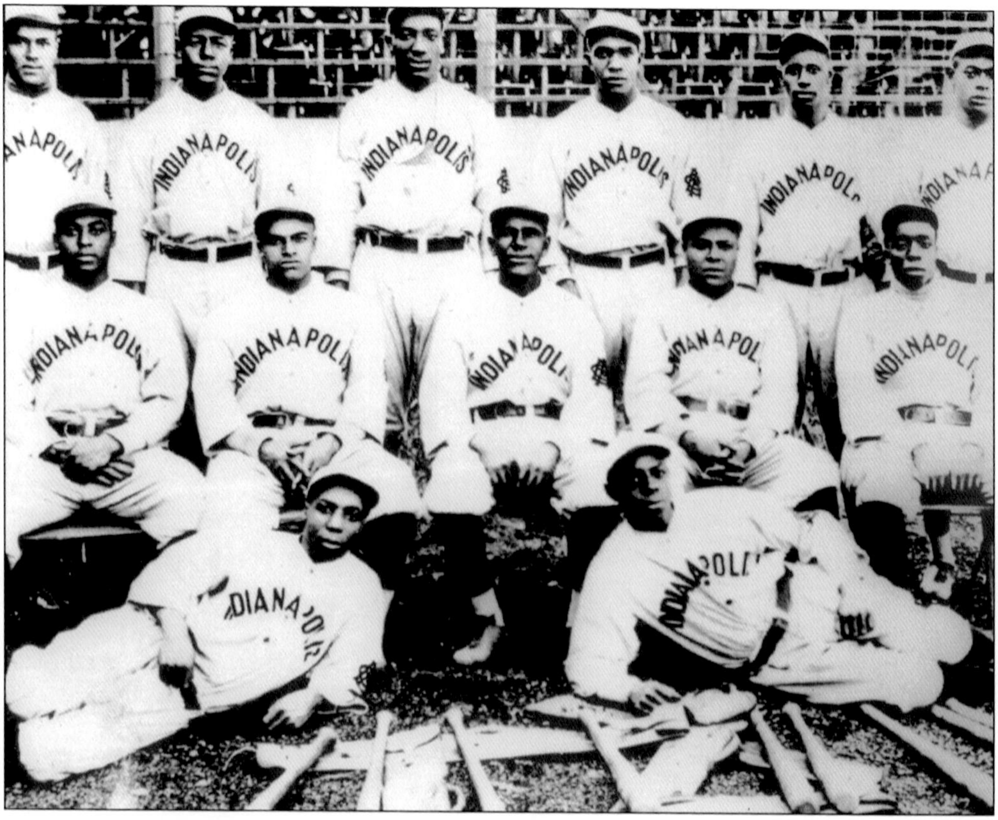

Charles Isam Taylor (center of photo), 1875–1922, was a player/manager in the Negro Leagues, 1904–1922. Known as C.I., he managed the Birmingham Giants until coming to Indiana to run the West Baden Sprudels and the Indianapolis ABCs. He was instrumental in founding the Negro National League and the National Association of Colored Professional Baseball Clubs. His grave is located in Section 29.

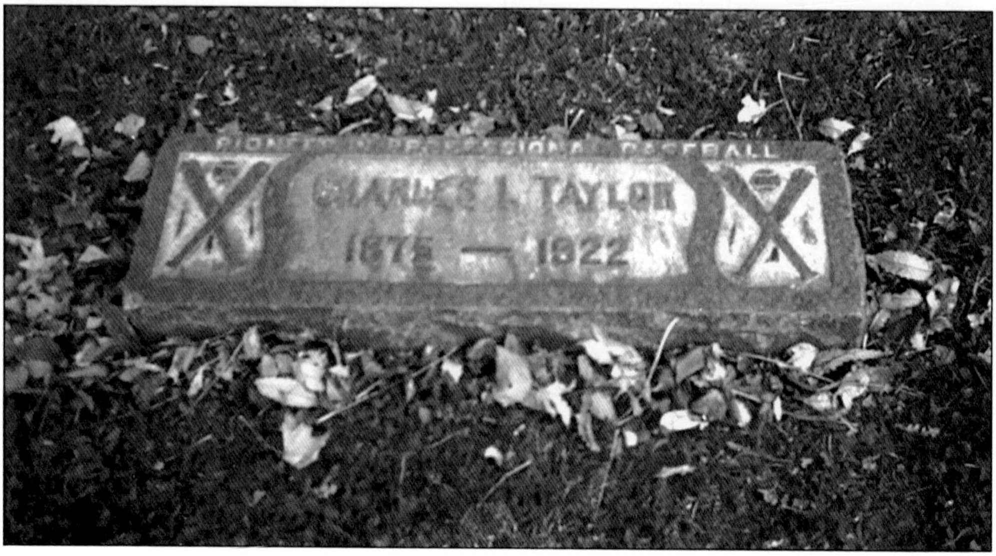

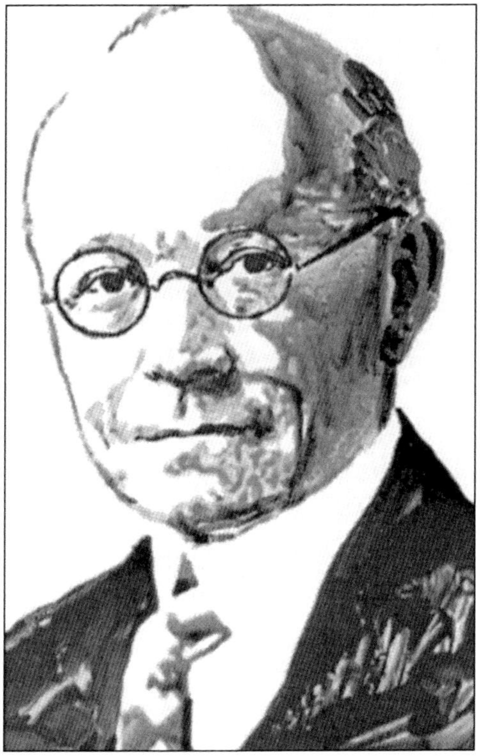

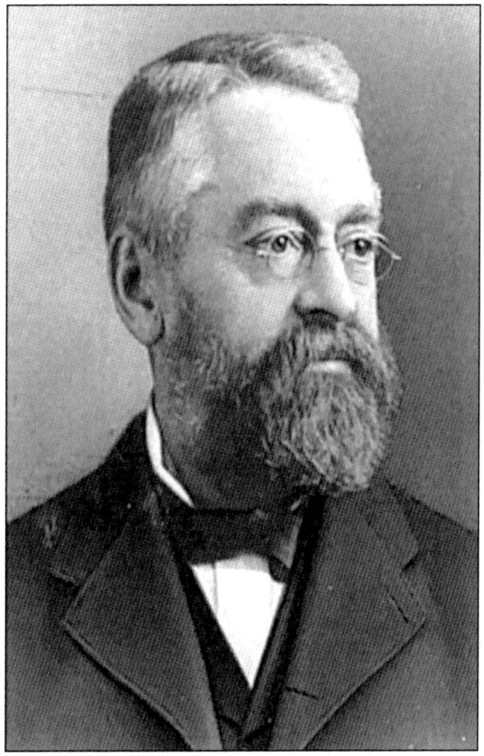

Walter Carpenter Marmon, 1872–1940, (*left*) directed the Nordyke & Marmon Company in Richmond, Indiana. The builders of flour milling machinery turned to automobile manufacturing, and one of his cars won the first Indianapolis 500 race in 1911. He also helped organize the Marmon-Herrington Company in Indianapolis. His remains are located in Section 29, Lot 44. Other Marmons buried in Crown Hill include Franklin, 1899–1924, and Howard, 1876–1943, and Daniel W. (*right*).

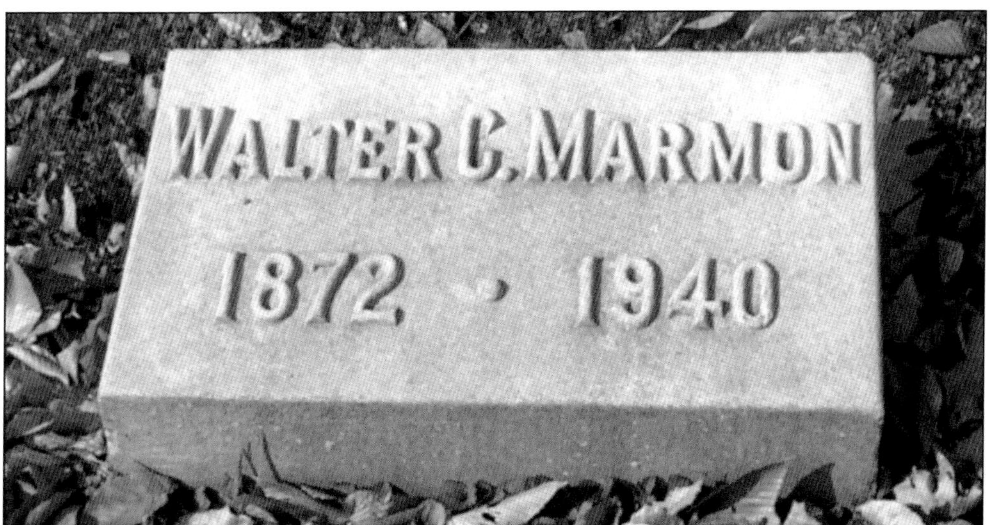

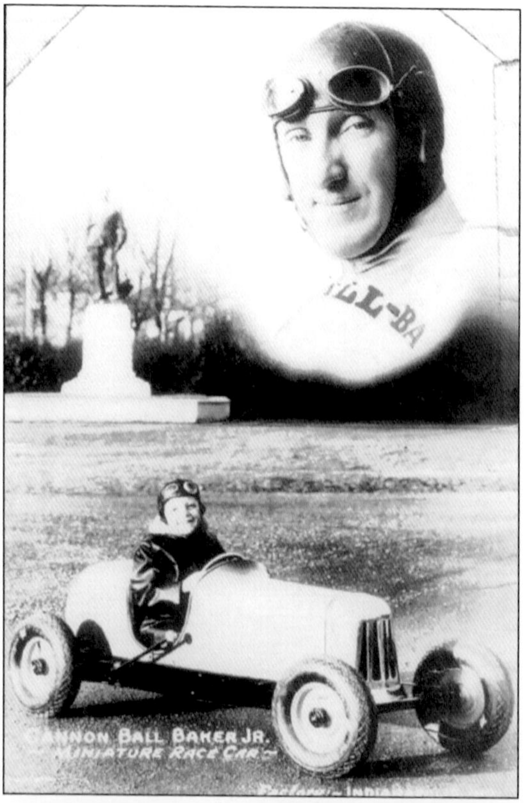

Erwin George "Cannonball" Baker, 1882–1960, was a race car driver who chalked up five-and-a-half million miles of racing during his career. He began as a motorcycle racer for the Indian factory team and won the 10-mile national championship at the new Indianapolis Speedway in 1909. He also drove in two early 500 races. "Cannonball" became his nickname after he drove a Stutz Bearcat from San Diego to New York in 11 days, 7 hours, and 15 minutes in 1915. He was also the first commissioner of NASCAR. He once held more auto and motorcycle records than any other driver. This postcard shows him as a child and an adult. He is buried in the Section 60, Lot 150.

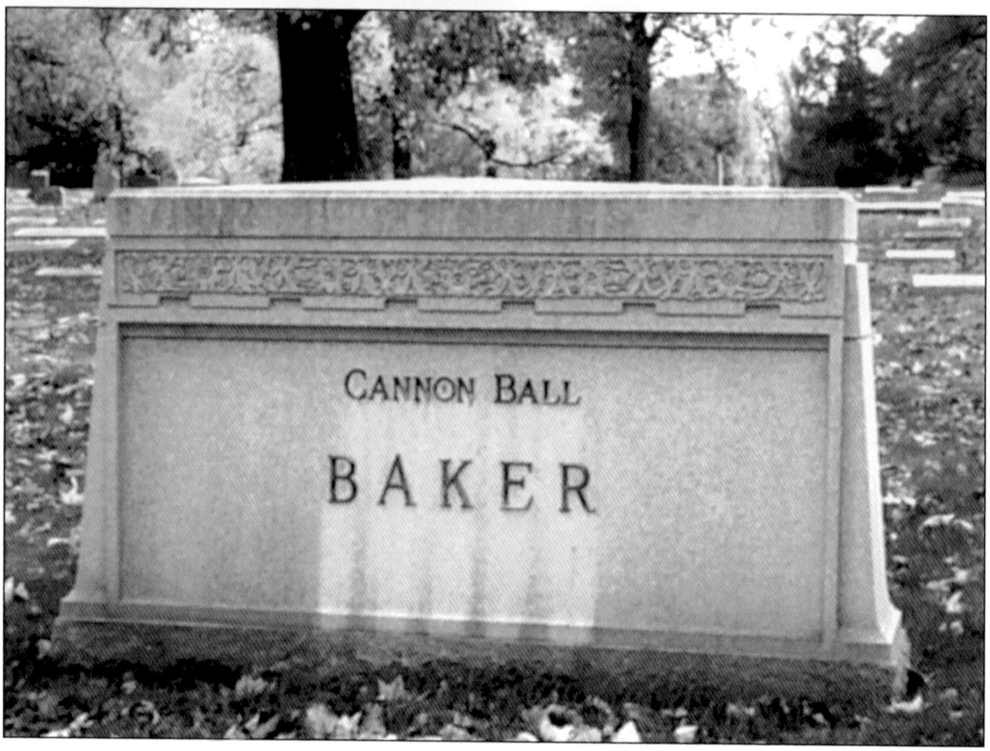

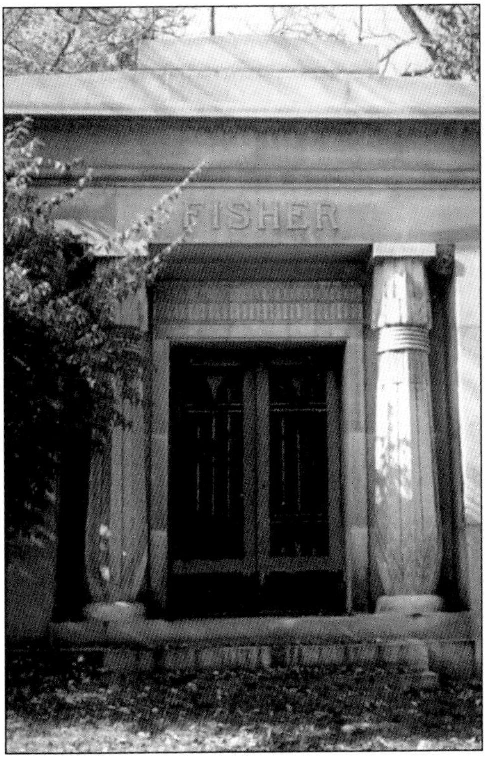

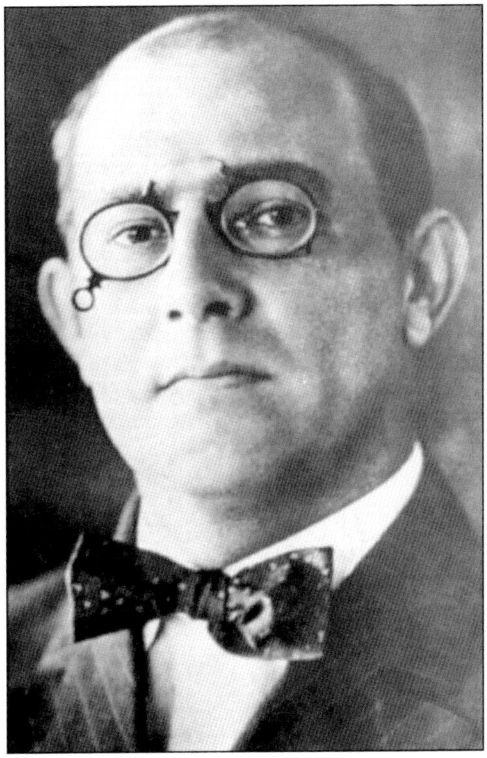

Carl G. Fisher, 1874–1939, conceived the Indianapolis Speedway and was its first president. Later in life, he founded Miami Beach, Florida. The automobile racer and dealer founded the Prest-O-Lite Company and pioneered cross-country highways. First, he developed the Lincoln Highway from New York City to San Francisco. Then he developed Highway 1 and the Dixie Highway from Indiana to Florida, where he developed Miami Beach and became a rich man until a hurricane and the stock market failure ruined all of that. He died as a poor man of cirrhosis in Miami Beach. Several of his motor speedway partners—James Allison, Authur C. Newby, and Frank Wheeler—are also buried at Crown Hill. His remains are located in a mausoleum in Section 13, Lot 42.

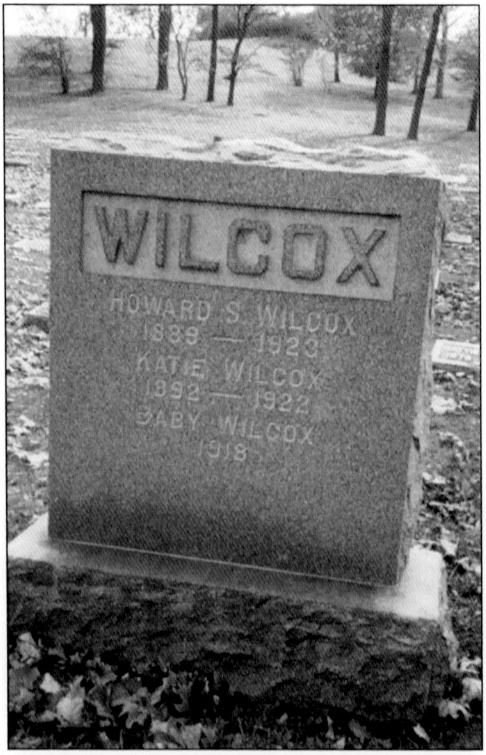

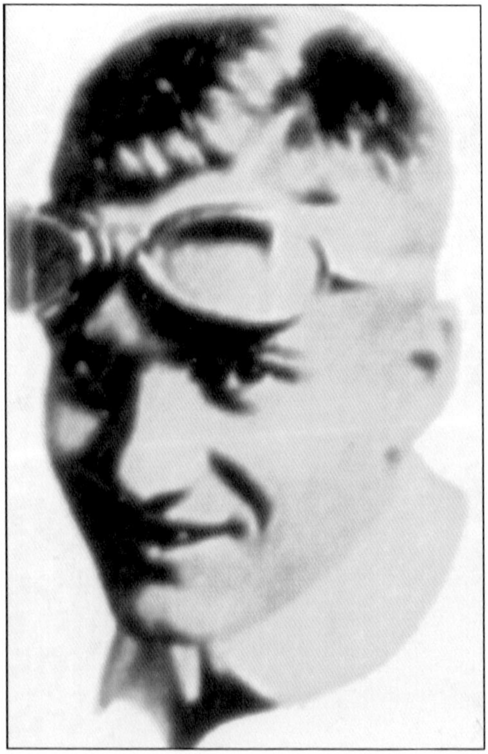

Howard S. "Howdy" Wilcox, 1889–1923, won the Indy 500 in 1919 and had five top-ten finishes in the race as well before he died racing in Altonna, Pennsylvania. He was the first 500 driver to break the 100 mph barrier. His son, who was the founder of Indiana University's Little 500 bicycle race and instrumental in found the Indianapolis 500 Festival, is also buried in Crown Hill. The racer is buried in Section 56, Lot 240.

Frederick, 1876–1932, and August Duesenberg, 1879–1955, created the Duesenberg Motor Company and entered Duesenberg-powered cars at the Indy 500 from 1913–1934. They were elected to the Indianapolis Motor Speedway Racing Hall of Fame in 1962. The brothers moved their company from Des Moines, Iowa to Indianapolis in 1920. In 1921, seven of the first 10 finishers at the Indianapolis 500 were Duesenberg racers. On three occasions, Duesenbergs won the 500. Fred Duesenberg (*right*) died of complications following the crash of one of his cars in the Pennsylvania mountains. Augie died of a heart attack. Frederick is buried in Section 104, Lot 294, while August is interned in the Community Mausoleum, D-2-NN.

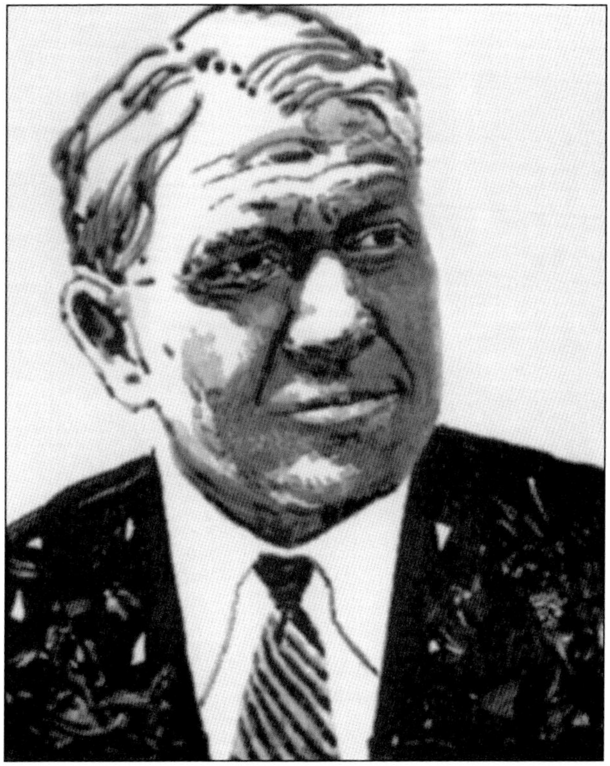

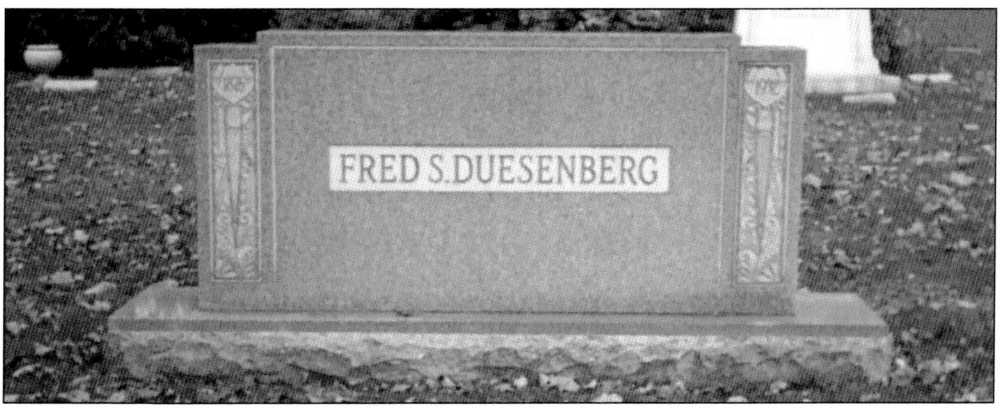

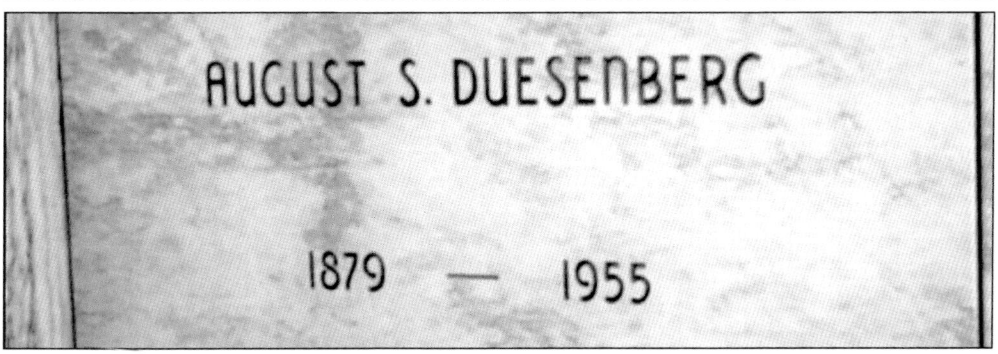

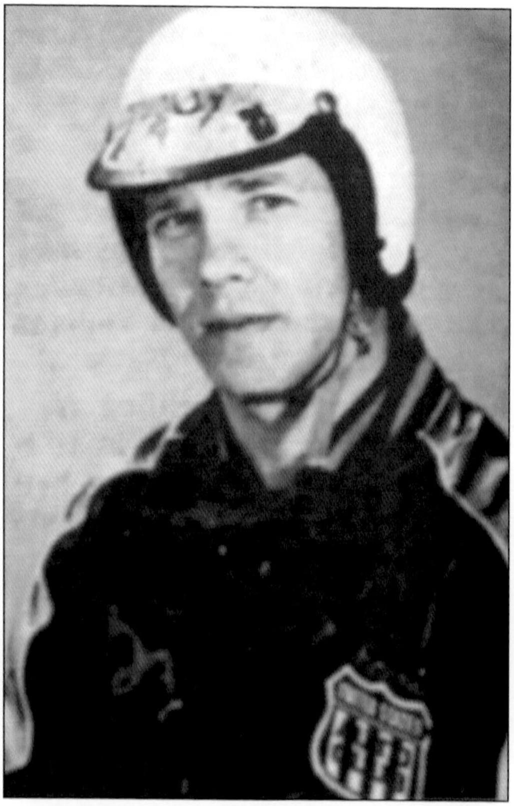

Ronald B. "Ronnie" Duman, 1929–1968, was a local driver who raced in five Indianapolis 500s, 1964–1968. He survived a fiery crash in 1964 at the Speedway, but he died in another crash when he was competing in the Rex Mays 150 at the Wisconsin State Fair Grounds in 1968. He died of massive head injuries suffered in a third lap crash. He is buried in Section 224, Lot 106.

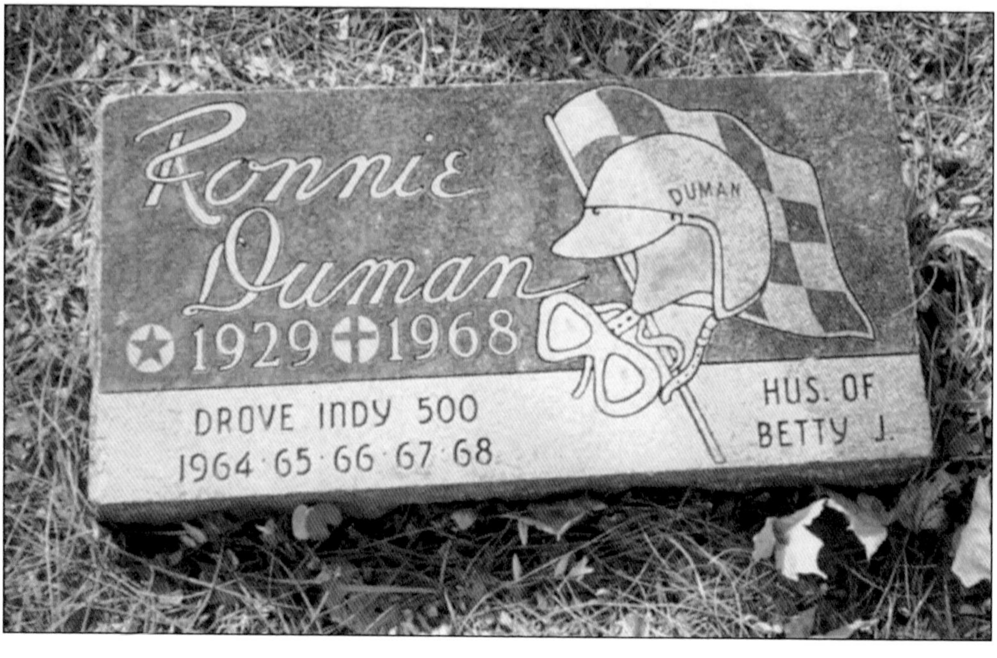

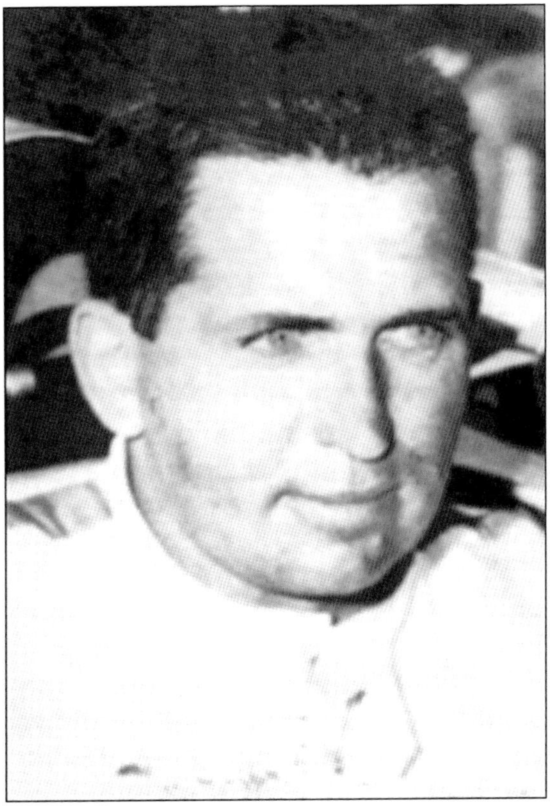

Jim Hurtubise, 1932–1989, raced in nine Indianapolis 500s and was named rookie of the year in 1960. He was in the front row in 1961 and 1962, but mechanical breakdowns kept him out of victory lane. He nearly died from a crash in Milwaukee in 1964, but he recovered and returned to racing the next year. He created a car he called the Mallard in 1968, which became the last front-engine car to compete in the Indy 500. He died from a heart attack on January 6, 1989. He is buried in the Community Mausoleum, D-8-2DD.

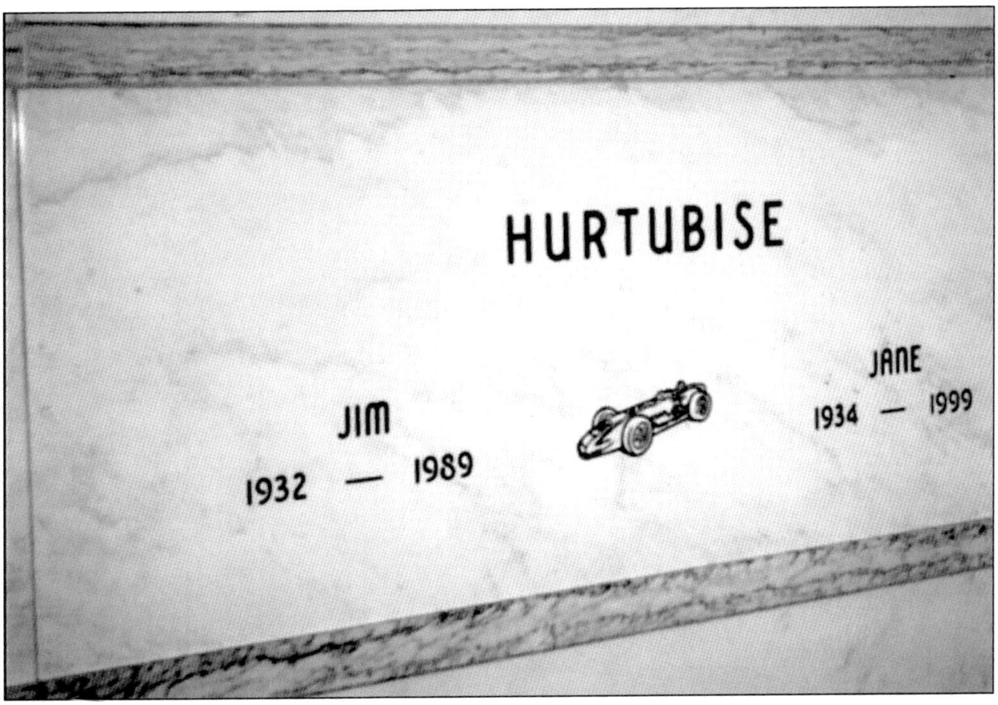

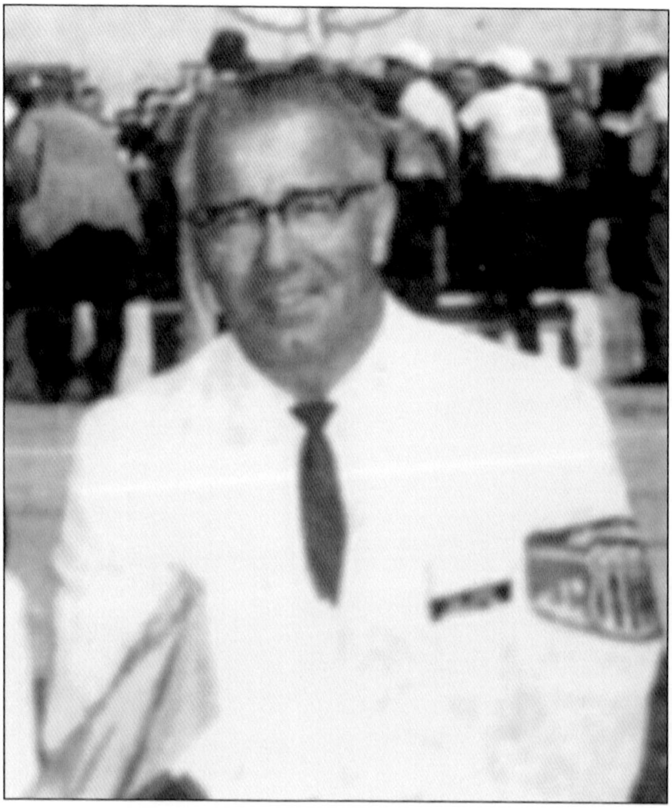

Pat Vidan, 1914–1983, was the chief starter at the Indy 500 from 1962–1979. His grave is located in Section 224.

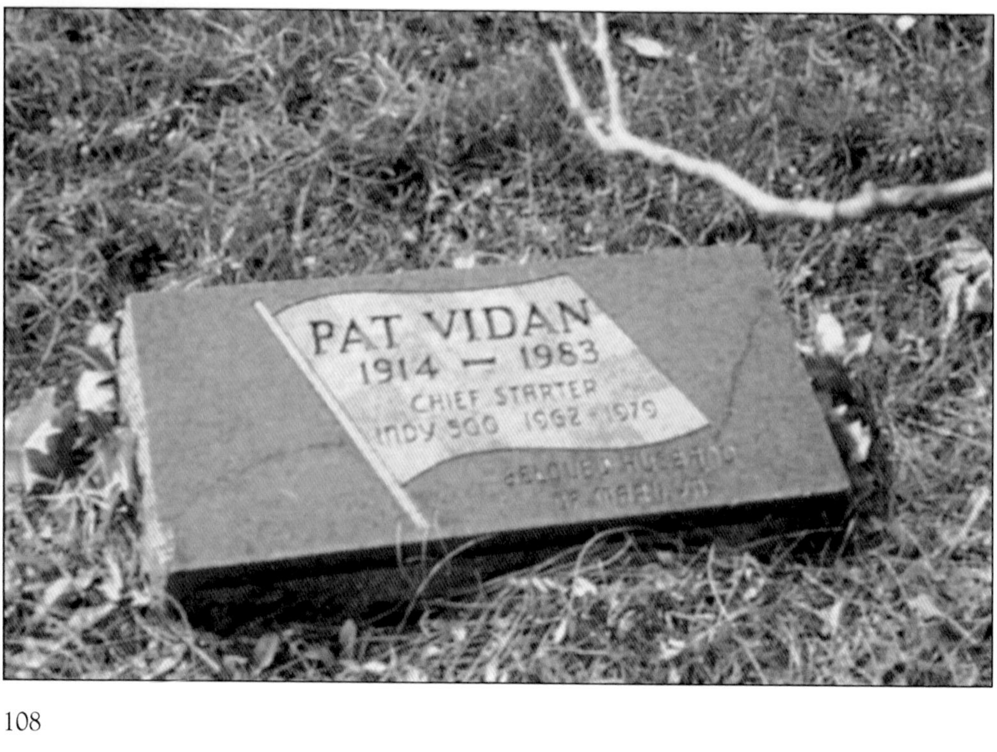

Seven

Other People

The people buried at Crown Hill come from all walks of life, from the distinguished to the undistinguished. Many famous educators, physicians, engineers, and architects are buried there, as well as criminals. The famous bank robber, John Dillinger, resides there. Some are buried in unmarked graves, while others reside in mausoleums. Regardless of their stature in life, they are all equal when they arrive at Crown Hill, their final resting place.

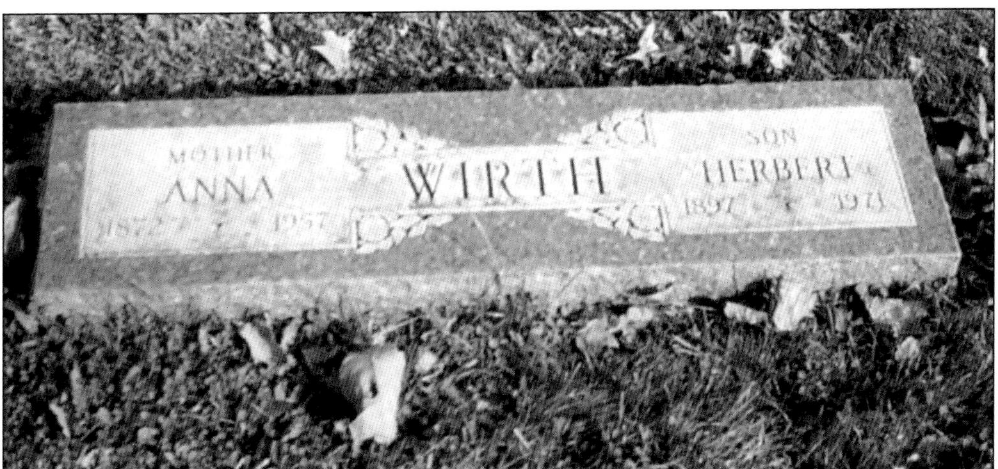

Herbert A. Wirth, 1898–1971, was a common man who received an uncommon burial. The door-to-door peddler was well known to residents on the north side of Indianapolis. When Herbie died, the *Indianapolis Star* wrote a feature article on him. The article explained how the lonely, gentle man asked only that someone come to mourn his passing. More than a thousand turned out for his funeral, which was one of the biggest funerals in the cemetery's history. His remains are located in Section 78, Lot 89 alongside his mother.

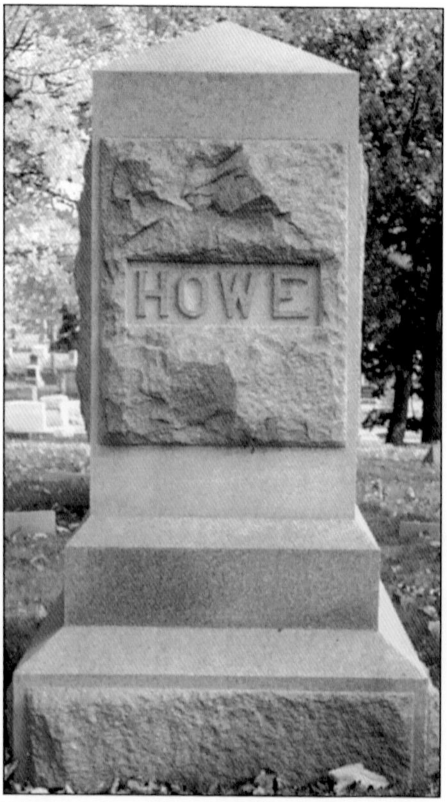

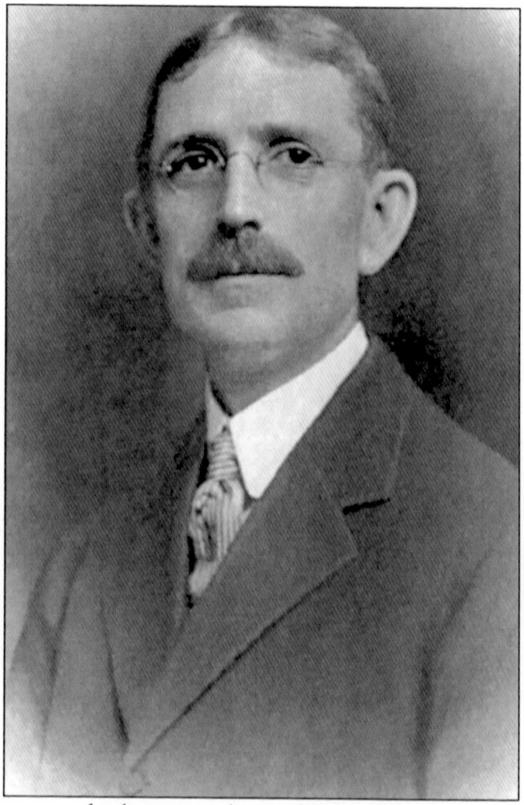

Thomas Carr Howe, 1867–1934, was an educator, and religious and civic leader. Born in Clark County, Dr. Howe graduated from Butler University in 1899 and became a professor there. He took over as the president of Butler from 1908 to 1920. He later became the president of the Pension Fund of Disciples of Christ Church and first president of the Indianapolis Boy Scout Council, which he helped organize in 1914. Irvington High School was named for the educator. His grave is located in Section 36, Lot 8.

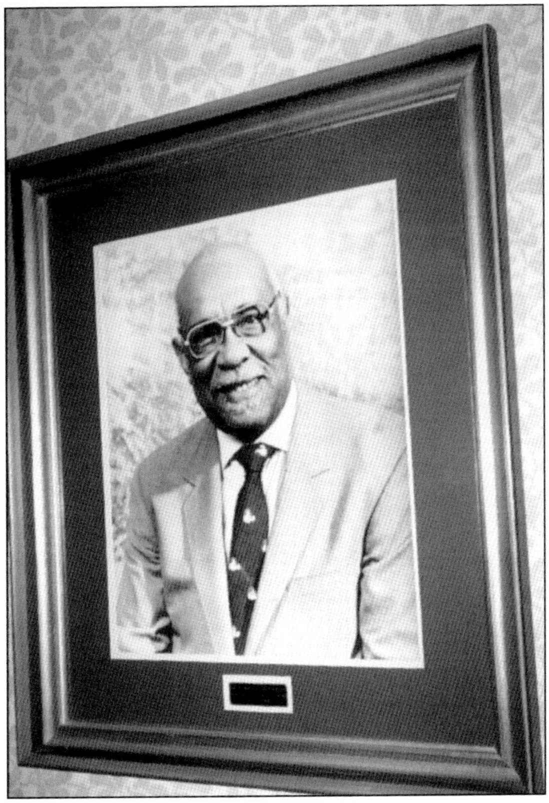

Rev. Mozel Sanders was a local minister and civil rights activist. He used to hold a Thanksgiving dinner for the community each year and that tradition continues today. His remains are located in the Community Mausoleum, D-13-2A.

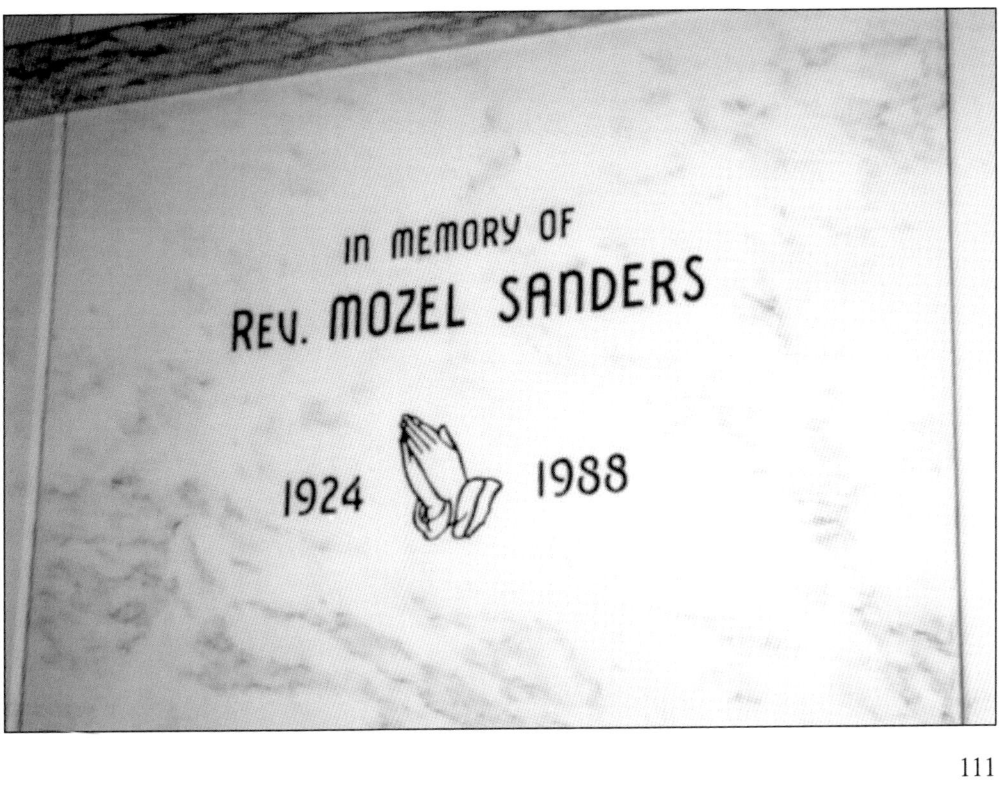

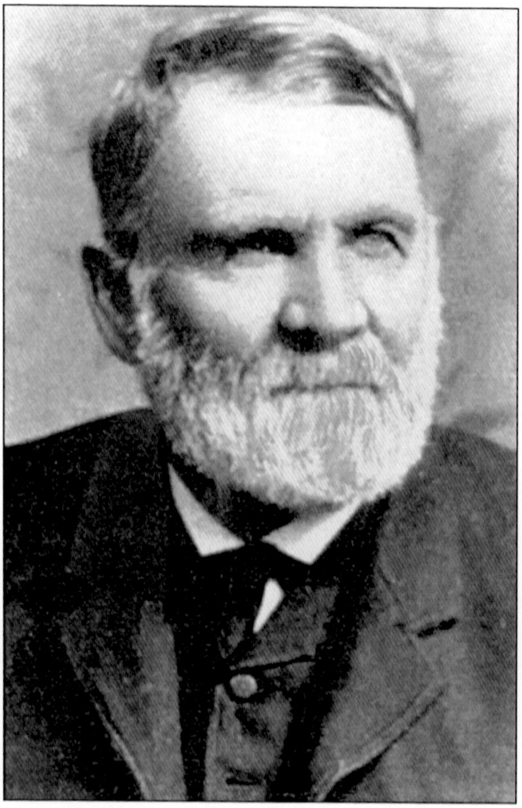

Dr. William H. Wishard served two years as a volunteer surgeon during the Civil War. Then he was elected as coroner of Marion County and served as superintendent at the City Hospital, which was later renamed Wishard Hospital, but that was after another doctor by the same name. Wishard practiced medicine for more than 50 years. He is buried in Section 78, Lot 108.

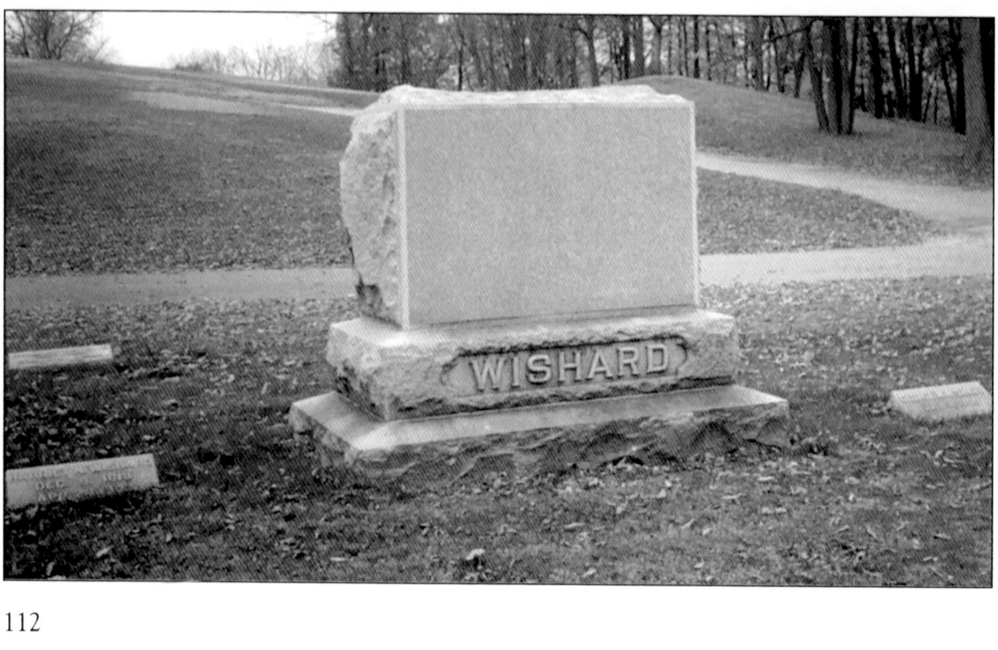

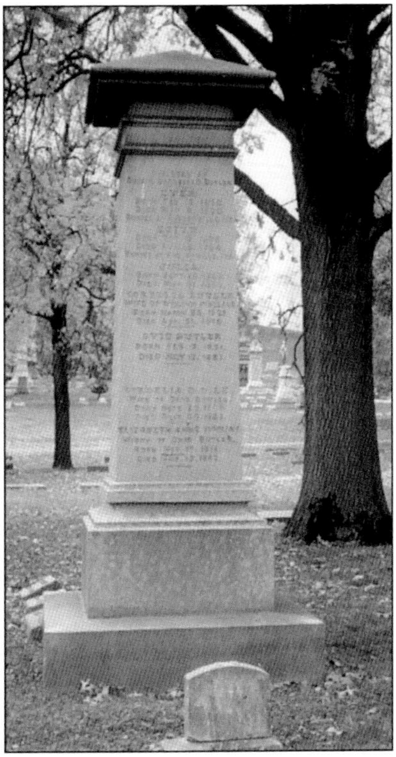

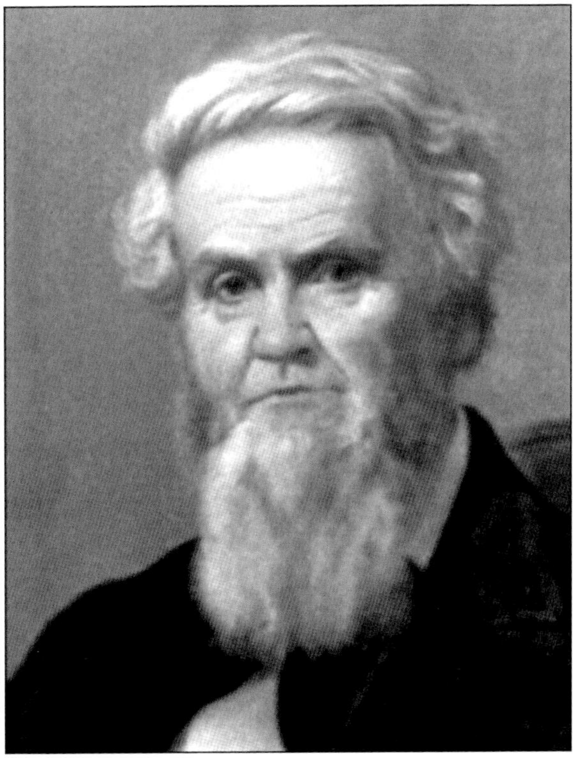

Ovid Butler, 1801–1881, was a pioneer lawyer in Indianapolis and for whom Butler University is named. In 1849, he established a paper called, *Free Soil Banner* in Indianapolis. It was a political paper with much emphasis on anti-slavery. In 1849, due to bad health he gave up his law practice bringing an early retirement. He turned his attention to raising money to establishing the North Western Christian University, which was later renamed Butler University. His son, Scot Butler (1844–1931), who also is buried in the family lot in Section 6, twice served as that institution's president.

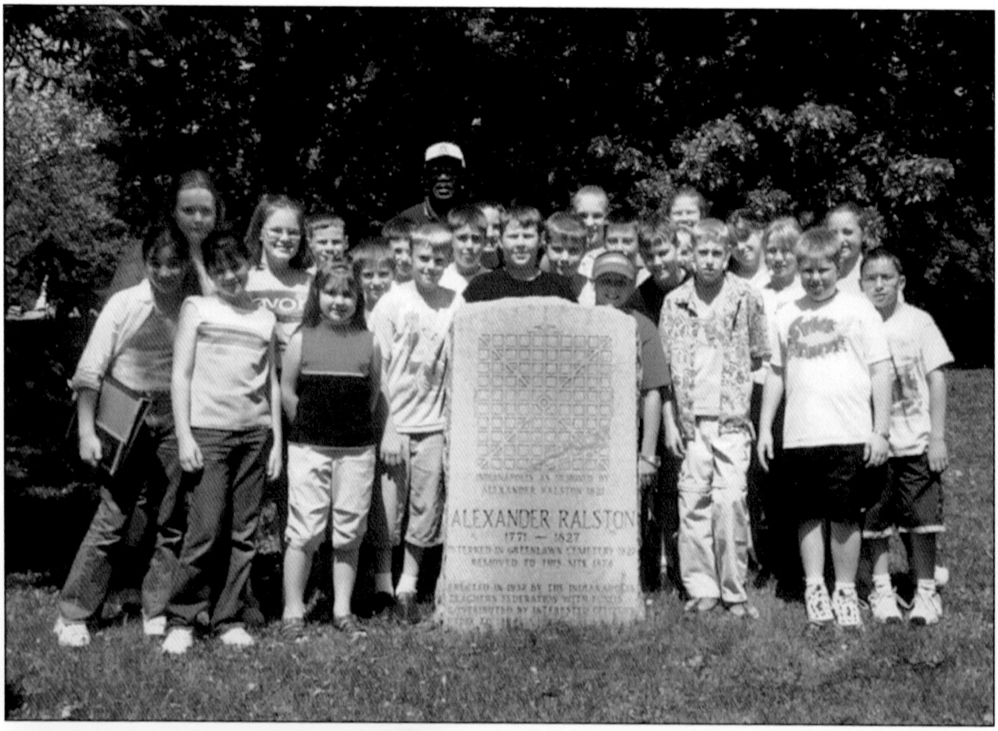

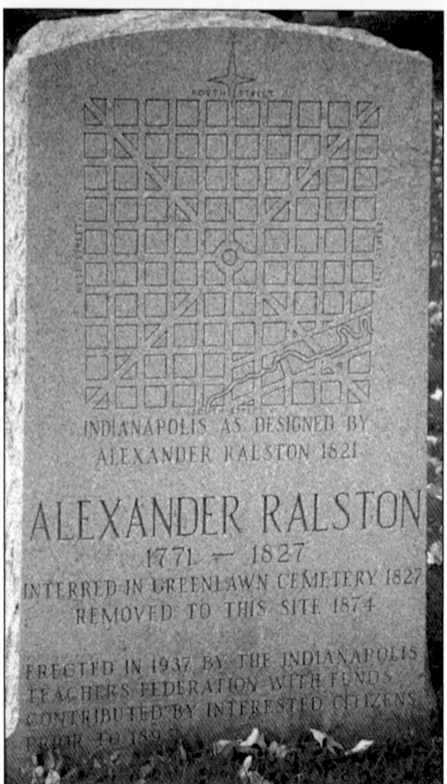

Alexander Ralston, 1771–1827, laid out the first plot of Indianapolis. His mile square, which was similar to his design in Washington D.C., is inscribed on his monument, surrounded by youngsters from Avon in this photo by Marty Davis. Ralston was buried in this charity lot in Section 3, which was reserved for "Destitute Instructors of Public Schools" in 1874. By the way, Indianapolis is second to Washington D.C. in the number of monuments dedicated to the military.

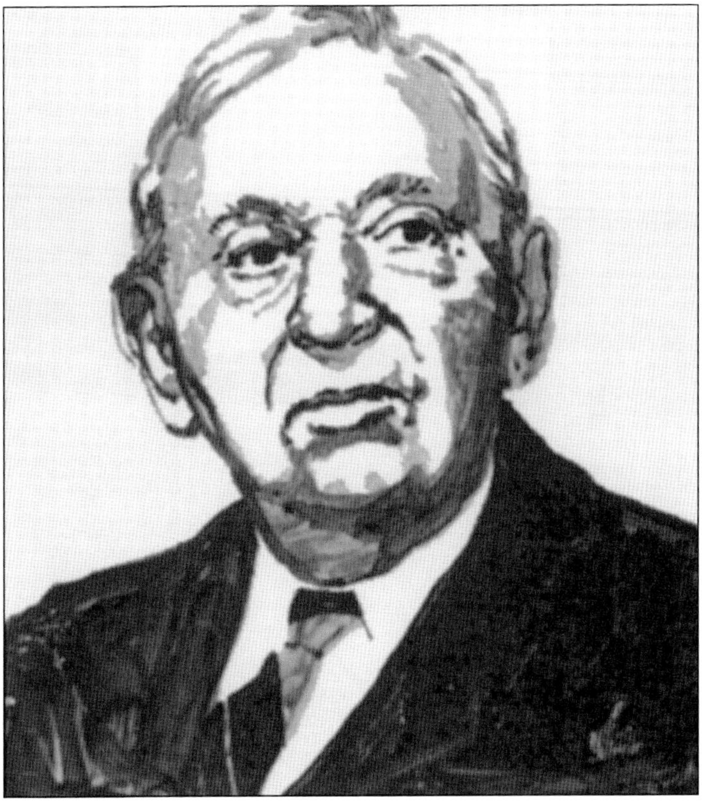

William Lowe Bryan, 1860–1955, was president of Indiana University, 1902–1937. He was a scholar, philosopher, progressive administrator, scientist, author, and public speaker. His grave is located in Section 42, Lot 181.

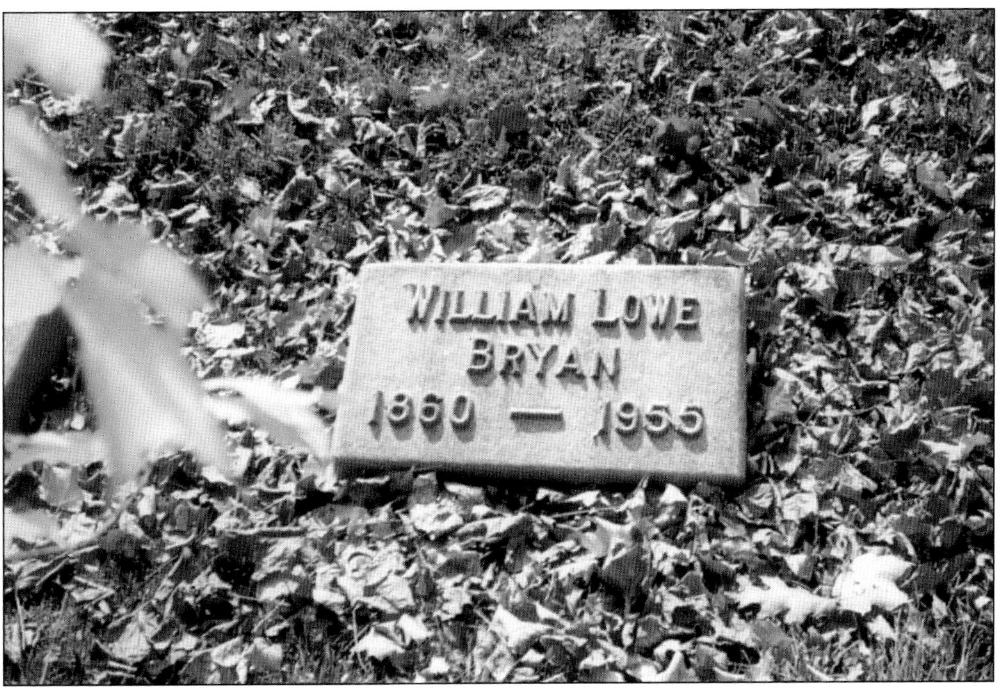

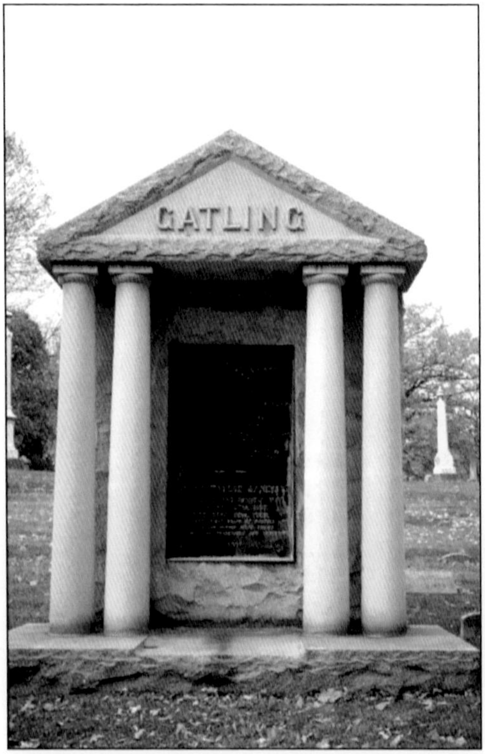

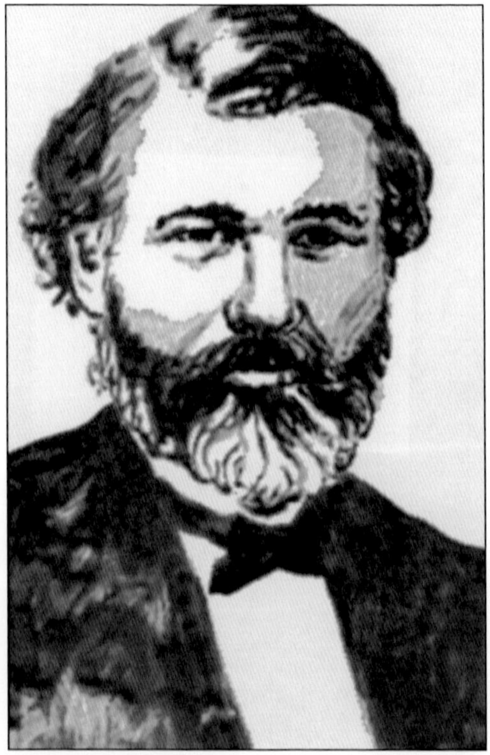
Richard Jordan Gatling, 1818–1903, was the inventor of the Gatling gun, which preceded the modern machine gun. The resident of Indianapolis conceived and built the first model in 1862. He also invented many types of agricultural machinery and owned several patents. His grave is located in Section 3, Lot 10 in a family plot.

The most asked for grave in Crown Hill is that of John Dillinger, the famous bank robber of the 1930s. He was born in a middleclass Indianapolis neighborhood on June 22, 1903. He was killed by federal agents at 10:40 p.m. on the night of Sunday, July 22, 1934 in an alley outside the Biograph Theatre in Chicago. Some 15,000 people went to his wake. He was buried in Crown Hill three days later and a couple of days after that an elaborate protection of concrete mixed with scrap iron and chicken wire was placed at staggered levels above the coffin to protect the grave from any attempt to vandalize it. His grave is located in Section 44, Lot 94 in a family plot. A special stone sits next to the family plot monument and says, "Our hearts still ache with sadness and secrets still flow, What it meant to lose you, no one can ever know."

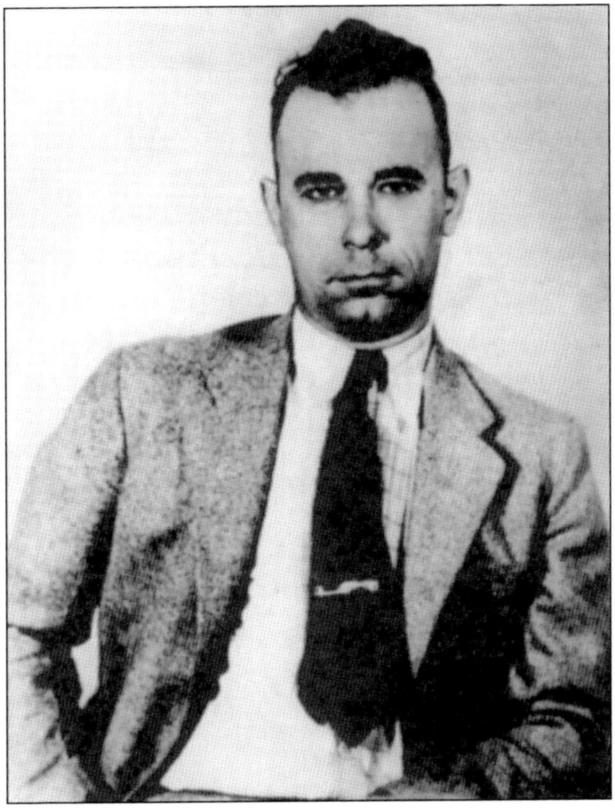

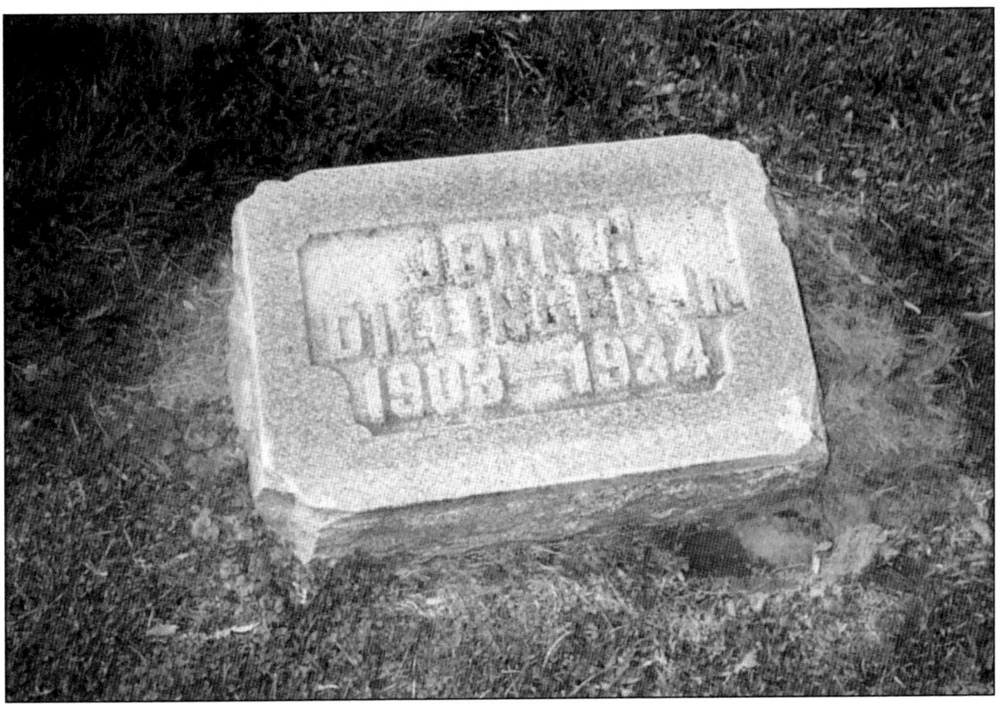

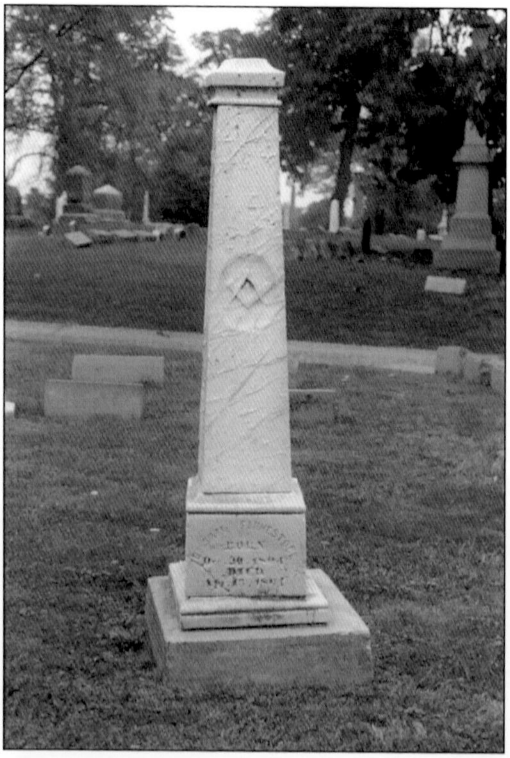

Dr. Samuel Fahnestock, 1804–1864, met his fate to guerrillas in Louisiana when he journeyed there to care for liberated slaves. The volunteer physician with the Christian Commission was the third interment in the cemetery. His upright obelisk with a Masonic insignia is located in the northeast corner of Section 4.

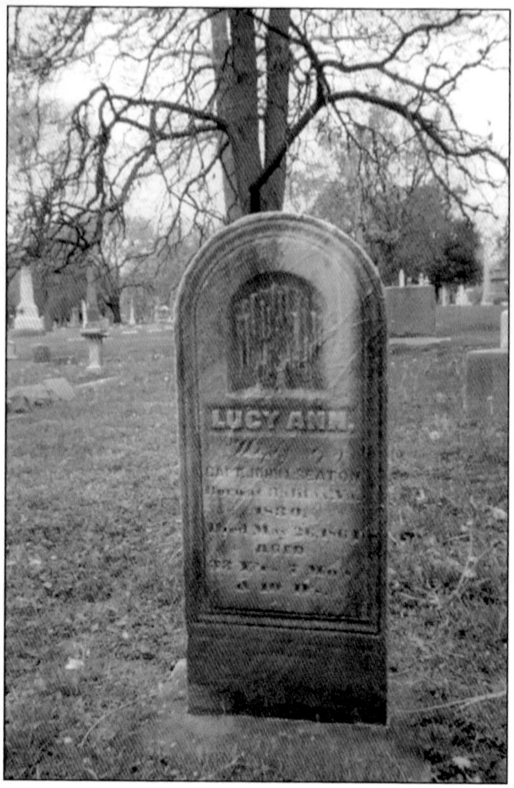

Lucy Ann Seaton, 1831–1864, was Crown Hill's first burial. Born in Virginia in 1830, she was the wife of John L. Seaton of Paducah, Kentucky. She died of consumption (tuberculosis) on May 31, 1864 and was buried two days later. She is buried in Section 4. (Photo courtesy of Marty Davis.)

Eight

Funerary Art

The cemetery is a fascinating encyclopedia of funerary art with many different forms of monuments and memorials to those who are interred within its grounds, from angels, lambs, and children carved in stone to obelisks, gravestones shaped like tree trunks, and private mausoleums whose stone and stained glass magnificence reflect the grandeur of past generations.

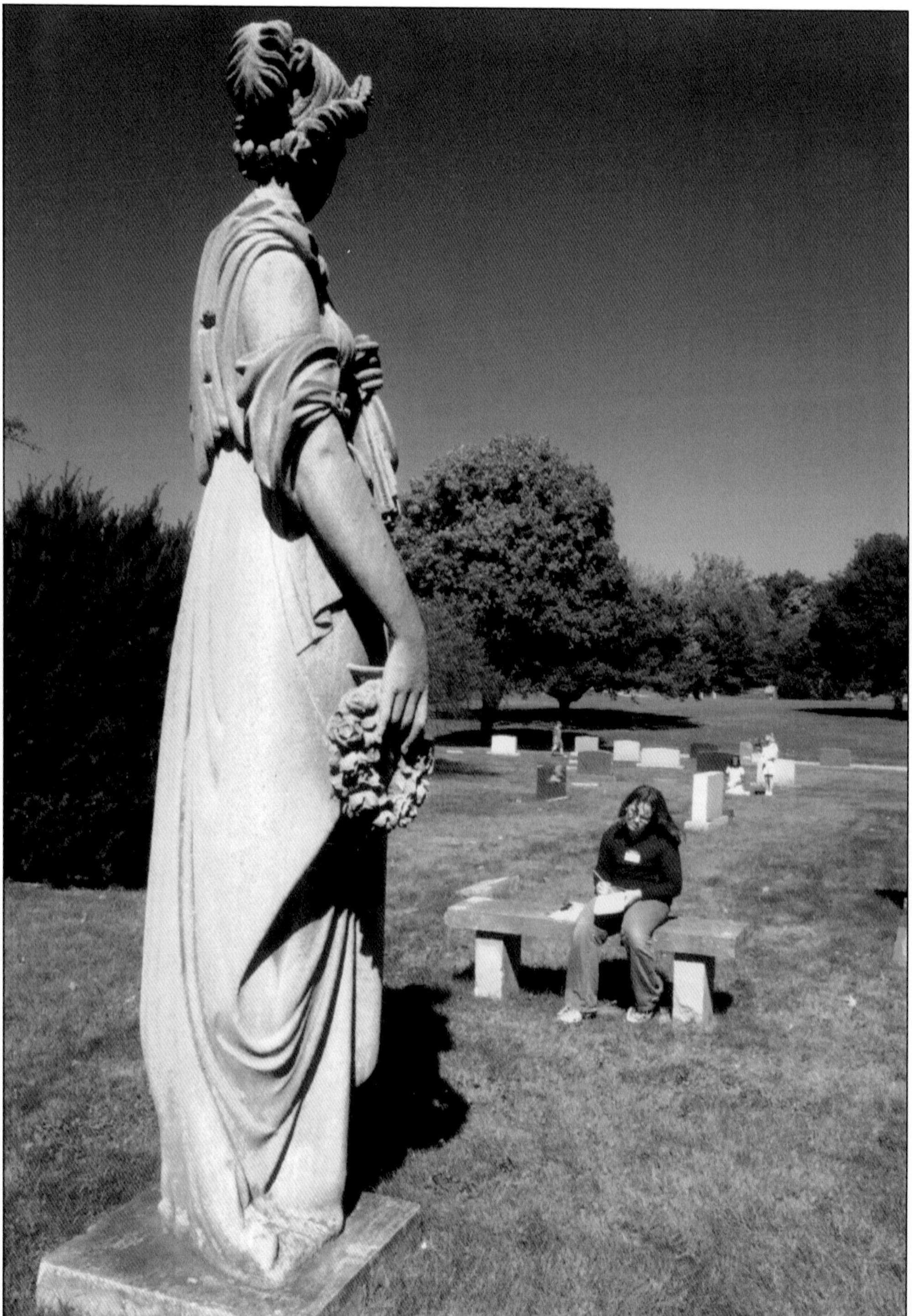

A high school student draws from the Demeter statue, the Greek goddess of Agriculture. She stands in Section 46-B. The statue comes from the old County Courthouse, which was razed. (Photo courtesy of Marty Davis.)

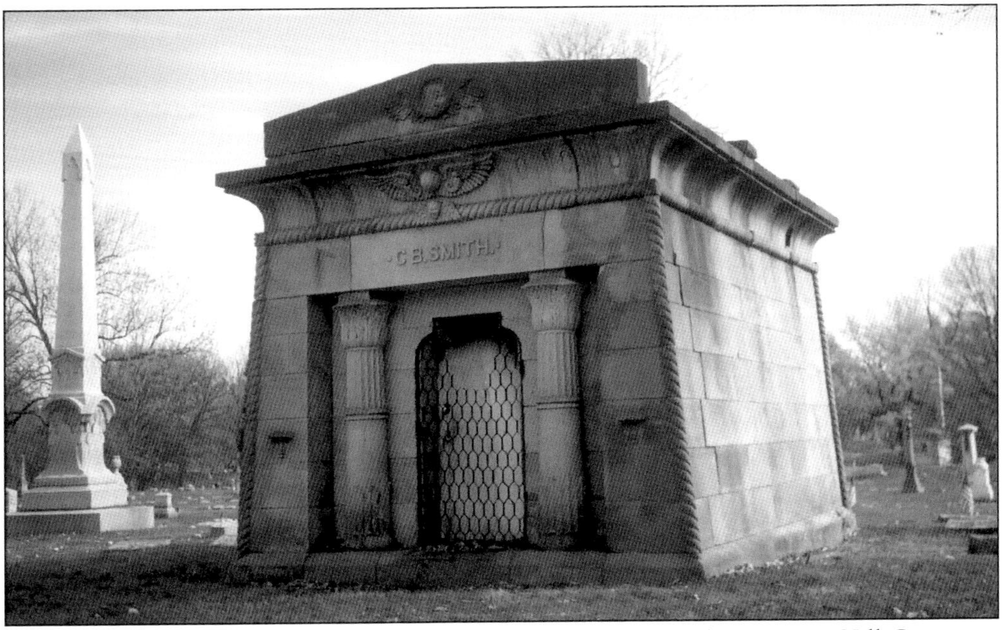

The C.B. Smith Mausoleum was the first private mausoleum built at Crown Hill Cemetery. Ironically, Caleb Blood Smith, who was a lawyer, editor, and politician, was never entombed in the mausoleum. Several myths surround the reason. One reason was that hijackers stole the judge's body from the hearse en route to the cemetery. Another is that Smith's widow buried him in secrecy at the City Cemetery in Connersville. However, entombed in the mausoleum are his two children and Mrs. Smith. Another myth surrounding the mausoleum is its appearance. It looks as if it was blackened by fire, which supposedly came from the black community setting fires around it to keep the spirit of a conspirator in the Abraham Lincoln assassination from coming out and haunting the city. Smith was Lincoln's Secretary of the Interior. It is located in Section 5.

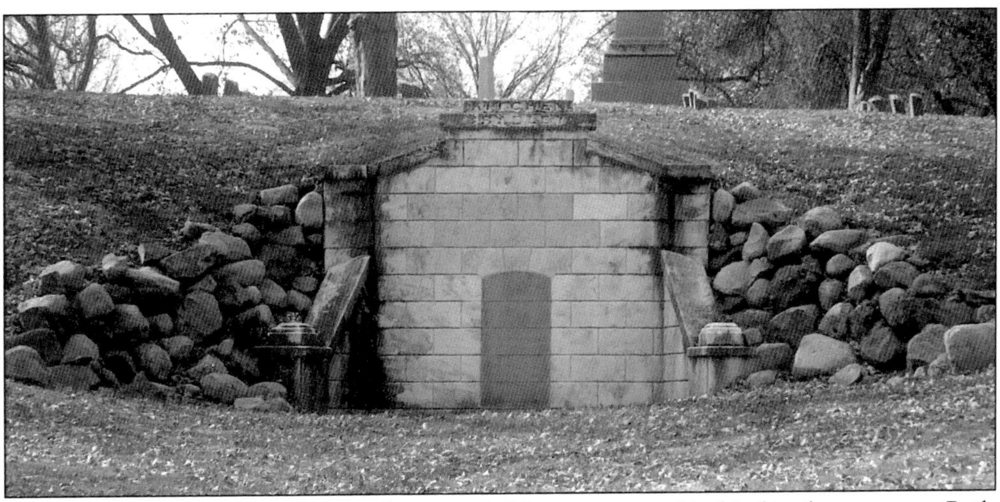
The Kitchen-Bradley mausoleum is the second oldest structure of its kind in the cemetery. Built in 1866, it was sealed in the late 1960s. One of the persons buried there is Dr. John M. Kitchen, 1827–1916, who was a prominent Indianapolis physician. He helped create the Indianapolis Medical College. It is located in Section 6.

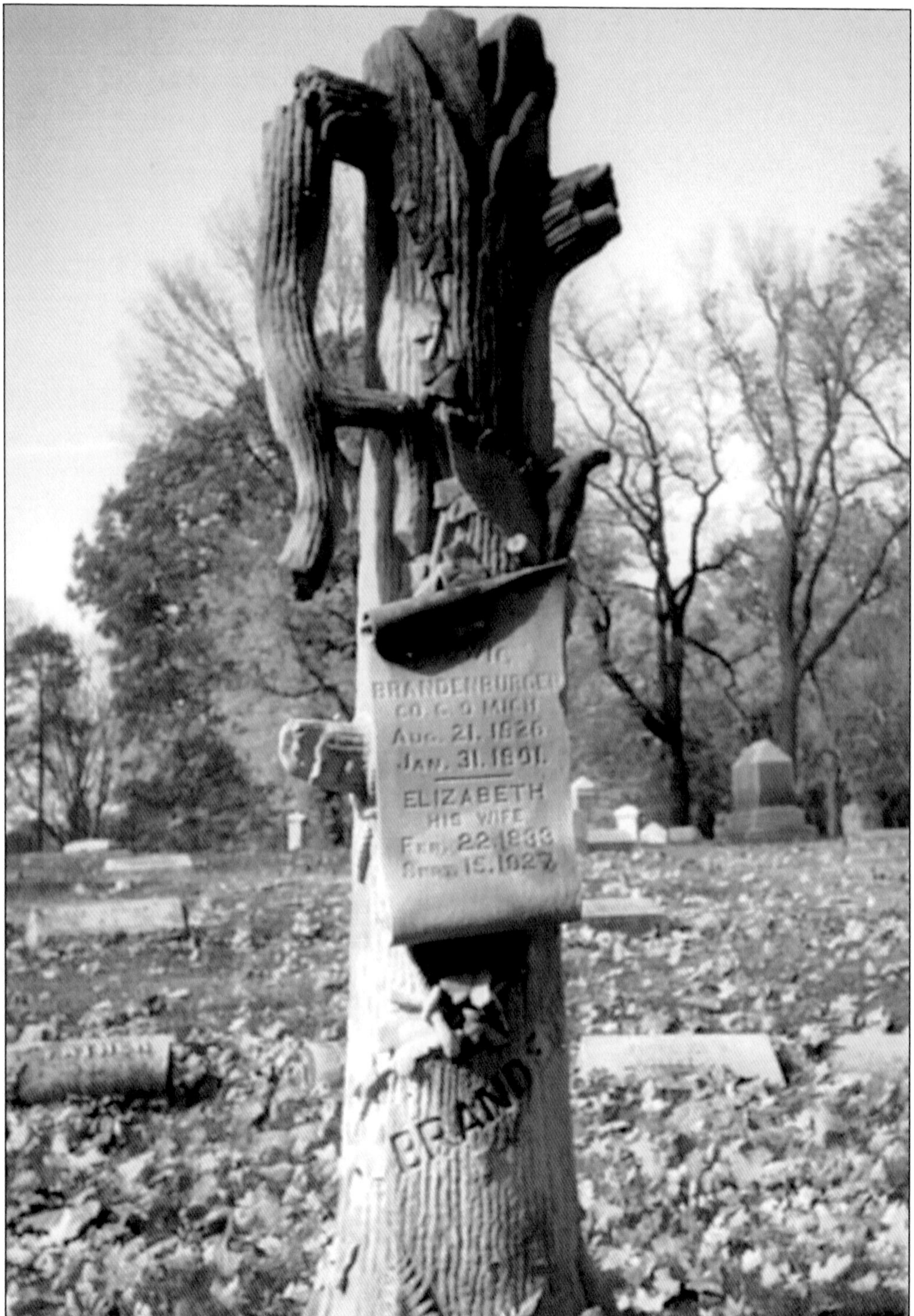

Tree stumps, which indicate that life ended prematurely, are prominent throughout Crown Hill. This stump marks the graves of Ludwig Brandenburger, 1826–1891, and Elizabeth, his wife, 1833–1927.

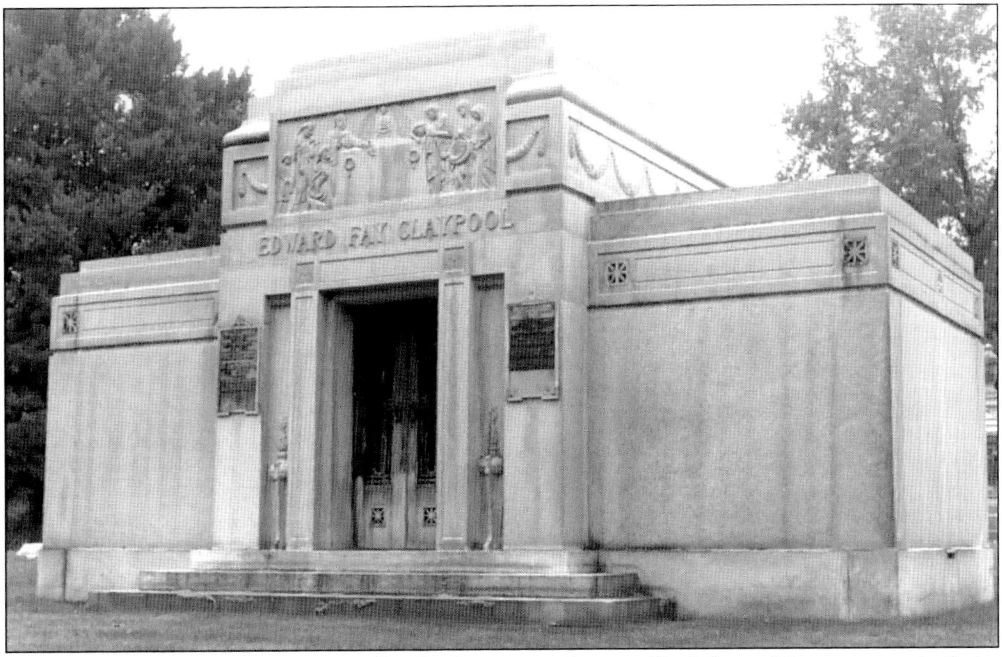

Mausoleums are very expensive and only the very rich can afford them. This one was built by Edward Fay Claypool, 1832–1911, an Indiana banker and investor. He financed the purchase of the old Bates House on Washington Street and converted it to the Claypool Hotel, which stood until 1969. Today, the Claypool Court sits on the site. The mausoleum, which contains 17 crypts, is located in the northeast corner of Section 29 near the Gothic Chapel.

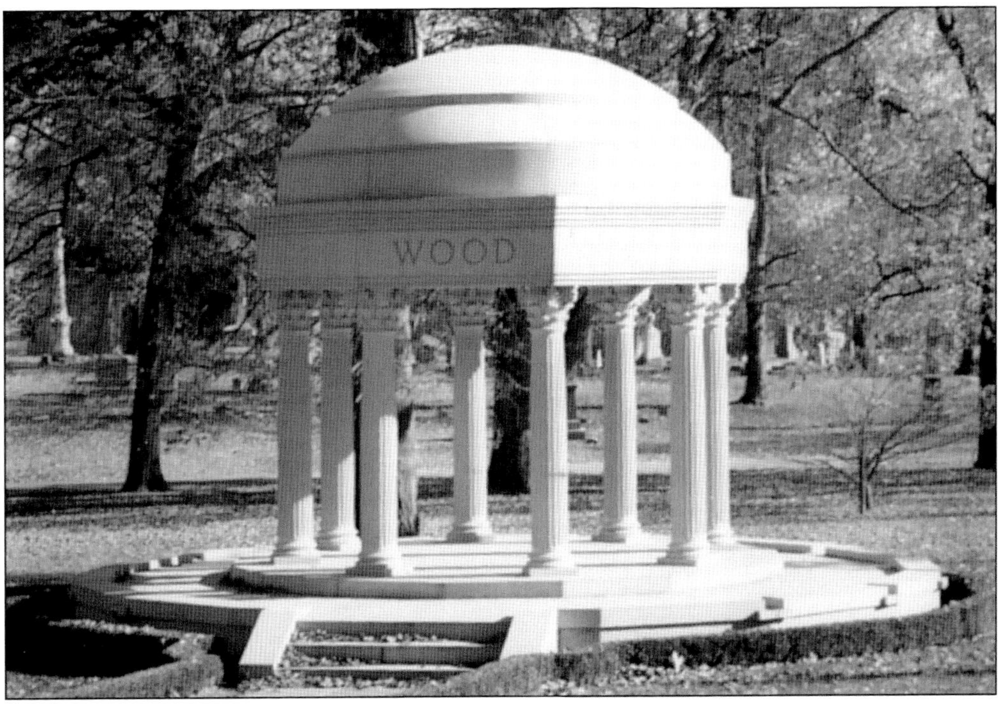

The latest monument to be built at Crown Hill is the Wood Memorial.

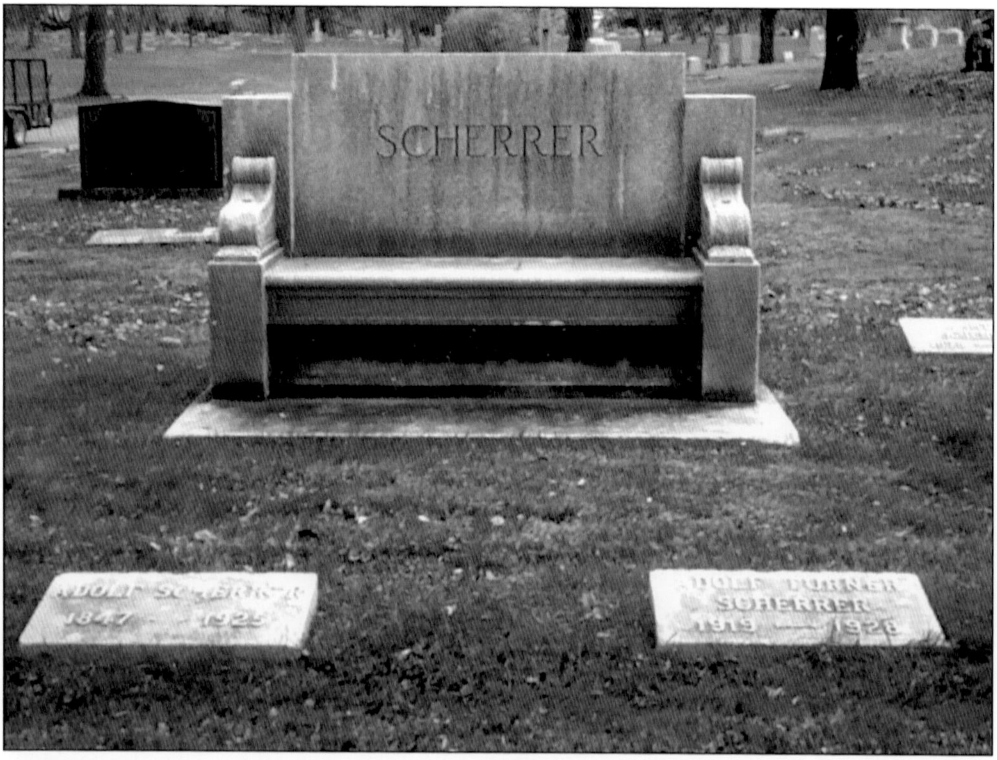

Benches are popular and can be found throughout the cemetery. This one honors Adolf Scherrer, 1847–1925, the architect.of the 34th Street Archway Entrance and Administration at the cemetery. He also completed work on the current Indiana State Capitol Building. His bench monument is located in Section 53. The other one honors the Aufderheide family.

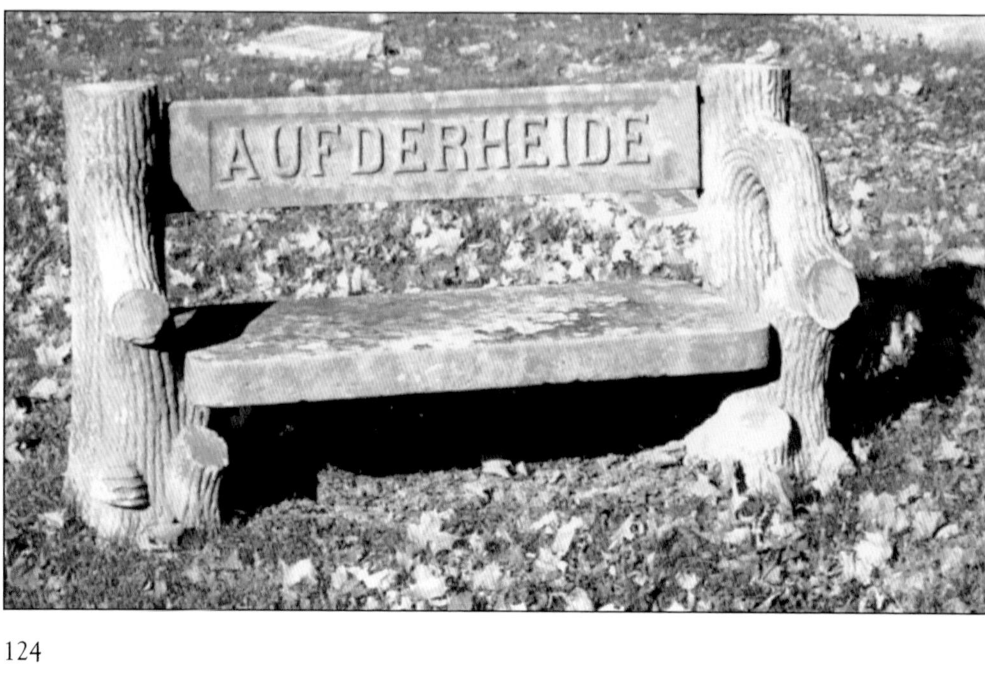

Probably the most popular funerary art at Crown Hill is the angel. Angels can be seen all over the cemetery.

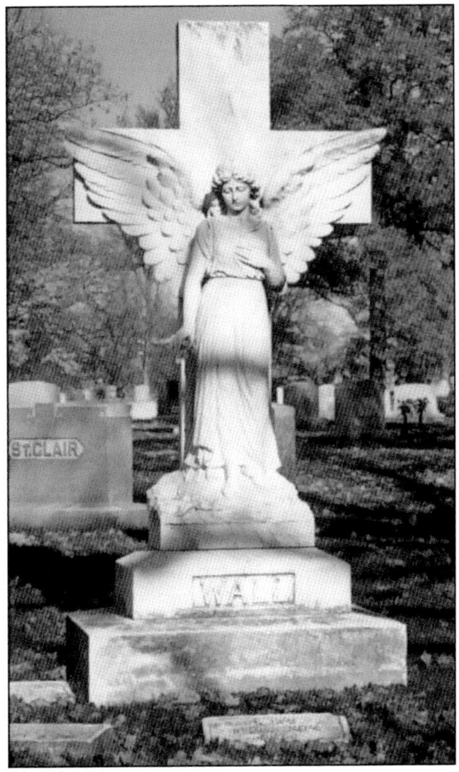

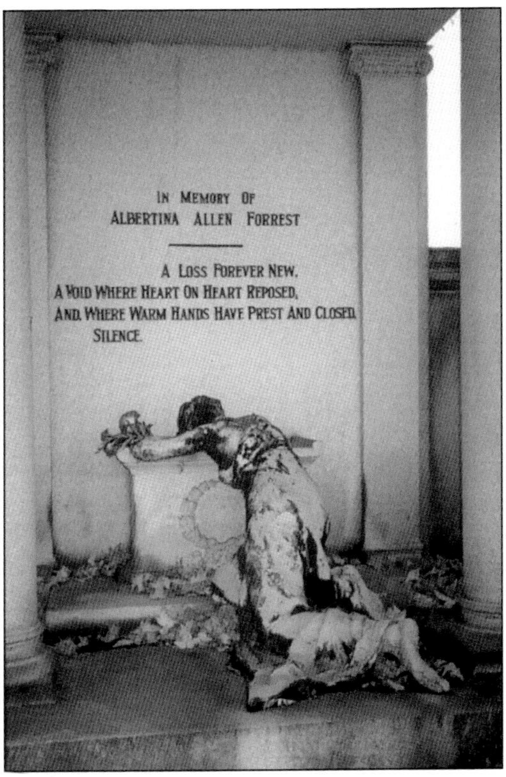

A woman in repose is the subject of this bronze statue created by noted sculptor Rudolph Swartz. She can be seen at the monument for Albertina Allen Forrest, 1872–1904, who was a professor at Butler University. It's located in Section 25.

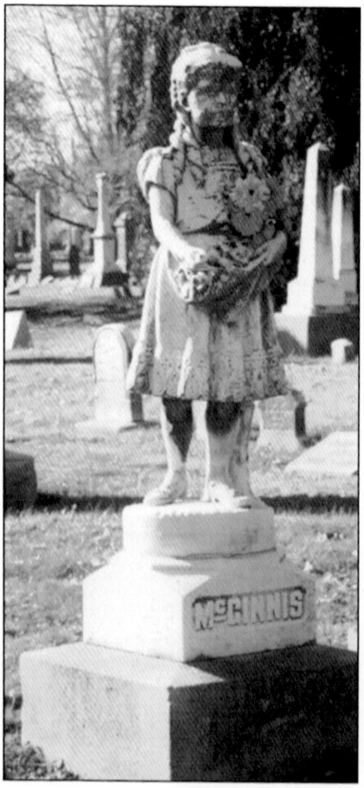

The beautiful statue of Mary Ella McGinnis is the second one made. The first was made by Lorado Taft, a Chicago sculptor, but it was refused by the family, who had a second likeness of the little girl carved in Italy. It has stood at the grave for more than 120 years. She died of lung congestion at age five in 1875.

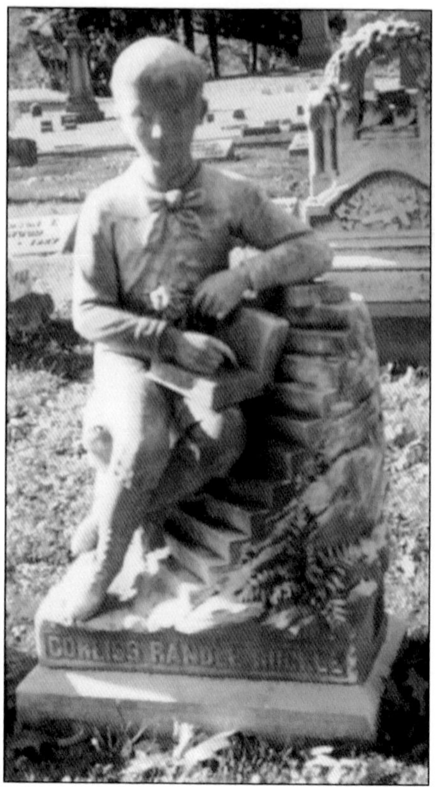

Another life-like statue of a child is that of Corliss Randel Ruckle in Section 12.

The archway of William R. Amthor in the National Military Cemetery includes a glass mosaic.

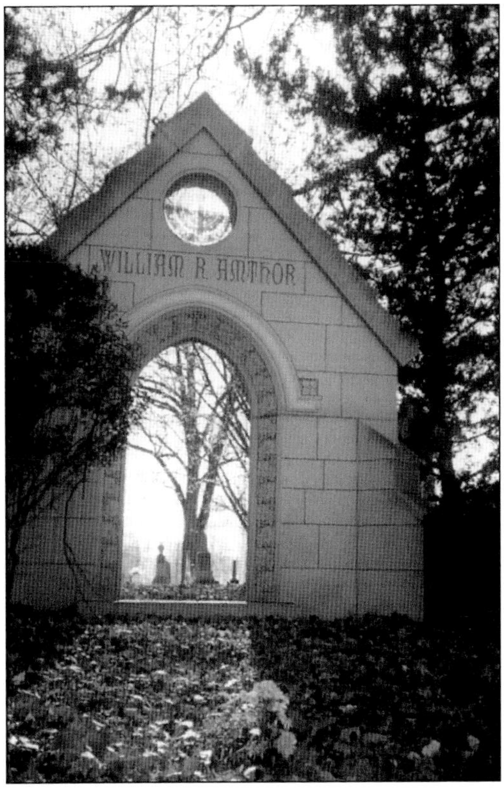

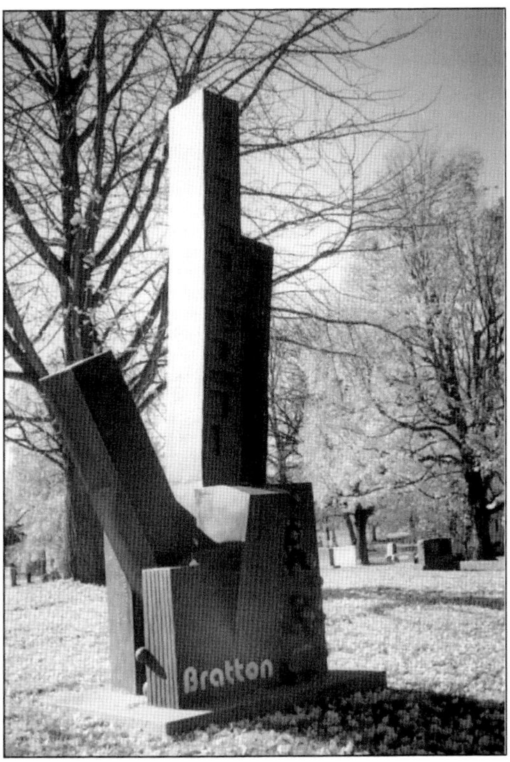

The Bratton memorial shows the influence of modern design at the cemetery.

BIBLIOGRAPHY

Indianapolis and its Resources, The Indianapolis Sentinel Company, 1891.
Nicholas, Anna, *The Story of Crown Hill*, 1928.
Pictorial & Biographical Memoirs of Indianapolis and Marion County, Indiana, 1893.
Sanford, Wayne L., *Memories of the Past: A Tour of Historic Crown Hill Cemetery*, 1996.
The Encyclopedia of Indianapolis, Indiana Press University, 1994.

www.angelfire.com/in4/jimmydaywalt
www.ata.com
www.baseballlibrary.com
www.canadiandriver.com
www.celebratetoday.com
www.crimelibrary.com
www.desmoinesregister.com
www.fctucker.com
www.findagrave.com
www.hickoksports.com
www.indymotorspeedway.com
www.indygov.org
www.indystar.com
www.mrl.lib.in.us
www.stutzclub.com
www.statelib.lib.in.us
www.4reference.net/encyclopedias